Out of Print

Out of Character

ALISON STEADMAN
Out of Character

A MEMOIR

From *Abigail's Party* to *Gavin & Stacey*,
and everything in between

WITH FIONA LINDSAY

HarperCollins*Publishers*

HarperCollins*Publishers*
1 London Bridge Street
London SE1 9GF

www.harpercollins.co.uk

HarperCollins*Publishers*
Macken House, 39/40 Mayor Street Upper
Dublin 1, D01 C9W8, Ireland

First published by HarperCollins*Publishers* 2024

1 3 5 7 9 10 8 6 4 2

A catalogue record of this book is
available from the British Library

ISBN 978-0-00-866540-1
TPB ISBN 978-0-00-866541-8

Printed and bound in the UK using 100%
renewable electricity at CPI Group (UK) Ltd

To my parents,
Marjorie and George Steadman

'Never say you can't. Always say you can and you will.'
Marjorie Steadman

Contents

This Is the Real Me

No. *Absolutely not. No. I can't wear this.*

I'm in the bedroom of my digs, staring at myself in the mirror. The reality of what is reflected back at me makes me recoil with embarrassment.

Earlier that day, the stage manager had stopped me as I was leaving rehearsals and said, 'Here you go, take this home with you and see what you think.' His jaunty enthusiasm should have aroused suspicion. And now here I was squeezed into a skin-coloured nylon body stocking like a very unappetising overfilled sausage, which is not a good look at any age and certainly not at twenty-three when you're about to make your professional stage debut. I looked awful. This was a big first moment and under no circumstances was I going to be impersonating a fry-up favourite. Without giving it a second thought or glance, I peeled off the offending sausage skin and chucked it to one side. When I returned to rehearsals the next day I told Richard Wherret, the director, 'I'll just do it naked.'

Richard was my tutor at drama school, and he had asked me if I'd play the schoolgirl Sandy Stranger in his production of *The Prime of Miss Jean Brodie* at Lincoln's Theatre Royal. The show would be taking place during our Easter holidays and I thought that it would be a brilliant opportunity to keep on learning before heading into my final term of training, so I said yes.

The Prime of Miss Jean Brodie gave me a chance, a first step, and it taught me that I was bold and brave, and would always do what felt right for the character, for the production and for me. That's why I made the decision to reveal all and be my naked self. It was 1969 and, despite the massive shift in what was deemed acceptable in culture and society, appearing naked was still a very rare occurrence especially so when the bare body was female.

Let me set the scene. Sandy is the sitter for a life study being painted by the school's art master, who is part of a love triangle with Sandy's teacher, Miss Brodie. Thankfully, due to the positioning of the chaise longue that I was seated on, the audience couldn't see too much, thank goodness, and the fact that I was lying on my side helped too. The back of the chaise was facing the audience, which meant that my naked twenty-three-year-old self was facing the actor playing the art master. During the run, my original bravura came and went, and I often felt far more nervous and exposed than I may have appeared on the surface. When that occurred I'd conjure images of my mum in my mind's eye (or should that be my 'mind's aisle', as Pamela Shipman would say) and her comforting and familiar phrase, 'Never say you can't. Always say you can, and you will,' which helped to settle me. To ease any awkwardness during the scene I tended to look upwards slightly, rather than directly ahead. On the press night I glanced up and got the shock of my life when I noticed a man staring down at me from a position high up on the lighting rig! It turned out to be a journalist who had got backstage unbeknownst to the stage-door keeper. I let them know and they threw him out. Ah well. Thank goodness I was young and there was something to look at in those days!

For the duration of the run, I was Alison by day and Sandy by night, quietly honing my Scottish accent by recalling the impressions that I used to do of our lovely Scottish neighbour, Mrs Grey. I began to settle into being an *actress*, the professional role that I was to play over the decades that lay ahead. It's interesting for me to think about Sandy now, with her overactive imagination and obsession with trying to understand human behaviour, and how she tipped from reality into fantasy. It's so close to how you need to be as a performer. Sandy was my first significant experience playing another person rather than just being myself.

There is always an 'other woman' in my life. My job is to get under the skin of another human being, a woman that isn't me, and to ask question after question about what it is that has made her how she is and who she is. We are all stories. We're knitted together from the lives of people that we've never met as well as those that we have. Our insides and outsides are testament to past and present times, good and bad, and we wear it all on our skin, as well as our hearts on our sleeves, at times. To know ourselves well we need to become like our own specialist archaeologists and dig deep into the personal, social and cultural landscapes that are layered within us. Becoming the other woman means I have been an archaeologist for nearly sixty years (gosh that sounds like a long time) gathering evidence that I use to interrogate the interior beings of the women I have become, looking to their age and physicality to determine how they might walk through their worlds.

It's the same as bird watching in a way. Being able to see beyond the robin's red breast and his little fat shape. Why is he plump? Why does he have a red breast? Both of my grandmothers loved birds and it's something that I've inherited from them. Grandma Evans (née Campbell), my mum's mum, would make bird baths from old metal bowls covered in cement that she'd then fill with water. She was constantly telling me to look out for the birds and she taught me how to properly observe them, as well as how to break up bread crusts into small pieces and then soak them before scattering to avoid any choking incidents. My induction into noticing detail and doing things carefully began early!

When I've worked out the part that I'm playing, it's as if Alison disappears for a while and the other woman reveals herself. For those that love me, and especially for my partner, Michael Elwyn, it's like constantly being in a ménage à trois! He might say it's more like a ménage à neuf, as I'm always adopting so many silly voices at home, which I think are amusing of course but he might find a bit tedious. He'll wake up and instead of hearing the soothing tones of Classic FM, he has me in his ear saying in my broadest Scouse, 'Alright, our Jo, cum on, lawve, let's be 'avin you sittin' up now. Cum on. Hey, La. Hey, our Jo, here's yer tea. You're alright, luv. Did you sleep? Oh, soft lad. You're a bit smelly. Don't you worry. We'll give you a nice wash down now and get you sorted.' It's not as if it's the first time he's heard this, and although he is really kind and tolerant with me, he does have a withering look that appears from time to time as if to say, 'Please just give me my tea. I don't need a one-woman show every morning.' Perhaps I take it too far. Who knows? When my boys were young and they were in the back of the car, I'd always be doing a full repertoire of different voices to entertain them. It was such fun to have a rapt audience who couldn't walk out on me, although they did leave a review! One day as we were driving along one of them said, 'Mummy, stop doing the stupid voices!' I can't say that I stopped completely but I did pare it back for a while, at least with them.

There's a reason for my lapsing into other voices though. Growing up it felt like I was an only child as my sisters, Pam and Sylvia, were ten and twelve years older than me. When they left home, I hated being on my own and so the daft voices would begin. I'd make up stories and characters and become other people just to keep myself company. It's not something that I've grown out of. Being on my own doesn't suit me. I can do it for a while but being in the company of others has always been something that I've loved.

Doing the job that I do, you need a huge capacity for empathy (note to self to restrict imposing my silly voices on Michael as he might not like it as much as I think he does) and be willing to understand a different point of view, another human being and what they are going through. It's never about imposing who you are on a part. You're not you, you're someone else. You're in a particular situation and you need to think, *Ah okay, I know why she might be feeling this way*, and make useful connections with your own life where you can.

In many ways, my education in being inquisitive and reading between the lines was directly related to my own Miss Brodie, Miss Davies, the deputy head at my secondary school and the scariest-looking woman that I'd ever seen. Her tightly curled hair looked like an untended, gnarled bush that was in sorry need of maintenance and her round thin-rimmed glasses, perched precariously on the tip of her nose, induced anxiety and amazement. She wore a long black gown and reminded me of the uncle in *The Magician's Nephew* by C. S. Lewis. Miss Davies was such a gift to impersonate, and I'd stand at the front of the classroom behind the rostrum, ruffle up my hair and stare menacingly at my friends, as she did, until someone said, 'Quick, get down, Miss is coming.' We were truly frightened of Miss Davies. That was until she took us for English and transformed into the kindest, funniest, warmest person that you could hope to meet, and we all fell in love with her. She would read poems aloud to us, and invite us to try and find connections between them and our own lives. We'd talk about the emotion that we felt and then go back into the poem. Keats was her favourite and the way she shared his 'Ode to a Nightingale' with us made a very deep impression on my fourteen-year-old self. She explained that when he writes of being 'too happy in thine happiness' it was about crying with pleasure not sadness and helped us think about things in our own lives that might have brought a lump into our throats because they were so thrilling. Remembering the way Miss Davies taught us Keats has always been so useful. It's about being curious and curiouser, and putting aside my own personality and beginning to see another face in the proverbial mirror. It's pretending to be another person but not actually being them. This might seem like a very strange way to earn a living, but at the end of the day you take off your costume, put your own clothes back on and you're you again and ready to take up the other roles that contribute to who you are. Hopefully.

The Prime of Miss Jean Brodie press night remains etched in my memory not just for the peeping paparazzi chap but also for my own unfettered enthusiasm. The show had gone spectacularly well and we were all thrilled. I was buzzing with excitement and eager to get off stage and into the bar to see everyone. *They're bound not to recognise me with my clothes on*, I pondered as I was leaving my dressing room, and so, out of character and giddy with adrenaline, I decided to adopt the catchphrase of the well-known Scottish comedian Stanley Baxter to ensure that my first post-show entrance to a theatre bar was a grand one. Stanley Baxter impression, *check*. Scottish accent, *check*. Cue, Alison Steadman, *check*. And with gusto I launched myself into the unaware and disinterested crowd with aplomb declaring, 'And this, ladies and gentlemen, is the real me!'

In many ways, it was. And still is!

CHAPTER 1

Waking Up

It's just gone 4.00 a.m. and I'm tiptoeing around the home that I've shared with my partner Michael for over twenty-five years. A car is coming in thirty minutes to drive me to the filming location for the BBC comedy *Here We Go* on the other side of London. I yearn to stay in bed for an hour or two longer, but that's not going to happen today as the demands of the filming schedule won't stretch to giving me more slumber time. It's dark and quiet, inside and out, as I go about my well-practised routine that makes sure I'm ready on time and I don't disturb the household. Michael is also an actor and so we're both very familiar with each other's early morning creep-abouts and quiet exits. I brace myself for a quick shower before slipping into the spare room where, the night before, I laid out all my clothes and other bits and pieces that I need for the day. Being organised like this is essential for me. I find it difficult to leave any mess or not know where things are. A quick cup of tea and a plain biscuit helps to give me the kick-start that's required at this preternaturally early wakening and they will have to do until I get the cup of strong coffee on set that will finally lift my fatigue. A faint mechanical purring noise breaks through the pin-drop silence as a car pulls up outside and switches its engine off.

There's something very special about this time of the day, as everything awakens. Standing in the kitchen not knowing if the now silent car is mine or not, I lift the blind and peer out. The ground is dusted with a soft covering of snow that glows in the rising light and makes everything seem brighter. Suddenly, there he is, stealthily rummaging around with his nose in the snow. He looks up and we lock eyes for at least a minute. He has a look of surprise that suggests he is wondering why the light is on and why on earth I am up. Then the headlights of the newly arrived car give a double flash and Mr Fox is off.

These are moments to cherish, and I'll never tire of them. Michael and I live surrounded by trees. Sometimes when I walk out of the house at this time of day the only sound will be a lone blackbird singing its morning aria, the high notes soaring over the treetops. Or, if I'm lucky, the owls in the woods on the opposite side of the road will be chatting to each other. It's the best part of the day for me, invisible threads of pure gold connecting us to an awakening world.

Getting up at the crack of dawn isn't my natural waking hour but, yawning, I tell myself that this break-of-day departure time won't go on forever. The car is warm and comfortable, and it would be so easy to snuggle into the seat and snooze for the duration of the journey. But I'm too concerned about knowing my lines to do that, and so the only thing that I make myself comfortable with is my script as we calmly make our way across the deserted streets of central London. This solitary, quiet time before arriving on set is a vital part of the process that I need to go through to take me out of myself and into the character that I'm playing, which in this instance is Sue Jessop, mum and grandma in *Here We Go* by the writer and actor Tom Basden. Learning lines is increasingly nerve-wracking. It takes me longer to get a full hold of it all and this worries me. There was a time when I could look at a script on a car journey, and it would all go in. All I'd have to do would be to have a quick check over it during the make-up call. Not now. I look at Katherine Parkinson, who plays my daughter in-law in the show. Her brain is how mine was years ago and I think, *Give me a bit of that back.* She's quick and word perfect whereas I need lots of time as my brain has slowed down. You never think it will, but it does and mine has.

At home, the desk that I work at faces out into the garden and my bird feeders are directly outside. If I'm finding it all a bit difficult, I stop and look out at the birds to take my mind off things and ten or so minutes later I go back to the words feeling much lighter. It can also be a convenient distraction from doing what needs to be done and sometimes hours can pass as I watch all the different species come and go. On rare occasions a bird that I've never seen before will turn up out of the blue, which always causes a stir. 'Michael, Michael!' I yell. 'Quick, quick, get the nocs! It's a blackcap! A blackcap!!!' And for a few moments it's like we're the presenters of those TV shows *Springwatch* and *Autumnwatch*, as we both begin to stare intensely and whisper to each other. Goodness knows why we whisper when we're inside! My aim is to try to encourage birds to make the area their home and so I experiment with different types of food to tempt them. Did you know that a way to a bird's heart is to feed them fat balls? I've always thought that this is a very unfortunate yet amusing name for mass-produced bird feed. 'Fat balls, Michael, fat balls!' is something that I'm careful not to say within earshot of our neighbours, although it does feel like something Pamela Shipman might! Sometimes it's hilarious watching a wren or a robin decide whether they want to have a bath or not. They step onto the edge of the large bird bath and dip their beaks into the water as if they are testing the temperature, *Hmm … shall I go in or not? Not, I think.* Then they do this very delicate manoeuvre to turn themselves around and walk in backwards. It's so funny to observe.

There must be at least six sets of 'nocs' in our house, but as a child I didn't have any. My dad had a pair of binoculars that were quite complex and instead of letting me use them, he bought me a small Grundig tape machine so that I could record the birdsong that I heard in the garden. We'd just watch and listen and watch and listen for hours on end. On summer nights, I'd put the microphone on the window ledge and record the evening's activities. Sometimes it was deafening. Listening so avidly I became quite an expert at identifying and impersonating the different birds' songs.

Once, when I was at junior school, we went on a trip to Durham and on the final evening we had a small party, during which the teacher said, 'Anyone who wants to get up and do a turn please come forward.' Well, I didn't hold back. Walking to the front, I cleared my throat and proudly began to impersonate a singing blackbird. It must have been so dull for everyone else as I stood there whistling my merry tune. Even more embarrassingly, thinking back, was that I was doing this in my homemade fancy-dress costume for a competition that was happening later in the evening. And, no, I wasn't, as you might be expecting, dressed up as a bird of the feathered variety. My *Stars in Their Eyes* transformation had been created by fashioning a long blonde wig out of crêpe paper and a bikini top and skirt out of the same. When competition time came, I did my best wiggly walk and impression of 'Sabrina from the telly'. Sabrina – real name Norma Ann Sykes – was a Barbie-esque actress and model who became a household name by appearing with the miniature comedian Arthur Askey in his 1950s TV show *Before Your Very Eyes*. My parents must have watched the show and allowed me to see it too. It was such an odd choice of fancy dress for a ten-year-old and I didn't win, alas. The girl that did had cut up lots of long pieces of green crêpe paper and layered it all over her to resemble grass! She was obviously ahead of us all and very environmentally aware – a deserved winner!

Back on our journey, as the day begins to break, the joggers appear as well as the occasional dog walker, and if I look up from my script and out of the window, I may be lucky enough to spot some birds begin their own journey for the day. How on earth do they do it? How does any tiny bird keep itself in the air for such long periods? How does it know which direction to fly?

A few years ago, I was filming in Ireland and staying in this big old house that had been converted into a hotel. It was all very informal, so much so that they gave me my room key and then just left me to find my own way. It was a case of up the stairs, down the stairs, around the corner, turn left then right and then down a few steps, and there was my room! None of that stuck though and, in the morning, I went down some steps, turned right then right again and down a long corridor, and I swear it took me twenty minutes to reach the breakfast room and a bowl of porridge. By the time I got there I was splitting my sides as the programme that I was filming alongside Stephen Mangan and Sue Perkins was called *All Roads Lead Home* and we were learning about something called natural navigation but, on this occasion, my own inner sat nav had completely failed me. How do birds do it?

As we near the filming location my earlier encounter with Mr Fox warms me. I think of the knowing look he gave me and how misunderstood foxes are. They get such bad press for being intrusive and the rest of it, but we very rarely stop to consider our own part in their evolved behaviour and our interconnectedness. A few summers ago, one of my sons was out with friends having an evening drink at the back of a pub garden in the middle of London. Emerging slowly out of the gloom, a fox appeared, grabbed a sandal that one of the girls had kicked off and ran back into the dark. The girl was upset but resigned to the fact that her shoe was lost forever. Anyway, the following week the exact same group was in the exact same spot at the exact same time and out of the night came the same fox with the sandal in its mouth. Everyone was very still as the fox placed the chewed shoe at the girl's feet. What an incredible moment for them to witness – I love that it can't be explained and is beyond our ken. The wonder of the natural world and our cheek-by-jowl existence with wildlife is constantly inspiring and intriguing to me, and I never take it for granted.

Talking about foxes makes me remember my time on the popular 1970s sitcom *Two's Company*. It ran for four series and took delight in the dysfunctional relationship between a London-based American author and the quintessentially English butler that she hires, and the banter that arises out of their miscommunication. Mine was a guest role, which I'd taken as an opportunity to work with the iconic Elaine Stritch and the silky-voiced Donald Sinden. Elaine was an extraordinary woman who had shaped herself an impressive career in Hollywood, on Broadway, in the West End and now as the lead in the long-running ITV hit series. She was tough but I guess she had to be to jump over the hurdles that the business presented to women of her generation. For a woman to survive and thrive in the entertainment industry in the 1950s took courage and tenacity, especially for comediennes, who were, radically for the time, breaking away from conventional expectations and forging a new path. Being a funny woman wasn't a laughing matter and they faced a huge amount of prejudice. Women like Elaine paved the way for me and

I hope, in turn, that I've done that too, over the years of my career, for those younger women who were rising courageously behind me. The filming was in front of a live studio audience, and I remember that Elaine fluffed her first line. Rather than cower with embarrassment and apologise, which was the mode that I went into whenever I made a mistake during my early TV career, she held her head high and said, 'Oh fuck!' What a fabulous woman she was.

Although I only appeared in one episode, I still had time to put my foot in it. Elaine had a tiny little dog that was by her side all the time. When she was filming, she'd put the dog into a small bag, and it would pop its head out the top. There was no need to zip the bag up as the dog was always so calm. However, one day, during rehearsals, the dog began to yap and yap, and Elaine, in her unmistakable, cigarette-flavoured drawl, said to the dog, 'You stop that or you will go in the bag.' The yapping went on and on, so Elaine scooped up the dog, put it in the bag and zipped it shut! We were all a bit stunned and obviously concerned for her furry companion. Anyway, after five minutes she unzipped it and the little dog's head popped out. 'Right now. You gonna behave?' The dog just looked up adoringly and said nothing, so we continued rehearsing.

My character was called Pamela, let's call her 'Fox Fur Pam', and I had to wear this real fox-fur stole, complete with a fox head, the thought of which now makes me feel dreadful. When we got to filming, Elaine and I were standing side by side waiting for the cameras to get sorted when a sudden urge came over me. I made this yapping noise and then looked at the fox head and said, 'You will go in the bag.' And then, another yap, 'You will go in the bag!'

Elaine looked at me sternly and her riposte put me well and truly in my place: 'Alison, no jokes about the dog!'

I was mortified to have offended her. 'Sorry, Elaine, okay, no jokes about the dog.'

Boy, have I laughed about that since.

The weather has turned wet and cold as we drive onto the lot where we're filming. The lovely location lady is there, guiding people as usual, waving her arms left and right, like an airport ground controller, to get us all to the right place. She notices me and waves. The second assistant shouts over, 'Morning, Alison, everything alright?' as I'm dropped off at my little caravan. And I mean little. It's no Winnebago but it does the trick. It's private, comfortable, warm and there's a loo, a washbasin and a kettle, which is all I need really. I head over to the coffee machine situated in the make-up area to collect a much-needed coffee – my order's always a decaf cappuccino with frothy milk – and carry my treat back to my home away from home.

Everything about *Here We Go* has developed so naturally and even though it's an intense and complicated shoot period it's always fun. Sue Jessop, my character, is as mad as a box of frogs and that's so liberating to play. She's a woman who knows how to have a laugh and doesn't take life too seriously. When Tom approached me to see if I was interested in the role, he suggested that I go back to my Liverpool roots and play her as Scouse. It's not something that I've done a great deal over the years of my career, as I've wanted to make sure that I am never typecast and always free to choose the sort of person that I want to play. But it's where I'm from, and I know that woman, so I said yes and it's been *a lorra lorra* fun so far.

Most of the cast are in most of the scenes, most of the time, and the writing is a tightly woven tapestry of emotional family dynamics, familiar banter and high jinks. It all spins on a sixpence and everyone must be fully switched on all the time. This is possibly easier for the younger actors than it is for me, but I'm up for the challenge and that's why the daily drive to the set is such an important time for me to get settled and become ready to take it all on. There's also an added dimension to this shoot as it's contrived to look as if it's all filmed by Sue's grandson, Sam, who originally needed to create a video diary for a school media assignment. This means we're all meant to look at the camera most of the time. It's not something that I've ever done, as I've been trained to never look down the lens, and early on in filming this felt so wrong to me. But I'm used to it now and it's actually great fun. Watching actors like Jim Howick, who plays Sue's son Paul, and Katherine Parkinson, who plays his wife Rachel, is a real joy as their timing is perfect, and the small flicks and kicks that they give to the camera are so skilfully done.

It's a miracle that I've managed to get through most of the series without dissolving into a puddle of laughter, which for good and ill has been quite a regular occurrence for me over the years. Very luckily the only time that I did was during that infamous watery scene when the family are all enjoying the warm waters of the pop-up pool that Granny Sue has bought them. They're all clinging onto its slippery sides trying to look as if they're enjoying it all when the water begins to change colour. Rachel puts her head under and her husband, noticing that he's now bobbing around in a mysterious brown liquid, turns his head and says to his wife in an incredulous voice, 'Is that? Have you—'

She looks at him and gives an indignant, 'Have I what?!'

It looks like a sewage leak or worse and the reactions of the family are priceless. The colour change begins slowly and subtly, but of course it's not a sewage leak or anything else, it's the dye from Rachel's hair, and the joke is that she's been denying dyeing her hair all episode. Katherine's face as the water turned brown around her made me laugh so much that I nearly slipped under and swallowed the murky stuff.

The rain has eased, and I head back to make-up just as the costume team arrive at my caravan to hang up what I'm wearing for the day's scenes. My character is very fond of wearing trainers, which is a relief as the idea of wearing high heels is out the window now as my joints are quite painful. It's not even 6.30 a.m. I've been up for over two hours and I'm hoping that the skin on my face has ironed itself out a bit now I need to look at myself in the mirror. Being on camera is like being looked at through binoculars and there's no covering up. The cameras turn over at 8.00 a.m. and my make-up needs to be given an hour so that the appropriate amount of Polyfilla, aka foundation, can be applied! We decided that Sue was the sort of woman that would go, *You know what? I fancy having a bit of pink in my hair. That'll cheer me up.* And so, that's what we did, and it stuck. So the morning make-up routine includes adding this too and then, depending on the scene and what the family is getting up to, we choose the colour of lipstick that feels right for the occasion.

It's not at all glamorous sitting in rollers at that time of day, staring at your seventy-seven-year-old face in the mirror. I much prefer observing others, whether that's people or wildlife. I'd much rather be staring at birds and foxes – and ants. Ants can stop me in my tracks, you know. If I see ants I'll pause what I'm doing and look. These tiny creatures always seem so purposeful and collaborative, and much more organised than us. People find them irritating but they intrigue me.

A few years ago, after a long stint of work, Michael and I treated ourselves to a holiday in Sardinia. We stayed in one of those places that has tiny lodges in the grounds, which makes you think that you actually live there and aren't on holiday at all. That notion was only scuppered by having to head out to the restaurant to eat every night. The place where we ate was outdoors and beautifully located, although the scenery was completely overshadowed by the waitress who was assigned to our table each evening.

She was a petite woman with tightly permed hair and glasses, and her formal black-and-white uniform seemed much too big for her, which made her seem even smaller. She was very good at her job and lovely with it. Each evening she would appear at our table and say in her lilting Italian English, 'Guuood eveeening. Ow r youuu? Ave youuu ad a guuood daiy?'

And we'd say, 'Thank you, yes, it's been lovely,' and I'd then ask, 'What's the fish on the menu tonight?'

And our waitress would say, 'Welllla, we ava—' and then she'd say the name of a type of fish that we'd never heard of.

'What sort of fish is that?' Michael would ask politely.

And no matter what sort of fish it was, each night she'd say, 'Eeets a leeeetle beet lika seeeeebazzzzz.' Each night, 'Eeets a leeeetle beet lika seeeeebazzzzz.' We both had to really steel ourselves, particularly me, because I knew that if I began to laugh, I'd have to run out before embarrassing myself. As you can imagine, I couldn't resist impersonating her.

Anyway, as I've said, this happened each night then afterwards we'd head back to our little lodge full up with fun and wine, and carrying a doggy bag of bread rolls. The rolls weren't for us, or the birds or the fish, they were for the ants! We'd sit on the terrace, sprinkle a few crumbs and out they'd come. They were much bigger than our ants at home and so we could see them more clearly, which was great. An individual ant would pick up a crumb and scurry it back into its hole. If there was a larger bit then a group would get themselves in line and march off with it on their shoulders in a brilliant display of ensemble work. Sometimes a pair of them would collaborate and we'd see their antennae moving rapidly as they communicated to each other. 'Alright, John, can you come over here and help out with this crumb?' It was brilliant. We'd sit there with a glass of wine, feeding crumbs and watching them for hours.

Watching ants is far preferable to looking at my much older face in the mirror as I have to do each morning on the shoot of *Here We Go*. It's odd being the age that I am, and I suppose staring in the mirror now makes me face myself in a way that I haven't before. Being older is something that I've not previously thought much about or worried over, but this is changing. On reflection, I think that there's a whole period of your life, growing up, getting married, having kids, getting divorced (although this isn't everyone) and working, when you're just going through it, getting on with it. Then you get to fifty or sixty and you say to yourself, *This is alright, I'm alright*, and you have a party. But things feel different now at this stage and the passing time can't be bartered with. As the Polyfilla-like make-up sinks into the life that's lined on my face, my blonde hair turns pink and the rollers come out to give a bounce to my hair that I need to put into my step, I lean in closer to the mirror to put on Sue's lippy. A lifetime of being other people, of looking at birds and other animals, flashes in front of me. The lives of all these women that I've inhabited are both there and not there, ghosts, in a way, from my past. Some have faded from memory far more than others but those that have left an imprint remind me of my own life story and the corners that we turn that can change the course of our direction. I have a fierce love for the women that I've played – the girlfriends, the wives, the sisters, mothers and grandmothers – and the glorious messiness and brilliance of their lives. They are within me for passing moments only, and they are not who I am, but I feel immensely lucky to have stepped out with them all, as well as always being able to return to me.

It's 7.45 a.m. I'm done. I grab another coffee and hurry back to my retreat on wheels to get into the costume for the day which is a flowery blouse, slacks, coloured trainers and a pink puffer jacket.

Today, Matthew, I'm going to be Sue Jessop.

However, dear readers, over the next chapters I'd like you to get to know me, Alison Hilda Campbell Steadman. Get your binoculars out! We're bird watching! This is the real me!

CHAPTER 2

Sent for a Reason

My heart was in my mouth, my chest felt tight, and I was doing my best not to show it. It was 1966. I was just twenty years old and properly leaving home and the city that I've lived in since I was born, for the first time. *Okay, keep walking, keeping walking, you've said goodbye, don't look back, try not to look back.* I looked back. My mum and dad were standing together tightly on the main concourse of Liverpool Lime Street Station, each clutching the other with one arm and waving enthusiastically with the other. *They're better actors than me*, I thought. One final wave before I boarded the train and we all put our best smile masks on. The station master blew on his whistle and gave a wave to the driver. We're off. A very posh sounding announcement confirmed that I was heading in the right direction. *Phew.* 'This is the 11.30 a.m. train from Liverpool Lime Street to London Euston with an expected arrival time of 2.00 p.m.' As the train drew away, my mum leant into my dad, and it looked as if she was saying something to him whilst they both kept their eyes firmly on me. There was a great deal of love in that moment. Years later Mum told me what she'd said in that railway-platform exchange.

'Oh, Dad,' which was what she always called him, 'I hope she doesn't grow away from us and does come home.'

My parallel thought was, *I can't wait to come back and see them soon.*

There were butterflies of excitement in my tummy about the thought that I was heading to London and drama school. This was it. I was also nervous and scared. *What if I'm rubbish? What if everyone is horrible? What if I run out of money? What if? What if?* I reminded myself of how proud my family were of me for getting this far and taking this step towards following my dream, and imagined my mum saying, as she always did in all my moments of worry, 'Come on, Alison, never say you can't, always say you can and you will.' I settled into my seat, clutching my bag of theatre books. *I can and I will*, I thought.

No going back now. I got myself comfy and closed my eyes as my mind began to wander as the rhythm of the train on the track gently gave my memory a shake. Over the years, I've become incredibly familiar with this train route and even now my heart still flutters as we cut through the sandstone on our approach to the station and a few minutes later I'm back. I'm home. These arrivals and departures are connected to so many important moments in my life. The clock in the concourse that was there when I left that first time is still there now which is comforting. Although I've spent more years away from the city that I have in it, there's a deep attachment that goes beyond my immediate family. I feel steeped in the history of the city as well as my own. It's where I'm from. It's in my DNA.

'She's been sent for a reason.' That's what Grandma Steadman used to say. It was August 1946 and people were slowly beginning to allow themselves to breathe out again after the trauma of the war years and the fear and sadness that had cloaked everything. Joy was beginning to seep into the nooks and crannies of day-to-day lives, and this is what I was born into. There was, quite literally, a boom in baby births in the years immediately following the end of the Second World War and so I'm officially a first-generation 'boomer'. How odd to be labelled before coming into being. On 26 August 1946, in the Liverpool Maternity Hospital on Oxford Street, Marjorie Steadman (née Evans) gave birth to her third daughter, ten years after her last daughter and twelve years after her first. Four years earlier, John Winston Lennon had been born there too, which was always a fabulous conversation starter when I was a drama student.

George Percival Steadman (usually George but sometimes Percy), my dad, wasn't at the birth. No dads were during that time, it wasn't expected or even allowed. He'd been hoping for a boy. He must have thought that my mum was a bit anxious when I wasn't because he said to her, 'You mustn't worry, girls are actually much better than boys. They'll look after you and be kind to you when you're older.' My grandma's 'sent for a reason' suddenly takes on a different meaning altogether! No matter, all the adults were thrilled to bits to have a new baby in the family, and welcomed the change and sense of a bright new future that it heralded. But it was an adjustment for the whole family, especially for my sisters, ten-year-old Pamela and twelve-year-old Sylvia. Sylvia thought that I had skin like a peach and was interested in me from the beginning. Pamela, however, thought that I was ugly. In fact she told my parents that I looked like a monkey, and only conceded reluctantly, twelve months later, that she thought I was quite pretty. Suddenly being thrust into the middle position must have been difficult for her as she'd had her place as the youngest in the family for such a long time.

I made my grand entrance into a family who were very close-knit. They had shouldered the experience of the war years with fortitude and resilience, as many families did. Liverpool, a major strategic port with dockyards, was attacked constantly and aggressively throughout the war years. There were days of constant bombing, so the road and rail routes out of the city were blocked on a regular basis. There were communal air-raid shelters that weren't fit for purpose and thousands of families were separated through evacuation and death. The 'blitz spirit' was a very real state of mind – everyone kept calm and carried on as they were instructed to. They came together and made the best of what they could, and this was no different for my family. But the impact of those years took their toll long after the bombs had stopped dropping.

My dad was on fire watch during the war. He wore a special rounded metal Zuckerman helmet and an armband marked 'SFP', which stood for Supplementary Fire Party. The helmet became part of my dressing-up box when I was younger; little did I know its significance. With this so-called protection on his head, Dad would head out to one of the Littlewoods buildings with their huge flat roofs and take up his position. There were men high up on rooftops on watch all over the city. Fire watch was a dangerous and essential wartime duty that was established in 1940 and taken on by volunteers who were compelled to do forty-eight hours a month on top of their day jobs. A fire watcher helped to smother flames to prevent fires from spreading, and if a fire had taken hold, they also helped to evacuate people from the building. It was a petrifying job in a city that was a principal target for the hostilities of the Luftwaffe.

Like many men, my dad was unable to participate in active service on medical grounds. He'd wanted to join the RAF, but as a young boy he had become critically ill with something that began as flu, then turned into pneumonia, and then became far more serious when he developed an abscess on one of his lungs and had to have a massive surgery to remove it, which took out most of his lung too.

The surgery initially began at home on the kitchen table and his sister, my Aunt Hilda, remembered picking up one of his ribs from the kitchen floor. It sounds horrendous. Can you imagine? I can still visualise the scar on his back that ran from the nape of his neck right down to his waist with huge stitch marks across it. He had another massive one under his arm with skin that folded in on itself, which is where they'd taken the parts of his lung out. The medical team saved his life, but he was extremely unwell and was at home and off school for a very, very long time, which set him back a lot. When he eventually returned, he had to work really hard to catch up. When he did, his efforts were rewarded with a copy of *Treasure Island* by Robert Louis Stevenson, which he put his signature in and cherished all his life before passing it on to me. I still hold it dear as a treasured keepsake of him. Sometimes I think that my dad was saved twice, once on the operating table and once when they wouldn't allow him to join the RAF. This was much to his annoyance, but not, I'm sure, to my mum's or his own family's, as he was grounded at home. Despite missing time at school, Dad was a very smart man who was good at many things and could have gone on to pursue his passions, but life was irrevocably altered for all the young men of his generation and class when Neville Chamberlain made his fateful announcement at 11.15 a.m. on Sunday 3 September 1939 that 'this country is at war with Germany'.

My family were able to stay together through most of the dark years of fighting, although my mum and sisters were evacuated to the coast further north at Southport for a bit of it as the bombing on Liverpool was incessant, which wasn't easy for any of them. When reflecting on that time, Mum, ever the optimist, would always say, 'We were so lucky, we had a home and so many people didn't.' Like all families at the time, mine was issued with an Anderson shelter to put in the garden and my dad, as instructed, camouflaged the curved corrugated roof with turf so that it wasn't visible from the air. Many years later he removed the shelter and turned the area into a rockery, which I'd play on, unaware of the significance of that part of our garden. Long after it had gone Mum would regale me with stories of urgent retreats to the earth-submerged shelter. 'I'd always have the pots and pans at the ready, a big one for me, a smaller one for Sylvia and the smallest for Pam,' she'd say, 'and we'd put them on our heads and make our way, mostly in the dark, to the air-raid shelter. We had to walk to it during the blackout and so your dad tied a rope to the handle on the back door and the other end of it to the shelter handle and we would follow along the line with the pots and pans on our heads.' I can't imagine how intimidating this must have been for my sisters who were young, but not young enough not to remember it or be affected by it. 'We'd get to the shelter,' Mum would say, 'and light the Tilley lamp, which kept us all cosy, and we were safe.' That was Mum through and through, always seeing the bright side and hoping for the best.

Once there was a tip-off that Liverpool docks were about to be bombed and if the ammunition didn't get moved fast it would all be lost. The stock was shunted away along a railway line that ran just one road away from ours. As bad luck would have it, the Germans got word of this and bombed the train. The bombs were wrapped in a cotton-like protective coating and when they detonated they sprayed out white confetti. Sylvia remembered that when Dad lifted the opening of the shelter the next morning the garden looked like Narnia. She told this story as if it was a wonderful, magical tale but I know it affected her deeply. It must have been petrifying and it's a sobering image that stays with me still. So much anguish and pain was absorbed by young children and the legacy of war that played out through my sisters' childhood was clear to see in their retelling of events. Pamela, who I later shared a bed with, was not able to go to sleep without protectively pulling the covers up over her head for as long as I can remember.

This was such a contrast to my own childhood as a baby boomer, growing up in the 1950s, a decade in which, as each year passed, everything got lighter and brighter. We all concurred with Harold Macmillan when he pronounced that: 'You've never had it so good.' It was all that I knew and how lucky I was to have been born when everything began to feel possible.

CHAPTER 3

Home Ground

'Oh, they've scored, they've scored,' Mum would cheer as the roar of the crowd from the Liverpool FC stadium on Anfield Road spilled out and over the rooftops. We could hear the game being played from our house on Sherwyn Road, and long before matches were televised, we'd know if we were the winning team from the noise outside. 'Oh, it's not us, it's them this time,' my mum would sigh. 'Never mind, there's still a bit to go,' as she willed her team to win. Our family home was a fifteen-minute walk from the famous football club, and once the ninety minutes of the game had played out, the streets would be awash with supporters re-enacting the theatre of the football match that they'd just experienced. Drama was all around me from an early age and perhaps this mapped out my road ahead. It was the men and boys that went to the match though (it only cost about sixpence, unlike the huge amount of money that it does today) and before and after each game, I'd look out of the window and see them all, in their thick overcoats that they'd pulled around for warmth, walking and chatting energetically about the game. The Everton ground was close too, but we were a family of proud Liverpool Football Club supporters through and through. Well, almost!

Is a love of football and a particular club something that's handed down from generation to generation? My mum was the biggest supporter of LFC in our house and she assumed that the rest of us, including my sons, would be too. On my eldest son Toby's tenth birthday she bought him a tour of Anfield as a special treat. The only problem was that Toby supported Manchester United so her gift hadn't landed as well as it might have with him. I hadn't plucked up the courage to let her know and so I said to Toby, 'Look, just thank Nana and we'll go along,' and he reluctantly agreed. The day of the tour arrived and off we went, with Toby doing his best not to feel that he was betraying his true team. It was just the two of us and the chap who'd been assigned to take us around was all puffed up and proud, giving it, 'This is the best club in the world … this is Kenny Dalglish's shirt … here's the cup that we won in 1965 …' and so on. He must have gone on for at least forty-five minutes before saying with a tremble of pride in his voice, 'And now,' fill in the drum roll, 'I'm going to show you the hallowed turf.' We went through the sacred tunnel and out into the stadium. Toby, who was stood looking at the hallowed turf with a nonplussed expression on his face, suddenly said, 'I'm a Man U supporter.' I looked at Toby, Toby looked at the ground and the chap looked at me, his face drained of all colour. There was a long pause before he said, 'And what do you think you're doing here then!' I jumped in and apologetically said, 'His nana bought him it as a birthday present as she's a HUGE Liverpool fan.' The chap gave us a contemptuous look and responded with, 'Right, there's the pitch, there's the Kop, that's it and that's that, time to go.' He walked away from us, and I looked at Toby and whispered, 'What did you say that for? You could have pretended!'

My ever honest ten-year-old replied, 'He was getting on my nerves going on about all the football shirts and how many cups they've won.'

He was right, it had been overly sentimental and not what a young Man U fan needed to hear. 'Well, just don't tell your nana,' I said, and we walked as quickly as we could out of the club and onto Anfield Road.

So, to answer my own question, a love of a particular football club isn't installed within the DNA of my family and handed down from generation to generation. But we are Scouse and proud of it. The whole extended family lived within walking distance of 'the hallowed turf' and each other's houses and this was our community. We were all on the same team.

22 Sherwyn Road, Anfield, L4 was home to me for twenty years. Built in the 1930s, our three-bedroom house was identical to all the other houses on the road, as well as all of those around it. The estate was constructed as part of a nationwide housing initiative that sprung up between the two world wars. The layout of each house was almost the same and with a garden at the front and back there was more outdoor space than many of the houses that are built today. There were three roads that looked exactly the same: Sherwyn, Berwyn and Corwyn, and the top and bottom of each was bookended by Hildebrand Road and Hilary Road. As children, we played outside all the time, which was safe as there were hardly any cars around. In fact, I think only two families on our road had a car. Mostly people walked everywhere or took a bus. Rounders was a favourite game; we used the gateposts as the bases and would bat the ball as hard and fast as we could to give ourselves half a chance of getting around our makeshift pitch. It's a wonder that no windows were broken during the action. In the winter, when it was icy, and it

was always much icier then than it is now, we created a slide on a section of the road and would slip and slalom up and down it at lightning speed without a care of breaking bones or doing any damage. There were lots of children of my age in the vicinity, all of us the result of the post-war baby boom, and so playmates were never in short supply. Our front door would be knocked at regularly. My mum would answer it and one friend or other would say, 'Is Ali coming out to skip?'

'Ali doesn't live here,' my mum would always reply, 'but Alison does.' I was mortified, but it was always Alison and never Ali in our house.

The war was still very present in people's memories and there were reminders of it everywhere, which must have been haunting for everyone who went through it. But for my generation, the rubble-strewn patches of land, where bombs had once wreaked havoc (including the huge bomb site that was the result of that dreadful night my sister Sylvia used to tell me about) now became our adventure lands. We'd play on them without a care in the world and with no understanding of the sacrifices that had been made just a few years earlier.

Our green front door, like all the green front doors, led into a small hallway and slightly to the left there was a flight of stairs. On the right of the hallway at the front of the house there was a sitting room that we only ever went into at Christmas and for special teas like birthdays. The room that we all congregated in, the dining room, was the next room down and then directly opposite the front door was the tiny little kitchen with a door and a few steps down to the garden. That was it, small and perfectly formed and home to the five of us. The upstairs was the same footprint as downstairs with a bedroom to the front that looked over the road, another to the back that looked out over the garden and then our box room, which had three little windows, and the bathroom next to that.

None of the radiator pipes in the house were boxed in and there was a hot water pipe that ran along the width of the bedroom that faced the garden. I wasn't quite tall enough to reach the handle that opened the window outwards and so I would place my feet on the pipe to give myself the extra bit of height that was required. There was always a dip in the pipe, which made me think that my sisters had stood at the same place a few years earlier. The house was telling its own story and it felt comforting to know that I was living amongst the history that my sisters and parents had carved out before I was born. Standing on the pipe I could see outside and, when I was a bit older, I would act out various characters to whomever was in the garden. One day, it must have been after the coronation, Queen Elizabeth II was pulled from my repertoire. I flung open the window and imagined that I was standing on the balcony of Buckingham Palace in front of a cheering crowd. 'My people, my people,' I declaimed, as I waved to the adoring masses that I imagined were standing below me.

'Alison, is everything alright?' Mrs Grey from next door had seen me and thought that I was calling for help.

I was so embarrassed and, uncrowning myself, said, 'Yes, Mrs Grey, everything's fine,' and shut the window.

While my communication from the back bedroom window might only be noticed by Mrs Grey, my parents' bedroom window on the front was to give me a means of communication to all my friends on the street. It was 5 November 1954 but I wasn't outside enjoying the fireworks or the bonfire with my friends as intended, but instead was in a very unfamiliar hospital bed having been struck down by scarlet fever. An ambulance had collected me a few days earlier so that I could be immediately isolated and quarantined, which is what they did before the arrival of antibiotics to avoid neighbourhood panic and the possibility of it spreading through entire schools. The nice ambulance man said, 'How old are you, love? Is this your doll?'

I nodded and then said, 'I'm eight.'

'What's your doll called then?'

'Nina.'

Nina was quite a big doll that looked like a toddler. She had been a present from Father Christmas the previous December and I'd grown very fond of her even though I had wanted another baby like my doll Jonny.

Jonny was a little boy (he may not have been, but I thought that he was) who was small and like a newborn to me. I cared for him as if he was real: feeding him, clothing him, telling him stories and giving him a bath every night. His arms and legs were attached to his body with elastic, and they filled with water during bath time and so there was always an unceremonious yet loving pulling of each limb and emptying of the water that was inside. Jonny was my surrogate baby and my friend. Pam, my middle sister, who was creative and artistic, would knit for him constantly, so he had a wardrobe of outfits, hats and woolly suits that made him the best dressed doll on our street.

When the ambulance arrived, the thought of Jonny coming to hospital with me was too much to cope with, and so I'd picked up Nina.

'I'm sorry, love,' said the ambulance man, 'but you can't take Nina. She's gonna have to stay at home, cos if you bring her, you'll have to leave her in the hospital just in case she's picked up a disease.'

I'd no idea what he was talking about and just nodded as I handed my second favourite child over to him.

And so, there I was in a cold, sterile hospital room on my own. It was Guy Fawkes Night and all that I could hear was the tantalising whizz and pop of fireworks as I lay on my back looking up at the orange ceiling, which was possibly that colour to induce joy and happiness but left me wrung out and cross with the world. *I need to get out of here.* In the heat of my fever I would fantasise about how to escape, but then I'd fall asleep and my bolt for freedom didn't happen until the very end of the month when I was officially discharged. My time in hospital had passed so slowly and the imposed isolation was torture for me. I have never been comfortable being on my own and even though it was just a matter of weeks it had felt like forever. The season had changed completely and it was cold and dark when I returned home. *Had anyone missed me? What has changed while I've been away?* I was desperate to reconnect with my friends and almost immediately, and with purpose, I went upstairs to my parents' room to signal to the street that, at long last, I was in residence again. Luckily for me, the change of air had steamed up all the windowpanes so they perfectly served my intention. I reached up with my right hand and, using my forefinger, urgently wrote and then underlined two words in the hope that my friends, who I'd missed with all my heart, would see and take note: 'Alison's Home'!

The garden at number 22 was small but well-tended and Dad, a natural gardener, had worked in it tirelessly to cover over any remnants from the air-raid days. The only clues that things may once have been a little different were to be found in his garden shed, a treasure trove, which I regarded as an extension of my play area. I made our shed into a little home and put curtains up on the windows. I rearranged all my dad's woodworking tools so that there was space to sit, which I made comfortable with old cardigans. I found all sorts of things in that shed including my grandma's beautiful Edwardian parasol made of cream cotton and lace and the small gas masks that were to be used in case of any emergency. It's hideous to think that these masks went from protecting two of the most important people in my life to becoming props for storytelling and my handmade adventures. I was still too young to know the facts and perhaps my family didn't want to travel back to that dangerous time, and so shutting things away from view in the shed at the back of the garden kept their unwanted memories at bay.

Dad loved his lawn and always kept it smart and framed with colourful shrubs. There was a beautiful laburnum tree at the bottom of the garden, which turned a glorious golden yellow when it flowered. The grumpy neighbour whose garden backed onto ours hated it and complained about the leaves and the petals falling over her fence and causing a mess. She went on and on and Mum said, 'You're going to have to cut that down, Dad.' He didn't want to but, in the end, he did. I'm still sad when I think about him losing his beautiful laburnum tree. Our garden was like Tom and Barbara Good's, full of delicious things to eat, and both of my parents were determined that ours would be a good life. Dad had a greenhouse where he grew tomatoes and seeded other things, and I loved going in there to get warm and to breathe in the smell of the sweet and earthy tomatoes, which told us they were ripe and needed picking. They always tasted delicious, tangy and sweet, and we ate them straight from the vine. Taking centre stage in the garden was the James Grieve apple tree, bearing fruit that was always slightly tart but perfect for apple sauce. The garden was a baker's paradise, and my mum was constantly making cakes and pies from whatever was available: rhubarb, raspberries, blackberries. In the early 1950s there was still rationing, and butter, sugar and margarine weren't readily available, but I can't remember a time when there wasn't a warm homemade cake or pie waiting for me.

We had a regular cycle of meals according to what Mum was able to buy with our family's rations. Our weekly menu included rich beef stews and there was always a pan of Scouse on the hob, lamb which was left to simmer in one pot alongside potatoes and onions so that it blended into a tender, tasty, complete meal that could be served straight on to our plates. On a Friday, Mum would poach fish in milk and we'd have it with creamed potatoes and vegetables. Sunday was a roast, usually lamb, and it was my job to make sauce out of mint leaves from the garden.

Food rationing ended in 1954 when I was eight and after that being in our kitchen was like being in cake- and pudding-making heaven with sticky syrup sponges, oozing jam roly-poly, stick-on-the-top-of-your-mouth fruit crumbles, creamy rice pudding and cinnamon bread-and-butter pudding on a constant loop, not to mention sponge cakes and scones. The buttery sweet aroma would waft through the house and teatime was always something to look forward to. The productivity was the same in most of the kitchens on the streets where we lived, and I suppose people were making up for what they couldn't do during the war years. Money was still scarce and there wasn't a great deal of extra, but Mum and Dad did what they could, and we never went without.

Our garden was my true happy place and during warmer weather and over the summer months I was out there constantly. Mum would drape an old sheet over the washing line and lower it down to make a simple tent. This was my den and I'd gather up my cat, Whisky, and my tortoise, Cocky, some jam sandwiches and water, and head to the tent. I loved Cocky and would pick dandelions to feed him – it always looked like he was smiling when I offered him one of the bright yellow flowers – and he would gratefully pop his little head into an egg cup of water to take minuscule sips.

Is a love of animals passed on from family member to family member? My dad's sister, my Aunt Hilda, who had a natural touch with animals and knew how to care for them, taught me a great deal. She had a budgie that talked incessantly. When my Uncle Cliff was returning from work Aunt Hilda would say, 'Oh, here's Cliff,' and the budgie would repeat, 'Here's Cliff! Here's Cliff!' and then go into a rendition of 'Georgie Porgie, pudding and pie', which I loved. Hilda also had a tortoise called Sammy that lived with her for over sixty years. He was only a little thing and his shell curled up at the back and there was a little hole just at the tip. Aunt Hilda would thread a length of thick string through it long enough for Sammy to be able to explore the whole garden without getting lost. When she became elderly and had to move from her house, her son took Sammy on, and they lived together happily for many years.

No strings were attached to my own tortoise, and he'd join me as I'd venture out from the tent to mooch around the garden to look for caterpillars. My favourites had thick, furry brown coats. When I was about five a workman came to repair the garden fence and told me that in Africa the caterpillars were so big that they were used as scarves and that the rhubarb leaves were so enormous that they were used as umbrellas. Even, then, I wasn't so sure he was telling the truth. Our Anfield garden was full of caterpillars and, later in the summer, lovely butterflies. I'm thrilled when I see a butterfly these days, which isn't often, and saddened that pesticides and weed killers have impacted on their numbers so greatly since my childhood.

With my sisters being so much older than me, I was alone a great deal, so comfort and company were found in the garden, its inhabitants and from my pets. From an early age, animals and nature were a passion, and at junior school I drew a picture of a cat trying to get into a rubbish bin for food, for the PDSA charity and wrote underneath it: 'Please Be Kind to Me and All My Animal Friends'. The more of a menagerie I could gather around me the better. I begged my parents for a rabbit, and they eventually gave in. Skipper needed his own home of course and so my dad made a hutch which had a run attached so that in good weather he was outside and when it was inclement, he joined me in the warmth and protection of the shed. Skipper was black and white and full of character, which translates as quite mischievous. In the summer he would dig his way out of his run and scamper up and down the garden eating all the newly sprouted vegetables. His favourites were the tiny new lettuces grown by our lovely Scottish neighbour, Mrs Grey. He was a grazer and would nibble off a tiny bit at a time from each lettuce. If only he'd eaten a whole one, no one would have noticed or if they did, they wouldn't have made a fuss about it. Not that Mrs Grey did. Grumpy, cross Mrs Burns from six houses away did though and sadly, after a slew of complaints, Skipper's vegetable nibbling had become too much so it was arranged that he would be taken back to the pet shop. If only I'd been old enough to argue his case based on him needing his five a day! Poor old Skipper was zipped into a shopping bag. Carrying the bag myself, I walked with Mum towards the pet shop. To get there we had to cross a small patch of open ground, and this was my chance to do my final good deed for Skipper. I quickly unzipped the bag and encouraged him to escape shouting, 'Run, Skipper! Run!' As quick as a flash, as if she had anticipated it, my mum grabbed the bag from me and firmly hooked it over her arm and off we went again. My escape plan for Skipper foiled, I tearfully handed over my much-loved friend and, in exchange, to cheer me up, I was allowed to choose something else, so long as it wasn't an animal. Indifferently I selected a brush to groom Whisky's long hair and refused to be happy about the very unequal trade-off.

As most of my relatives lived close by, we were often in each other's houses. I spent a lot of time in my grandmas' gardens, as both of them shared my parents' love, and my memories of them are always of sunny days and lupins. Grandma and Grandpa Evans' garden was small but cleverly paved to guide you around the elegant flower bed and there was a fence at the very bottom with a gap in it where I would peer out at the allotments, which had been so essential during the war. It's funny what the mind stores. I remember being four years old and trapping my finger in her kitchen door. It was the most painful thing I'd ever experienced, and the discomfort was persistent. Warm milk and being taken outside into the sunshine to smell the flowers was the best medicine.

When my Grandpa Evans became unwell, we'd often pop round to spend time at their house. One day I was taken upstairs to see him and then the next time we visited I wasn't allowed upstairs at all, and this confused me. My grandpa, Maurice Evans, had suffered a heart attack and had been told that bed rest was the cure. Nowadays he'd have been hospitalised and given tests but back in the late 1940s, bed rest is what was advised. My last memory of my grandpa is of standing by his bed and him reaching out and taking my hand, and us holding hands without saying anything, and me not understanding why he had been in bed for so long. It's the hand holding that I remember the most, even though his skin was tissue-paper thin, and his fingers so skinny compared to mine, his frail grip was soft and warm. He died suddenly and unexpectedly as my grandma was handing him a cup of tea. Our whole family was devastated. They didn't know how to tell me. I mean, how do you explain death to a young child? He was there one day and not the next.

It must have been very lonely for my Grandma Evans without her husband as in those days, apart from us, all she had for company was an old crackling radio which she'd put on for a couple of hours a day. Whatever we might say about television these days at least hearing other voices or becoming absorbed in a drama can bring comfort. The lively sound of others can fill an empty house and sadly Grandma Evans must have experienced some long and lonely nights. In her hallway she had a collection of pale-grey clay death masks hanging on the walls. They were images of her brothers who had died in the First World War. I can remember feeling scared and trying to avert my gaze. It must have made her terribly sad to be there all alone and with such powerful remembrances around her. Sometimes when I was about to leave after a visit, she'd say, 'Just hold on there for a bit,' and she'd go upstairs and take some loose farthings from a velvet drawstring bag that she kept under her bed, and, to my delight, give me some. She refused to believe that farthings were no longer legal tender and once she sent me on an errand to buy a small Hovis loaf clutching a handful of them. The lady in the corner shop wouldn't take the money and, on my bread-less return my grandma was cross, saying, 'That's nonsense, of course it's real money. Just go back and tell her that I say so.' I didn't go back, and she reluctantly accepted that farthings were no longer in use. On another visit to her house, I saw her combing her long brown hair. It was the first and only time that I ever saw it hanging loose, as usually it was pinned and rolled to the side. With it hanging down to her shoulders and centrally parted, my childhood imagination made me think that she looked like Jesus, although I refrained from telling her so. Grandma Evans wasn't overly religious, no one in our family was, but I can remember on one Good Friday seeing her weep about the suffering that Jesus had endured on the cross which I'm sure must have been linked to her own losses and her ongoing feeling of pain.

After a few years of her living alone it was decided that Grandma Evans would come and live with us at 22 Sherwyn Road. There was no choice really: she needed her family around her and her health had suffered. It wasn't ideal as our house was small and already crowded with all of us living there, but it was what had to happen. She shared a bed with me, and each night would rub her chest with Vicks VapoRub because she always had a bad cold or a chesty cough. The minty smell of camphor would infuse into the sheets. All that I can say in its favour is that it may have helped me from getting as many colds as I might have done!

It wasn't always easy for my parents as my grandma could be a little interfering, 'What time is this to get to bed?' Or, 'What time is this to get up?' Overall though it was fun for me as having her in the house offered another person to play with and to prod for stories. She was a trained milliner and after leaving school at fourteen had learned how to sew and make clothes, which she went on to do for my mum as a child, a teenager and a grown woman. Although my mum could cook and bake, she never learnt to sew because she hadn't needed to. My grandma was always on hand to hem a skirt or sew a button on a coat as well as to make copious outfits for my dolls.

Grandpa Steadman, whom I never met, died when my dad was fourteen, which was a huge loss for him, his brother Ron and sister Hilda. We were close to Grandma Steadman though. Although she never lived with us, Agnes Steadman, née Taylor, was a solid influence in my life and I could see so much of her influence on my dad too. Often, when we were alone together in the house, she'd read me stories and would always go to the funny section. Within moments we'd both be rocking with laughter, which, even way back then, I found hard to stop. I loved her story times. If it wasn't Grandma Steadman telling me stories, it would be my dad. He'd tuck me into bed, then pull out a Rupert the Bear annual, and we'd travel into Nutwood and the tales of Rupert, Bill Badger, Tiger Lily and their friends.

Grandma Steadman was a great cook too and especially famous for her puff-pastry mince pies which we looked forward to each Christmas. After Dad retired he started to cook. He was determined to make puff pastry as light and buttery as his mum's and we were subjected to endless rounds of sausage rolls. Each time he'd say to me, 'Now, then, what do you think, Alison, are these as good as the ones last week?

And I'd say, 'They're really good, Dad.'

Then the following week he'd ask the same question and I'd cheekily reply, 'Actually last week's weren't that good.'

He'd cheerily respond with, 'Well, why did you say they were then?' And out would come the mixing bowl, flour and butter, and he'd begin again.

He loved to cook; it was in his family and my mum didn't seem to mind at all when he spent time in the kitchen. She didn't feel like she was being pushed out; in fact she quite enjoyed it after years of being tied to the stove every day. Dad would cook at special occasions. At Easter he loved taking time to make a simnel cake in the proper way: soaking the dried fruits, candied peel and orange zest in brandy and leaving it overnight before adding the spices and other ingredients the following day. Years later, when I had my own family, my parents came to stay for Christmas. I'd made the cake and just needed to ice it. Dad said, 'Oh, are you going to ice the cake tonight? Can I join you?' He sat with me for a couple of hours in the kitchen, while I iced this cake. My boys were little, so I'd decided to make a fun snow scene rather than do anything fancy. There were snowballs, a snowman and children dressed in scarves and hats, which I created out of fondant icing and different food colourings. It was quite fiddly and at the end he said, 'That's really good, well done.' I could tell that he loved being part of it all and it's a memory that I cherish.

There's a great deal of talk about generational wealth these days, when assets are passed on down the line ensuring the well-being and security of a line and name. It's feudal and historically it's always been about property and money. For me, though, generational wealth is what I've experienced within my own family, and it comes freely. My grandparents offered kindness, laughter, instruction and love to their children, my parents, and in turn my parents did the same for Sylvia, Pamela and me. We didn't live in a huge house, we didn't have much, but we had a lot, and it was all contained within the four walls of our own hallowed turf at 22 Sherwyn Road. It was our home ground and we had scored.

CHAPTER 4

Dining In

One side of the freshly washed, and now, eventually, dry sheet, is dangling down from the top of the ironing board. It looks like a ski slope or a waterfall and each time my mum finishes pressing a width of it she eases it over the edge and begins on the new section and more crisp white fabric softly unfurls on the floor and edges closer to where I am sitting. We're the only ones at home. The dining room is warm and cosy as usual, and still has the old-fashioned mantle and steel fire with an oven inside it. There's a little ledge in front of the oven door and sometimes, because I am still small, I sit there as it is so lovely and toasty. Today though I'm sitting on the floor mesmerised by the billowing white material and the wooden criss-crossed legs of the ironing board that my mum is standing behind. Each time the hot iron presses down on the sheet I take in the deepest breath that I can, to suck up the fresh cotton aroma that is released from the freshly laundered bed linen. It's a heady sensation for me, but not so much for my mum I'm sure. I'm too young to realise how unfulfilling it must be for her to spend time routinely going between the dolly tub in the kitchen, where she washes and rinses all our clothes and bed linen, and the mangle, before folding the washing over the three long bars of dark wood that are attached by rope to the ceiling pulling them up high to hang there until they are dry enough to bring down and move onto the final stage, which takes place in the dining room. A washing machine didn't arrive in our house until I was in my teens and, looking back, I think about how tired my mum must have been keeping on top of looking after everyone, and how good she was at not letting us all know it. She always kept going and never made a fuss about things. *From rise of morn to set of sun. Woman's work is never done.*

Putting the iron down carefully on the metal cooling section at the wide end of the board, Mum walks over to the sideboard and says, 'Let's put the wireless on, shall we?' It is just after lunch, my favourite time of day, and my answer is always yes. The new programme, *Listen with Mother*, first broadcast in 1950, when I was four, must have brought a momentary peacefulness for mums all over the country, whose day to day was a relentless round of washing, cleaning and sorting everything for everyone, and without the mod cons of today. The radio makes a crackling noise before tuning into the right frequency and then the gentle sound of a piano flows over the radio waves and a friendly voice says, 'Are you sitting comfortably?' I respond that I am and then the very familiar, 'Then we'll begin.'

Our dining room was full of stories and was the heart of the house. People didn't go out to socialise as much then as we do now; even though the war was over, the early 1950s were years of austerity. Despite this our house always felt cheery and lively, and my parents would regularly get together with friends to share convivial nights full of humour and chat. These weren't raucous evenings and very little alcohol was drunk. My dad, on a very rare occasion, might have a whisky and my mum a sherry, but that would be it. One of their friends, always the same man, would instigate the singing. Everyone would join in together and the house would fill with the notes of optimism. These homemade evenings undoubtedly had an influence on me, and I'd often do my own 'turn' to entertain my family, on request, and sometimes of my own volition.

When there was nothing interesting to watch on the television that stood pride of place in the dining room from 1953 onwards, Mum would say, 'Why don't you just turn that off, love, and do Hylda Baker for us?' Hylda Baker, comedian, actress, music-hall entertainer, was my favourite TV performer and was well known for her catchphrase, 'She knows, you know.' She was incredibly funny and glamorous, and this combination was alluring to me, captivating my young imagination. I studied her in meticulous detail, from the sound of her voice, to how she walked, to what she wore and then, once perfected, like a butterfly emerging from a cocoon, I'd adorn myself with my mum's costume jewellery, her best coat and fox-fur stole, which I'd fling flamboyantly over my shoulders and then flounce into the dining room saying, 'She knows, you know.'

Another infamous dining-room turn was less an impression and much more of an improvisation (the first of many) that some might call a prank, and it definitely hadn't been requested by my parents. I loved pranks and would take any opportunity to play one. It was an ordinary evening at number 22, Mum and Dad were downstairs watching the television and as I was only nine years old it was time for me to head upstairs and to bed. At this time I shared a room with Pam, who was still living at home, but she was out. As I hated going to sleep on my own, I routinely tried to find ways of delaying the moment. I'd reluctantly done as I was told and was in the bathroom brushing my teeth when the idea came to me. Do you remember Gordon Moore's Toothpaste? I don't know if there as an actual Gordon Moore, but this was the name of a very fashionable toothpaste of the time. It was bright red and its claim to fame was that it made your gums turn pinker so that your teeth looked whiter. Not that I was bothered by any of this, but the redness of the paste flicked a switch in me. *It looks just like blood*, I thought. *It looks just like real blood.* Looking in the mirror, I held the tube up against the top of my cheekbone and gave it a gentle squeeze. It was runny stuff and came out in an enthusiastic spurt and then trickled quite realistically down my face. It looked brilliant and so I did the same on the other side of my face but a bit higher up. That was step one. Next, I tiptoed into my parents' bedroom across the little hallway and unzipped the make-up bag that was always on my mum's dressing table.

My mum loved her make-up, and the bag was a rainbow collection of eyeshadows and lipsticks. She'd always say, 'Put on a bit of lippy and you'll always feel better.' It's something that I took to heart, and no matter how early it is, I still won't leave the house without brightening my face with a bit of lip colour. After I'd left home, when Mum was visiting me in London, she would always get off the train and pop into the first chemist that she came across saying, 'I just need to nip in here,' and out she'd come with yet another new lipstick! She'd obviously ignored Grandma Evans' warning, who, when I was little said to me, 'Promise me that you won't wear lipstick, Alison. Don't you start to wear lipstick now. You put the lipstick on and by the end of the day it's gone! Where do you think it's gone to? Well,' she continued, 'it's gone into your stomach, so that means that you're eating lipstick every day! That's not a very good thing to do is it, Alison? If you wear it all your life, just think about all the lipstick that you'll eat!' This was possibly one of her prankish stories – of which more shortly. Clearly neither Mum nor I followed her advice.

I rummaged around in the make-up bag and found exactly what I needed, blue eye shadow, and pressed my middle finger into it. Lifting the deep-blue-stained digit up to my check I then blotched it into the drippy red toothpaste that was running down my face and smudged it in a bit, so it looked like purple bruising. The final touch was to mess up my hair before heading downstairs to make my entrance. The door to the dining room was slightly ajar and I could hear voices from the entertainment show that my parents were watching on TV. There was clapping and it sounded as though it was coming to an end. This was useful to me as it would cover the noise of my footsteps on the slightly creaky staircase. All set, I positioned myself carefully out of sight – it was a bit like being in the wings of a theatre – and waited for my moment. It came somewhere between the end of the short news bulletin and the beginning of the next programme, and, on cue, before Mum got up to put the kettle on the stove, I let out a blood-curdling yell, hurled myself into the room and fell dramatically onto the floor. It felt so good, and I was positive that it would delight my parents. Mum jumped out of her seat and began screaming and crying. This wasn't the response that I'd anticipated. My euphoria evaporated, and I swiftly came out of character and rushed to comfort her whilst bursting into tears at the same time. It then went from bad to worse and became a true comedy of errors as the red and blue runny paste from my face was now on the carpet as well as Mum's Saturday-night blouse, as I had pressed my head against it as she'd opened her arms to me. It wasn't quite the grand entrance that I'd planned, and reviews weren't favourable for the toothpaste turn.

I'd inherited the prank gene from my Grandma Evans. She loved to perform and make up characters and I think this influenced my own love of telling stories without me realising. She also loved to dress up and have fun with people. One day, so the story goes, after baking an apple pie, she decided to change into my grandpa's clothes from top to toe, from his cloth cap to his working boots, and then head out to visit my parents who lived about a ten-minute walk away. It was twilight, foggy and gloomy, and the street lighting wasn't as bright as it is today. So when Grandma Evans knocked at my parents' front door and my dad opened it, all he saw was a shadowy figure who then tried, with a freshly baked apple pie in hand, to push past him. My dad, George, was an incredibly mild-mannered man and never raised his voice to anyone, never mind his hand, but here was a scally, or so he thought, trying to break into our house and so he bopped them on the nose. He and Grandma Evans had stern words after that apparently as she was always convinced that he knew it was her!

Grandma Evans and I weren't the only performers in the family. Once, when I was playing in the shed, I found an old violin. I picked it up and went back into the house to ask about it. My dad was in the dining room listening to an opera on the gramophone. I'd no idea what opera was at the time and other than being told that the lady singing was called Maria Callas, and that the singing story he was listening to was called *La Traviata*, the high notes passed over me. Clutching the neck of the violin in one hand, I prodded Dad, 'Whose is this?'

'It's mine,' he said. 'I used to play it when I was a young lad. Not as young as you are now, maybe the same age as Pam is, about fifteen.'

This was all news to me. My dad only listened to music, he didn't play it, but now he was telling me that he did, and I was enthralled.

'I joined an amateur orchestra,' he went on. 'The violin wasn't an easy instrument to play, and they used to give us hard pieces to learn. I practised and practised then during the rehearsal we got to the most difficult bit and I heard this terrible screech. It was coming from my violin!' Keeping me hanging on his every word he continued, 'The conductor stopped us all and the room became silent until I held up my bow and said, "It was me that made that noise, sir, I'm sorry, I'm sorry."' I felt so terrible for him. '"No need to apologise, George. In fact, well done. You were the only boy to try and play that difficult bit and you should be proud of yourself."' Everyone else had mimed the section, hoping that their neighbour would cover them, and my dad was the only one that had continued to play, which summed him up to a tee. No matter what he did, even though it might not have been what he wanted to do, he'd do it to the best of his ability.

While my dad's operas were what I heard most often on the gramophone, on other occasions my sisters Sylvia and Pam would take over the dining room and play their records. Sylvia was a huge music fan and she'd have all the latest albums by people like Perry Como and Glenn Miller. Pam loved Bill Haley and played 'Rock Around the Clock' whenever she got the chance. On a Saturday night, when they were getting ready to go out on the town, they'd put their favourite tunes on the gramophone, hot iron their starched underskirts so that they stuck out, roll, set and style their hair with bobby pins and hairspray, and then put on their make-up. Their weekly transformations entranced me, and I'd just sit, listen, watch and absorb, mesmerised by it all. I loved it. Whenever I hear the opening beats of 'The Chattanooga Choo Choo', one of Sylvia's Glenn Miller favourites, I'm taken right back to those dressing-up days.

By the time I was at school my sisters were in their late teens and thinking about leaving home and preparing for marriage. In some ways, it was a bit like having three mums. When they weren't at work or going out with their boyfriends, they'd look after me and get me ready for bed. I shared a room with Pam but in the middle of the night I'd sneak into bed with one or other of them as I hated lying on my own. Feeling their warmth and breathing as I snuggled up with them always brought five-year-old me great comfort and security. They might not have felt the same aged fifteen and seventeen! The house was always bubbling with sound and laughter when they were around and when they left home for good, I was devastated and felt terribly lonely.

Sylvia, the eldest, was the first to get married. She met her husband-to-be at one of the dance halls in Liverpool. He was in the Merchant Navy; the boats would dock in Liverpool and the sailors would disembark for some R & R – and sometimes stay for longer! After her wedding we were all standing in the street waving the newly married couple off as they drove away at 10 p.m., which to me felt very late. I can clearly remember saying to my mum, 'When's our Sylvia coming home?' and being heartbroken by my mum's, 'She's not, love. She's married and is going to live in her own house.'

Pamela was still at home though to have as my night-time companion and make cakes with. Pam was an amazing baker. Every Sunday we'd get out the mixing bowls, measuring jugs and wooden spoons to make a chocolate cake that was topped with lusciously thick chocolate-flavoured icing. 'You make the best sponge out of all of us, Alison,' she'd say, 'because you're little and don't mind whipping up all the ingredients until it's a perfect mix. Mum and I just do it dead quickly now, but you put in the time.' Praise indeed for doing the hard mixing that ensured that the cake was light and airy.

Pam always let me get an advance taste of what was to come by licking the bowl clean. Those Sundays were a very special time together, but within a year Pamela was gone too, and it was all change for me.

Story time has finished and the ironing and folding of sheets continues. As the last bit of laundry is ironed and added to the folded assembly of sheets and towels that tower on the table, Mum engages in her usual few wrestling rounds with the ironing board as she fights with its legs to try and get them to collapse and lie flat, before standing it firmly in a corner and then turning the radio off until the next day. This is our daily shared couple of hours of toil and tales, and Mum's labour of love never falters as she smooths over the linen and any worries that we might have had.

Listen with Mother was fifteen minutes long and I loved it but the tales that I most wanted to hear were those told by my family about times gone by. 'Where did you meet Dad? Was it love at first sight? Was it romantic?' I'd eagerly ask, trying to distract my mum long enough from what she was doing to answer and tell me the real-life story. 'Well, I used to see him walk past my house each day, she'd say. We lived quite close to each other, and he would walk past at the same time each day of the week so I looked out for him. Don't tell him that I did, mind. And the more he walked past, the more I fell for him. I don't know if he felt the same at first, but I knitted him a long dark-blue scarf and gave it to him, and then we started going out together. It all felt very romantic to me and when he asked me to marry him, my answer was yes. I was nineteen years old when we got married, and so was he, and even now I think that I couldn't have married a better person than your dad.'

Sometimes on *Listen with Mother* there was a story that was set in London. The presenter would say, 'And along comes the big red bus.' I used to think that this was strange, *Why was it red?* All the buses that I'd seen in Liverpool were green, not red, so it made London seem very odd and far away, not a real place at all. Green was the familiar and comforting colour of my early childhood. It was the colour of buses, the colour of our window frames and the colour of the front door to the home that I lived in for twenty years, 22 Sherwyn Road, where my love of storytelling and performing began.

CHAPTER 5

History Repeating Itself

At last we'd reached the Palace. I stood in front of the huge black gates looking up with awe and wonder as my imagination and curiosity kicked into overdrive. There was *the* actual balcony that I'd seen on television when the newly crowned Queen had come out from the privacy of the rooms that lay behind. The balcony that I had pretended I was on in our back bedroom window. I was ten years old and my aunt had treated me to my first ever day trip to London. There was a lot to take in. The buses really were red for one thing! Without my parents, it was just my aunt, my cousin and me, and my excitement level was dialled up to the highest frequency. There was no chat about where we wanted to head to first, we all knew, and so that's how we found ourselves standing there looking straight up at Buckingham Palace through the enormous black gates and above the bearskin caps of the Queen's Guard. *Oh, my goodness. This is where the real Queen lives.* There was a momentary strange feeling of being caught up in time and history.

My childhood fascination with the Queen began when I was six going on seven, during the year of the coronation. My parents had bought a television, our first, especially for the occasion and one of my strongest memories is of the newly crowned Queen Elizabeth II, looking like a fairy-tale princess, waving from the most beautiful golden carriage that I'd ever seen. In fact, the only golden carriage that I'd ever seen. It was magical and I fell in love with all of it: the romance, a queen, a bejewelled and glittering crown, a sparkly dress, a palace and a golden carriage.

Large marquees were put up in Sherwyn Road and all the neighbouring streets. In the weeks before the coronation we were all given crêpe paper to make red, white and blue flowers. I spent hours cutting out crêpe paper circles and then folding them in half and half again before tying the bottom with string and opening it all out to reveal a crinkly flower. We garlanded the windows and the street to transform it into a celebration of our nation and the momentous and historic event that we were all going to be a part of. 2 June 1953 was a day for all of us and whether you were English, Scots, Welsh or Irish, in Liverpool there was a coming together and spirits soared. The sun shone and I was dressed in a new frock and my hair was adorned with bows. All the children who lived on the street were gathered and put into three rows to have our photograph taken to mark the special day. My friend Hilary, whose dad Joe had been at school with my mum, and I were sitting next to each other and full of excitement when the photographer asked us all to stare straight ahead and look at the camera and say cheese. It was the first time that I'd been asked to say cheese to a camera, and I was completely perplexed, and it shows on the photograph, which you can see later in this book, which I still have today.

For weeks after the coronation, on the wall of my classroom at Pinehurst Infants, there was a poster of that golden carriage, and it transported my six-year-old self to a land of princes and princesses and knights in shining armour. On the last day before the summer holidays the teacher said, 'The pupil that can sit quietly and not move and not make a noise and not giggle for the next ten minutes until the bell goes can take the poster home.' The not giggling bit was my challenge – it was the gauntlet thrown down in front of me – but inwardly I said, *That poster's mine!* I took a deep breath, prepared myself, stared straight ahead and didn't move an inch. Everyone else began to twitch and laugh but I sat stock still and straight faced saying to myself, *Don't laugh, don't laugh.* The bell went and I let out a huge sigh, and then a squeal of delight as the teacher said, 'Alison, the poster is yours, go and collect it from the wall,' which I duly did. I took it home and hung it in pride of place on my bedroom wall where it remained for years.

As I was standing outside the Palace, out of the corner of my eye I suddenly saw the curtain of one of the smaller square windows above the famous balcony being pulled open to reveal the outline of a person. I can still see it now. *Who's that? It's not the Queen I don't think. But who is it?* The swell of excitement at being this close to the Palace and by extension the Queen and therefore the golden carriage, coupled with the fact that I'd almost seen someone who worked there, made me fit to burst and I stored the memory carefully so that I could embellish it and share with friends back home.

Our next stop was the zoo in Regent's Park and then fish and chips wrapped up in newspaper as our teatime treat before we headed home on the train. Tea wasn't as tasty as anticipated as due to the fact I was still bubbling over with excitement from the twitching curtain moment at the Palace, I had put sugar on my chips instead of salt. But not even that could spoil my near royal encounter.

The cars turned into the courtyard and drew up beside the doors to the room where we needed to register our presence. The instructions and schedule were very precise and, so far, all was going to plan. It was my second visit to the Palace, forty-four years after the first. However, this time I was going *inside* the building and would be meeting the real-life Queen, the Queen in the golden carriage, the Queen from the telly, the person whose wave and voice I'd perfected an impression of as a child. It was the year 2000 and there I was, aged fifty-four, about to receive an OBE for my services to British drama. It's a huge moment for me and my family, and once again I'm fit to burst. *I must remember this; I must soak it all up. This is once-in-a-lifetime stuff.* We were all dressed in our Sunday best: me, my partner Michael, my sisters and my son Leo. Toby, my eldest, was in Japan, as he'd taken a year between school and university to see as much of the world as he could. I had a hat on and looked like I was going to a rather posh wedding. What do you wear to meet the Queen if you've never met the Queen before? The dress code had said formal not long, avoid wearing anything that exposes your arms, and jeans and trainers are unacceptable. Heels, not stilettos, were recommended. As we stepped out of the car, I gave everyone a quick glance up and down and felt happy that we'd scrubbed up well. My eldest sister Sylvia and I caught each other's eye, and my mind went to my parents who were, sadly, no longer with us. *They would have loved this; they would have been so very proud.* I gently cast aside the feeling of sadness that washed over me. *This is a happy day.* Had Mum and Dad been alive I knew they'd have dressed up to the nines and enjoyed every moment of it.

Dressing up smartly and taking a trip into Liverpool city centre was a frequent occurrence during my childhood. In fact, apart from when he was gardening, I can't remember a time when my dad wasn't dressed formally. He always looked very dapper in his sharply creased trousers and a perfectly ironed shirt, never without a tie. Mum loved her clothes, and her fashion sense was sharp. She'd keep up with the latest styles of dresses, blouses and skirts, which my grandma would make for her using *Vogue* pattern books, whilst she was still able to. When we went out on our trips, Dad would wear a beautiful over-coat and Mum would always wear a hat, gloves and her special brooch. Keeping her permed hair in haute coiffure style was impor-tant to Mum too. There were always hairdressing scissors in the house, and she'd say, 'Go on then, give us a little trim will you? It'll perk me up.' My middle sister Pamela, who went on to become a hairdresser, had relocated to live in Swindon and was too far away to do my mum's hair on a regular basis, so I would cut and set her hair for her. Mum was very particular about hair and if ever I had an unfortunate cut or perm, and there were a few of those, she'd say, 'What have you done with that hair? Goodness me you look like a fright on a dark night!' Then she'd phone Pamela. 'Can you tell our Alison to do something with her hair? Tell her will you?'

My own haute couture and coiffure weren't as sophisticated in those days and, like lots of girls at the time, my smart outfit was a kilt. This was enhanced by a going-out bonnet made for me by Mrs Ross from up the road. My dad then adorned the bonnet with a bit of tartan plaid – one of my middle names is Campbell after all. Dressed in our respective finery, we'd make the twenty-minute jour-ney on the number 14 green bus into the city centre and go for afternoon tea in the café of one of the big stores such as Blacklers, Owen Owen or TJ Hughes. A great deal of Liverpool, as those store names suggest, was built by the Welsh and often when we were out shopping, we'd come across groups of women, who, if they thought that we were listening to their chat, would switch into speaking in a sing-song lilt that none of us could understand. 'They're Welsh women,' my mum would say, as if it was like belonging to a special club. We'd also see groups of long-skirted women, with their hair scraped back into buns. 'They're the Mary Ellens,' which was the nickname given to the groups of mostly Irish women who would work on the city-centre market stalls come rain or shine, and often try and persuade my mum to part with some pennies for a rose.

During our café pit stop we would fuel ourselves with warm, gooey, toasted tea cakes, fruit scones with jam and a cup of tea, before heading off to shop or, if I'd been good, to St George's Hall to watch the Punch and Judy show. St George's Hall, which stood just outside Lime Street Station, seemed massive to my five-year-old eyes and its Victorian grandeur was a dramatic backdrop to the slapstick and sometimes shocking puppetry that took place within the colourful booth.

My favourite big shop was Blacklers, which was on the corner of Elliot Street and Great Charlotte Street. The store closed its doors for the last time in 1988 but not before acquiring a well-deserved reputation for having the most sumptuous Christmas grotto in the city and the one that we all wanted to visit as part of the festive season. On one occasion I was taken to see Father Christmas and, sitting on his knee, I pulled at this long white beard to see how it was attached – that didn't go down terribly well. Blacklers also became well known for being the place of work of a young apprentice electrician called George Harrison. He didn't hang around though! The shop's third floor, the children's clothing department, was where I always wanted to go as there was a huge white rocking horse. It looked so real and, because it was so enormous, it looked scary and formidable too. This didn't prevent me from sitting on it and giving it a hug and stroking its mane before rocking to and fro. It was another, if-you're-a-good-girl treat and I loved it. There was always a big queue and sometimes, after getting off the horse, I'd want to queue up for another ride.

Many years later, in 2011, I was invited to the opening of the new Museum of Liverpool that is situated on an impressive site at the Pier Head. It was amazing to walk around this architecturally stunning building and immerse myself in the city's evolution and history. Little did I know that I'd also come face to face with a moment from mine. Walking around the museum, I turned the corner and there, facing me in a huge glass case was the Blacklers rocking horse. For a moment, I thought that it couldn't be the same horse but as I kept looking the memories of my dad lifting me up and sitting me on the top of the horse came flooding back. It was an emotional coming together of past and present, as I'm sure it was for the many of the children who had visited Blacklers before it closed. Knowing that Blackie, as the horse was called, had given so much pleasure, the owners of the department store gifted it to Alder Hey Hospital, and many more children had been able to enjoy it before it was donated to the museum.

With so many childhood memories tied to Queen Elizabeth II, it was strange to be standing in the courtyard of Buckingham Palace and about to meet the reigning monarch. I needed a moment to take it all in.

Luckily, by the year 2000, there had been many opportunities to say cheese and smile on cue, and I was determined that any photographs of this occasion wouldn't have me gurning into the camera as I did on the coronation day. There was such a formality to it all that I'd coached myself to make sure that I didn't have an inappropriate fit of the giggles or find myself needing to go to the toilet at an inopportune moment. We were ushered into the Throne Room and invited to sit down. Possibly sensing my nerves, one of the Queen's equerries looked over, smiled and nodded as if to say,

'Everything's going to be fine.' And then the large double doors opened, the National Anthem began to play and the Queen entered the room. *Oh, how my mum would have loved this.* It all had such grandeur and sense of ritual and tradition. The equerry gave me my cue to join him and walk towards the Queen. After, years of working in live theatre, I was good with cues and so this felt much more like familiar territory to me. 'This is the actress Alison Steadman, ma'am.' The Queen smiled, looked at me and asked the question that all actors dread, 'What are you working on at the moment?'

My mind went blank before hastily remembering what it was that I was up to as well as thinking, *Thank goodness I am working at the moment.* 'I'm doing a series for Yorkshire Television,' I said.

'Oh, Yorkshire,' was her succinct reply, then she turned to the equerry and took the medal from the case that he was holding. 'Now then, I've got to pin this medal on you.' I noted that she said the words as if fresh minted, as if she'd never said the line before, which takes some doing given how many thousands of times that she must have said the self-same thing to others. Having pinned my medal on, she reached out her white-gloved hand and took mine, and then I felt a very gentle push of her hand against mine. They had told me to expect it. The push was the signal to begin walking backwards then, after a respectful distance, turn and walk away.

Walking backwards in heels requires all the focus that you have, so it was a relief to turn and walk out of the majestic room into one of the antechambers where my family was waiting for me. The adrenaline had kicked in and I was looking forward to a glass of champagne to celebrate. Sylvia gave me a huge hug and said, 'Well done, we're so proud of you and Mum and Dad would be too.'

'I wish Mum could have been here.'

Sylvia released herself from our hug and pointed down to the lapel of her dress jacket. I had to steel myself from dissolving into tears. 'You're wearing Mum's special brooch,' I said.

'Yes. When I put it on this morning I said, "Come on, Mum, you're going to the Palace."' I am still so grateful to Sylvia for doing that, and how lovely it was to have Mum there, dressed up to the nines, at least in spirit, to mark a moment of our own family's history. And she'd have been delighted that I'd had my hair done especially!

CHAPTER 6

Alison Is Performing

Long before everyone was singing 'Ferry Cross the Mersey' and a trip on a Mersey boat had become a tourist attraction, my family would be jumping on the ferry at Liverpool's Pier Head and taking the ten-minute journey to the attractions at New Brighton. It was like having a holiday destination on your doorstep, which was handy as we didn't really go on big holidays when I was little, apart from the Isle of Man from time to time or North Wales. From the minute the ferry began to chug out of the dock and head out to sea, it felt like we were on our hols. It was the same for hundreds of families, who'd pack picnics, swimming costumes, umbrellas and deck chairs to head out for a day at the seaside. The New Brighton ferry stopped running in 1971 but not before we'd taken many weekend trips on it.

New Brighton didn't feel like Liverpool at all. With its sandy beaches lining the edge of the mouth of the Mersey as it opened out onto the vast expanse of the Irish Sea, it felt more like another country to me. It was named *New* Brighton in an attempt to attract the gentry by making an association with the Regency glamour of the older Brighton, much further south on the warmer coast. I always looked forward to our trips there and time spent at the fairground and the open-air pool, as well as on the long sandy beach.

The Art Deco pool was the largest open-air lido in Britain and was in use for nearly sixty years before it was damaged during a storm in 1990 and later demolished. It was a sea-water pool, with a saltiness that made you forget that you were in a pool at all. As a young girl, I didn't have the bravura that some other children did and couldn't just jump right in or run in fast so that I was out of my depth suddenly. I was always tentative about things that I didn't know enough about, but the pool at New Brighton was perfectly designed for a novice like me and I wanted to give it a go.

The person who had designed the open-air pool at New Brighton was obviously keen to avoid anyone stumbling into the water and getting into difficulties, so there was a gentle slope that you could lie down on, still within very shallow water, that would make you feel like you were swimming when the swirling water lifted you off the incline and your body floated, but your arms were still firmly anchored to safety. Slowly, as my confidence grew, I'd release my arms from time to time and copy the actions that I'd seen other people do in the water, until the day came when I could turn myself around, let go of the slope and begin to swim out into the deep end. What a feeling that was. Learning to swim is about getting into water and using your body in a certain way, and therefore not drowning. It's such a good metaphor for life.

Making the decision to give something a go is the first step that we take along a pathway that may lead to exciting adventures. In my case, that chance happened when I was around nine years old, at the end of the school play at Pinehurst Juniors. The play had a Scottish theme, and my well-practised line was, 'Hey Boatman, do not tarry, for I'll give ye a silver crown if you row me over the ferry,' which I delivered in my best Mrs Grey (our Scottish neighbour) accent. The show must have had something to do with Flora MacDonald and Bonnie Prince Charlie as one of my classmates, on discovering that my middle name was Campbell, completely out of the blue decided to take a real dislike to me because her name was MacDonald. She told me she hated me, which left me shocked and puzzled as it seemed a rather unfair reaction to my having one of the best parts in the play. After the performance, my mum was politely talking to my teacher and her husband, who had helped to direct it. Hovering beside them all and pretending not to listen, I overheard the husband mention, 'Alison's a good actress you know. I actually think that she could be one.' Aged nine, I'd no idea that this play acting that I was doing and enjoyed so much could be a job and I replayed his, 'I think she could actually be one,' in my head. It was the first time that I'd heard anyone say anything about my future and I held onto it. It's no coincidence that around this time I began to step up my impressions of Hylda Baker and my homegrown improvised pranks, as I began to realise that I could entertain people.

It wasn't something that I expressed overtly at Childwall Valley High School for Girls, as there were so many other things to be getting along with when I moved there two years later, such as maths, which I hated and was useless at, and art, which I loved and was quite good at. And then there was English. Long before we had Miss Davies, our once-scary deputy head teacher who taught us to think and feel at the same time, we had a much lazier teacher who would just set up improvisations for us to do rather than teach us. This didn't bother me though as I loved pretending to be other people and began to recognise that there was a way of getting people to laugh by altering my voice and changing my physical shape. Spending forty-five minutes making things up was a comfortable place for me as I'd always got nervous about going into any English class because I knew that we might have to read aloud. It was the worst thing about school for me, having to read aloud and so even though I loved English as a subject, I used to dread it too. 'Why don't you do the next bit, Carol?' the teacher would say after reading some of the novel aloud herself, and then Carol would take over and I'd think, *Please don't look at me, please don't pick me.* But no matter how invisible I tried to make myself she'd always seemed to say, 'And now, Alison, will you carry on?' It wasn't a question to answer and even though my inner voice was screaming, *No, I will not carry on,* the class heard me stutter and stumble over every word. It was dreadful and carried on like this for many years and long after I'd left school and drama school.

At the beginning of my career, I had to attend read-throughs and the familiar feeling of dread would always be there. It was almost impossible for me to sight read as all the words would jumble in front of me so that I was unable to read smoothly or coherently. It was important to find the reason for what was happening and to try to fix it, in the privacy of my own company I'd try to read aloud. It became clear that there was a disconnect between my mind, my eyes and my mouth. Rather than take the script word by word, step by step, my brain would keep jumping ahead, which made any hope of getting to the end of a line without sounding like I didn't understand what I was saying impossible.

I'll never forget going to the first read-through for the Dennis Potter TV drama *The Singing Detective* in 1986. I'd been looking forward to it, as I'd done a thorough scan of my role, Mrs Marlow, and was prepared to read aloud in front of everyone. Then, just as we were all getting settled and comfy, the director, Jon Amiel, said to me, 'Oh, Alison, will you read in for us as one of the cast isn't able to join us until after lunch?' Again, like the request from my English teacher, it wasn't a question and my inner voice once again yelled, *No, I will not read in*, whilst politely I said, 'Of course, happy to, of course.' It was such a horrible experience stumbling through a part that I'd had no time to prepare and worst of all, at the end of the read-through, Jon said, 'Thank goodness we didn't cast you in that part.' I wish that I'd spoken up for myself and explained things but instead I laughed it off, as I knew how to, and thought, *Please ground, swallow me up right now.* It took some time to realise that my brain was so involved in working out each word to read that I couldn't look ahead to the next word, which is what you must do. I subsequently discovered that I had a minor form of dyslexia and that it runs in the family. It took some time to train myself, but with work I managed to overcome it.

The language of Shakespeare got under my skin almost as soon as I encountered it. We read the plays around the class and, contrary to how I usually felt, speaking Shakespeare aloud was something that I looked forward to. It must have been the drama within in it all. Not that any of us understood anything much about it at that stage, but the sounds in the language did something to me. I didn't fully understand Lady Macbeth when she said, 'I would, while it was smiling in my face, have plucked my nipple from his boneless gums and dashed the brains out, had I so sworn as you have done to this,' but those guttural sounds within the words helped me make a connection and, unlike many of my classmates, I was hooked.

Drama wasn't offered as a formal subject at school. All opportunities to act took place in the English classes and I'd take any chance that I could to perform. We were introduced to *Romeo and Juliet* when I was about thirteen, which is the perfect age to engage young teenagers in a story of massive crushes that are mistaken for love, gang fights, arguments with parents, gatecrashing parties and tragic outcomes. Reading the play around the class had taken some time but it still gripped me and so when our teacher said, 'Alison, will you take on the role of Romeo?' I didn't hesitate, my inner voice was singing, *Yes, I will take on the role and any other that you might want to give me.*

At the end of the play, Romeo enters the tomb, not knowing that Paris is there, only to discover Juliet's body. He thinks that she's dead, then Paris, with very bad timing, reveals himself and, in a fit of rage, Romeo kills him. Totally distraught, Romeo then swigs down the potent concoction that the apothecary has given him and utters the lines, 'O true apothecary! Thy drugs are quick, thus with a kiss I die.' That whole section, from Romeo entering the tomb, to seeing Juliet's body, murdering Paris and then killing himself was all mine. Just reading it made my temperature rise and I was so caught up in it all that, when it came to uttering that final line, there was no messing, I clasped my chest, let out my final breath and threw myself, in a proper death drop, onto the grubby hardwood floor of the classroom, which hurt far more than I could show, as I was meant to be dead. All of it unrehearsed I might add. It was a properly dramatic moment, and, in my mind, flowers were being thrown onto the stage and everyone was up on their feet giving a standing ovation, but the reality was that the whole class erupted into laughter and at me and not with me. Still on the ground I was thinking, *Why are they finding this funny, it's so sad, he thinks that the love of his life is dead and he's so distressed that he had to kill himself. It's not funny. It's tragic. Of course, he falls to the floor like I have done.* After what felt like forever, the teacher said, 'Okay now, everyone, stop laughing. Alison is performing,' and I stood up and gave a mock bow to my friends and joined in their laughter.

'Alison is performing' as a notion began to stick to me and so when our headmistress, Miss Brown, announced in assembly that anyone could join the newly formed Liverpool Youth Theatre, it felt like someone was pointing me in that direction. Hundreds of teenagers from schools all over Liverpool put themselves forward and so LYT decided that they'd only give out two places per school, and the successful applicants names would be drawn from a hat. *How daft is that? What if the person they pick is rubbish and doesn't really want to go? What if this is my only chance of becoming an actress and I know that it's the only thing that I want to do.* It felt like a completely ridiculous process to me and when my name wasn't picked out of the hat I thought, *Well, that's that.*

Fortunately towards the end of the Easter term, there was another announcement that was to open a door to a world of possibilities that I couldn't even imagine. A couple of the teachers at school had decided to form a holiday drama club and anyone that hadn't been picked first time round, and who still wanted to get involved, now had the chance. It was free and everyone was accepted. It went so well that the teachers decided to expand things and established a weekly youth theatre on a Friday night in a room in Anfield Road School, which coincidentally, was the school that my mum had gone to. It was a no-brainer for me, and I was off.

The old Victorian building, with its impressive bell tower, felt like a suitably dramatic place to learn the rudimentary skills of performance. Even though it was a big old building, we only used one room. With its dark wood flooring and stark lighting, it was perfect and all that we needed. The youth theatre was a game changer for me, and every Friday night I'd rush down to Anfield Road to take part in the improvisation classes that they taught to us all. Without any pressure to perform to an audience or learn lines, we'd just play, and, over time, our confidence grew. We walked in the shoes of anybody and everybody. I can remember building up the character of a very elderly woman and after the improvisation the tutor saying to the group, 'Can someone take that poor old lady and help her to the post office to get her pension.' That made my week, that did.

The youth theatre was led by the wonderfully encouraging Jim Wiggins, who was such a good person. It was a fair, open place where there wasn't a question of who had the poshest voice or who could afford things. There were no auditions, anyone could turn up and everyone was given a chance. That's all anyone needs isn't it, a chance?

CHAPTER 7

Working Things Out

'All off for the shoplifters' paradise,' yelled the bus conductor like a Scouse tour guide on a mission, as we turned into Church Street. He said it every time we took the trip on the number 14 into town: 'All off for the shoplifters' paradise and C&A Modes. It's the next stop, young ladies. Off you all trot.'

C&A Modes, which opened its first ever UK shop in Liverpool, advertised itself as being a specialist clothes store for 'Ladies, Maids and Girls', although by the time my friends and I would frequent it in the early 1960s, the word 'maid', which surely must have been maid as in old or unmarried, had been dropped. The shop, with its bright blue-and-red oval logo, would be our weekend shopping destination of choice and we'd head there to look at the latest fashions. We'd tootle about inside for hours, trying things on and amusing ourselves with the fantasy that we could buy anything we wanted. That very rarely happened though as money was extremely tight, and if there was something that we liked the reality was that we'd have to save up for weeks and weeks or persuade a relative to buy it for us as a treat. I'd return from most shopping trips empty handed but full of stories about how gorgeous the clothes were and 'if only I could afford to buy a thing or two,' which my no-nonsense mum would respond to with 'Well, you'll just have to get a Saturday job and save up.' My dad would say nothing but several days later there would be a shopping bag waiting for me and Mum would say, 'I knew he would, I just knew he would. That's your father for you, that's your father!' Dad bought me all sorts, including my first pair of stiletto heels, which I'd stagger around in feeling very sophisticated. Meanwhile Mum would be ironing one of my underskirts, which she'd then dip in flour and water and leave to dry so that it would stick out and look much bigger and wider than it was. Once it was set, I'd put it on, slip a dress over it and with a click of my heels I was all ready for a night at Billy Martin's Dance Club.

The fashions were changing though, skirts were getting shorter, and I knew that if I wanted to keep up then I'd have to get myself a Saturday job as my mum had suggested, so I did. George Henry Lee's on Basnett Street in the city centre was regarded as *the* posh shop and even as a Saturday girl I had to arrive for the day formally attired in a black skirt and top. It was a big store and I worked across the different departments including the menswear department where I was told that the most important thing was to be observant and look out for the aforementioned shoplifters – 'They'll put the bag down there, see, and crack on that they're looking at the shirts and then just drop one in the bag when no one is looking' – and the perfume section, or 'Fumery' as it was known, where there was a ferocious woman in charge. There was nothing sweet smelling about her at all. Working on a shop floor wasn't an ideal job for me, and I'd panic anytime anyone wanted to buy anything as this meant dealing with the convoluted, cashless system that the shop employed. You'd have to put some paper inside a machine, which would print off a chitty, which you'd then give to the customer to do something with. It sounds simple but it was beyond me, I just couldn't get the hang of the machine. I soon decided that my days of having to stand straight with my hands behind my back were over and I swiftly moved on to the café, which continued to give me some pin money to buy clothes from time to time and to go out on a Saturday night to dance with the boys.

Childwall Valley was an all-girls establishment but luckily there were lots of boys around the same age as me that lived on Sherwyn Road and we'd all grown up together and always been friends. My favourite, Roger Thompson – we are still great friends – lived next door. Perhaps because he was an only child and I was the only child at home for most of my childhood, Roger and I spent lots of time together. He'd knock at the door and say, 'Wanna come out and play?' When we were a bit older, but not old enough to go into the city at night, I'd go over to his house, and we'd put Bill Haley's 'Rock Around the Clock' on the turntable and feel quite adult. When we were about fourteen, we both thought it would be a good idea to learn how to smoke properly before braving doing it in public. This was long before smoking had any cautionary health warning attached and I can remember feeling so sophisticated and grown up as I nonchalantly blew cigarette smoke up the Thompsons' chimney. During another attempt at being grown up, Roger and I decided to venture into the world of cocktails, and we clinked our cut-glass crystal tumblers that were full of Martini before taking our first sips. The liquid had no sooner entered my mouth before I spat it out very inelegantly onto the log fire that was burning. The grate began to spit hot sparks out my way as bright-orange flames soared up the chimney before dying down again. I was lucky that my dress, with its sticking-out skirt, didn't go up in flames too. We both longed to be out dancing and yearned for the time when we could spend a Saturday night at Billy Martin's Dance Club or, as we knew it, The Club.

Billy Martin and his wife Pauline opened Martin's Dance Centre on Derby Lane in the late 1930s, in a tall and imposing Victorian house. They ran dance classes for all ages. For us juniors, these were held in the front of the house but if we graduated any further, then we'd move through to the grand ballroom that had been added on at the back of the building. Each Saturday afternoon, my mum would take me and a friend down the Derby Road and we'd be put through our paces learning the moves for the quickstep, foxtrot and waltz. As we made progress, we'd take exams, and those students who showed promise were invited to join the formation teams and enter competitions. I got to the tango stage, which is quite an awkward dance for fourteen-year-olds to do together and the feedback on my performance reflected my shyness. 'Alison needs to give more commitment to the dance and make more hip contact with her partner.' The last thing that I wanted at fourteen was more hip contact with my partner! When we turned fifteen, we could return on a Saturday night and dance the night away in the ballroom, which they would transform into a club for teenagers. The room was edged with bentwood chairs and we girls would sit there and wait, as we'd been told was the form, until some young lad would cross the room, hold out his hand and ask, 'Are you dancin'?' It was a searingly exquisite and painful pleasure sitting there in my sticky-out frock with my curled hair and high heels, waiting for an invitation to take to the floor with a young man. It was a long wait before anyone did the asking though, the reason being that none of the lads knew how to dance. So, being ever resourceful and putting my years of dance lessons to good use, I held jive classes in my front room for anyone that wanted to come along so that we could all shake, rattle and roll together. As the 1950s became the 1960s, things loosened up and we'd all get up and dance together in unison, singing along to the latest hits and a group called the Beatles, who had begun to play regularly at the Cavern Club and had just hit the charts with their song with 'She Loves You'. It was a joyous and heady time that was fuelled by orange juice, that was until we were old enough to have a beer beforehand at the local pub. So many boys and girls met their future husbands and wives on a Saturday night at Billy Martin's but even though I had a lovely boyfriend called Jimmy Ford, who could play the guitar and sang to me in a voice like Frank Sinatra, I knew that my heart lay elsewhere.

Saturday nights were for dancing, but my Friday nights were still faithfully given to attending the youth theatre in the Anfield Road School, where I was buoyed by the encouragement of Jim Wiggins and the other founders, Tony Joy and Mildred Spencer. I was slowly realising that performing was the thing that I was good at and loved more than anything else.

So I had no doubts about what to say when, towards the end of my time at school, there was a session with a careers advisor and our headmistress, Miss Brown. I went into the meeting totally prepared for the first question. 'So, Alison,' said the careers advisor, 'what ideas have you got about what you'd like to do with yourself when you leave school?'

I steeled myself, took a deep breath and said as confidently as possible, 'Well, I'd like to be an actress.'

It was like I'd said, 'I want to take a ride on a flying carpet to the moon.'

She looked straight at me but said nothing. There was a heavy and embarrassing silence until Miss Brown chipped in with, 'Ah, yes. Alison is very good at acting, you can ask her to play any part and if you ask her to read some Shakespeare, then she's just wonderful,' and continued, 'Ask her to write an essay about it on the other hand, well, she's not so keen on that.' It wasn't said in a nasty way at all. In fact, she was spot on. I wanted to act and that was that.

The careers advisor looked down at her sheet and the list of options that were on it – teacher, nurse, children's nanny, secretary – and then looked up at me and said nothing apart from, 'It's been very interesting, thank you and good luck.' It was short and not so sweet, but I didn't leave dispirited as I had Jim Wiggins and the other teachers at Anfield Road.

Nowadays there are so many more opportunities to join drama groups but back in the 1960s youth theatres were a fairly new concept and people from my background didn't think that actually earning money from acting was possible. I'd watch people on TV and at the cinema and think, *That's someone else's world, not mine.* But Jim encouraged me to think otherwise. I went from front-room entertainer to class performer to youth-theatre actress without really being aware that I was making a set of choices. All I knew was that acting was what I loved and that I wanted to get better at it. It was very much a case of right time, right place and right people. Mostly.

Mildred Spencer took me under her wing, directing me in plays and giving me great acting notes that I'd devour. Decades later, I was doing some filming on the Isle of Man. When I arrived back in my hotel room one evening, I noticed that a card had been popped underneath the door and was lying there on the carpet. It was from Mildred, who was originally from the Isle of Man and had moved back there when she'd retired. It was an invitation for tea and cake and later that week we had a wonderful evening sharing smoked-salmon sandwiches, strawberries and cream, plus a bottle of red wine, as we reminisced about our Friday nights in Anfield Road School, and how important it had been for us all.

It was Jim Wiggins, though, who said to me, at around the same time as I had the disastrous meeting at school, 'You know what, Alison, I think you should go to drama school when you leave Childwall Valley High.' The notion of going to drama school had never crossed my mind. In fact I'd no idea that such a thing even existed. I was sixteen and living in Liverpool and hadn't any idea of what opportunities there might be in another part of the country. 'Alison,' he said, 'you've got to tackle this properly, work it out. I can't bear the thought of you not doing this and in thirty years' time stirring a pan of stew saying, "If only if I'd gone to drama school."' That made me sit up and was enough to make me persuade my mum and dad to come down and have a chat with Jim.

Many parents wouldn't have even considered supporting their child in pursuing their dreams as an actor during that time in Liverpool. They couldn't. Things were tough and so many people had nothing. Families had very little security as some of the main manufacturing industries, and many of the dockyards, began to slope into a decline which would lead to an enormous crash in the 1970s. However, George and Marjorie Steadman, my mum and dad, having not been born during a period that enabled them to pursue their own dreams, wanted to make sure that I was able to have a go at trying to turn mine into a reality. And so, on a Friday night, dressed smartly for the occasion, they arrived at Anfield Road School, just as our improvisation class came to an end. This was such unfamiliar territory for my parents but Jim was wonderful at making them feel as comfortable as possible. 'We don't know very much about any of this,' said my dad. 'Do you think it's the right thing for her?' said my mum. None of us, apart from Jim, knew terribly much. There was no internet to quickly check things out and, apart from that, we were still living during a time when to aspire beyond your class was just regarded as foolish and the thing of dreams. 'Does she have enough talent to get into drama school? Is it safe to move away from Liverpool at such a young age?' My parents were anxious to learn the reality of what was being proposed, and Jim was brilliant at assuring them that he had, as they did, my best interests at heart. 'Okay,' he said, 'this is what we'll do. I'll get in touch with the lot at the Liverpool Playhouse as they'll have actors there in their season who will have trained at a drama school, and we might be able to get a bit more information.' And that's what he did.

But I was only sixteen, and Dad, full of common sense, said, 'Look love, you can't go off to drama school in London or anywhere else, at least not until you're seventeen. C'mon now, think sensibly, you might go and then end up with no work at all. You need another string to your bow just in case. Why not stay here in Liverpool, continue your drama classes and do a course in shorthand or something. Then get a job in an office for a while and see how things go?' It wasn't what I wanted to hear but in my heart of hearts I knew that he was right.

Of course staying in Liverpool in the 1960s meant I was absolutely in the heart of its glorious surge in youth culture. The emergence of Merseybeat and the Liverpool poets meant Liverpool was firmly on the map.

'Bye, Mum, I'm off,' I said dashing out the door before she could stop me, quickly adding, 'I'm just heading into town for lunch,' hoping that this would prevent any questions about exactly where I was going.

'Alright, love. See ya. But don't you be going down to that Cavern place and if I find out that you have, there'll be trouble. Alright?'

I had once asked my mum if it was okay to go to the Cavern Club and had been met with short shrift, 'You are certainly not to go to that place,' she'd said. 'It's all underground and only has one entrance and exit.' The firmness of her response confirmed my decision not to ask again and to find a way of going there anyway.

So, I'd head into town with my friends Hilary, who I'd known since I was young, and Barbara, who I'd met at secondary school. After getting off at the 'shoplifters' paradise', we'd mooch around C&A Modes for a bit before crossing over town and walking down the cobbles of Mathew Street, and to a lunchtime session at number 10, the home of the Cavern Club. Going to see a band on a Saturday afternoon was massively popular and there was always a queue of people, mainly teenage girls like me, waiting to get in. We'd give our money at the entrance of a narrow passageway and then head down the steep dark steps to the cellar at the bottom without a care about there only being one way in and one way out. Descending into the gloom, breathing in the very distinctive smell of rotten fruit and disinfectant that clung to the walls, we could hear the buzz of voices and the sound of the regular compere, Bob Wooler, saying, 'Remember all you cave-dwellers, the Cavern is the best of cellars.' Each time we ventured into this new experience it felt like we were part of something exciting, that we were exploring uncharted territory and that this was something bigger than us. The beat was loud and throbbing, and I could feel my heart pound in my chest as we all squashed into the sweaty vaulted space.

The Cavern had only been open a few years at that point and was still finding its feet but there was something in the air at that time and the narrow, brick-walled space struck a chord with poets and musicians. It began to establish itself as the new mecca for British pop, featuring regulars such as Cilla Black, the Searchers, Billy J. Kramer, Gerry and the Pacemakers and, of course, the Beatles. The small wooden chairs would be set out in tight rows, and we'd shuffle along until we could find a seat. Then bowls of tomato soup and rolls would be handed out as part of the ticket price, making me feel a lot better about not telling my mum the whole truth, *At least I wasn't telling a fib about going out for lunch.* The atmosphere was electric and the squished-together rows of chairs would pulsate in unison as we all tapped our feet and danced as much as we could with the upper parts of our bodies. It's funny to think about how formal it all was and how impeccably behaved we were too.

'Oh, hi, everyone,' said Paul as the band came onto the small stage at the front of the cellar. 'Say hello to Ringo Starr. He's playing the drums this week because Pete Best can't join us. Let's hear it for Ringo.' It was the middle of August and even hotter and sweatier than usual down in the Cavern. We all looked over and saw this chap take his place at the drums, none of us knowing that this would be a defining moment in the band's history, and in poor old Pete Best's. '"Red Sails in the Sunset,"' said Paul. 'One, two, three, four,' and they'd be off. It was one of their most popular cover songs and no matter how many times its fast-paced beat burst out, I'd be swept up and away in the excitement of it, and all of this before 3.00 p.m.!

The Beatles became our band, and we were smitten. All of us who went to those lunchtime sessions were their first fans. After one session, emboldened by there being three of us together, Hilary, Barbara and I decided that we'd get their autographs. It was a drizzly afternoon but we were very determined, so we kept waiting and waiting by the door for what seemed like an eternity, not caring that we looked like drowned rats. Just as we were about to give up and try our luck another day, out came John and Paul. Paul stood there for a moment and put up his big black umbrella, then they both started walking down the street together, heading towards the city centre. Wasting no time, we began to follow them. 'John! Paul! Hi!' we began shouting out, trying to get their attention as they marched on. John turned round and gave us a nonplussed look while Paul raised his umbrella up a bit and said, 'Hiya, girls', but they kept on walking. We kept on following them. They finally stopped at the Liverpool Central Post Office on St Thomas Street and went inside. Naturally, we followed them inside too. Paul sat down at a big oak table and began to fill out a form, which he then took to the counter before coming to stand by John who was filling something out too. 'Go on, go on, now's your moment,' said Hilary, pushing me forward. With my autograph book in hand and not feeling quite as brave as I had done on the street, I tentatively edged a little further forward and said, 'Excuse me, Paul, can I have your autograph please?'

And he turned and went, 'Oh yeah, love. Yeah. What's your name love?'

'It's Alison,' I said. And he took my outstretched book and the pen that I was offering and wrote 'To Alison, Love Paul x' and handed it back to me.

'Hang on a minute, give us that back will you?' Taking the book from me, he added, in brackets '(Beatles)'. Looking up at me, Paul said, 'I thought I'd better put Beatles because in the future someone is going to look at that and think, who the hell is Paul!'

This was at the very beginning for them. They were just starting out and hadn't recorded anything at that point so their regular sessions at the Cavern Club were their main thing. Riding on the wave of his willingness I said, 'Can I have John's autograph please?'

And passing the book to John he said, 'Hey, sign this for the girl, will you?'

John didn't look up but scribbled 'John Lennon' and handed it back to Paul who handed it to me.

'Oh, take no notice of him,' said Paul, 'he's always like that,' and with that we took our cue and moved on. Years later, once they had become world famous, I told my mum about this innocent encounter. She listened with crossed arms and said firmly, 'So, you did go down to that Cavern, didn't you?!' And then, like a teenage girl herself, 'What was it like?'

CHAPTER 8

Rite of Passage

I was too young for drama school but old enough to do a shorthand and typing course when I left school in the summer of 1963. I needed to earn a wage and be able to contribute a bit to my family, as well as learn something that I could fall back on if I didn't make it as an actress, as my dad had suggested. So my Friday nights continued to be spent doing what I loved at the youth theatre, Saturdays I was at the Cavern Club in the afternoon and then Billy Martin's in the evening, while the rest of the time I was learning how to do a job that I hoped that I'd never have to do. It all felt a bit pointless. Wasn't it all just time-filling? I can remember saying to my mum, 'Well, I'm not working in a shipping office,' which is where many of the girls that did the course ended up. I'm not sure quite why I was so against it.

Mum responded with, 'You'll work wherever you get a job and earn some money, never you mind,' then turning to my dad, 'Have you ever heard the likes of this? "I'm not working in a shipping office!"'

As luck would have it, I got wind that a job was coming up in the local probation office, which sounded much more interesting than sitting behind a desk all day not talking to anyone. *I'm bound to meet interesting people in a probation office*, I thought, so I jumped at the chance of an interview, and got the job which, given that I was only seventeen and just out of secretarial college, was quite lucky. 'You're very young to be working in a place like this,' the lady said. 'You might see a few things that will shock you. You really shouldn't be doing a job like this until you're twenty-one.' Walton Probation Office was indeed an eye opener for a girl like me who'd led a very safe and protected life in my small area of Anfield. We all sat behind a hatch and there was a window that could be opened to call people up from the waiting room. Most of the people who came in were young lads that had been in borstal for things like theft, but there were also couples, as the office, quite strangely, was also a marriage counselling service. It was always the women that called up and it was quite distressing to listen to it all. The lady who'd said that I was too young was possibly right. There were fun times too though with lots of laughs, mostly provided by the senior probation officer Jack Cogley, a tall, clean-shaven man in his fifties, who'd look at the waiting room and say to me, 'We've got to bolt down that furniture to the floor, Alison, cos some of these lads, they'd nick the blue out of your shirt.' It was a brilliant place to work, answering phones, typing up court reports, and being exposed to people and stories that gave me a fuller understanding of the world. During those late teenage years I witnessed very different lives and soaked up the emotional fragility of other people. My colleagues were a great bunch, who took me under their wings and helped me to grow up.

Money was always an issue. It very quickly ran out and I was often left short before the end of the week. One such week, not wanting to bother my parents about such things, I went to the bank and, in a very grown-up fashion, took my turn at the counter and said, 'I'd like to take out one pound please.'

'A pound?' the bank teller asked.

'Yes. A pound.'

The chap cleared his throat, 'Well, I'm afraid that you can't have a pound because you haven't got any money in your account.'

Undeterred I said, 'The thing is, I'm getting paid at the end of the week but it would be really helpful to have a pound now.'

Looking directly at me he said sternly, 'I'll say this again, you haven't any money in your account and so you can't have a pound.'

I still didn't really understand why but I headed back to work and asked one of the girls that I'd made friends with if she would lend me a few bob, which she very kindly did.

I didn't hide the fact that I wanted to train to be an actress and even though this was such a strange thing for my colleagues to consider, they were always egging me on and encouraging me to keep going. My immediate boss, Gerald Gordon Hamilton Elliott Brown, who had the longest name in the history of long names, or at least of all the names of people working in the probation office, was such a great support telling me, 'You mustn't stay here and get stuck, just look at me. You must leave and do something better.' It certainly wasn't an awful place to work, in fact it taught me a huge amount, but Gerry was right, I mustn't get stuck there.

Jim Wiggins kept to his word and got in touch with 'the lot at the Liverpool Playhouse' and a meeting with David Scase, the director, was arranged, 'What sort of actress do you want to be?' David asked me. It wasn't something that I'd ever considered before, but my answer prompted him to say, 'I think East 15 is the place for you. It's new and progressive and based on Joan Littlewood's work. I think you should give it a try,' He wrote down the name of the school on a piece of paper and put it into my hand. As I left his office and walked out of the Liverpool Playhouse, I looked down at the crumpled piece of paper that held my hoped for future. East 15. It sounded like the name of a rock band or the code word for a rendez-vous. Regardless of not knowing anything other than it was a place that someone who knew more than me thought that I should go, I decided to write a letter and request an audition.

I'd never auditioned for anyone or anything, and the process felt alien and extremely daunting. The trip meant that I needed to take time off work, so I asked for two days' holiday leave rather than explain where I was off to. *Who knows what is going to happen. I might not get into East 15 and then I will still need the job.* I also didn't want to jinx it. Mum and Dad were rooting for me and very gener-ously gave me my fare for the trip south.

East 15 was in Loughton in Essex, on the edge of Epping Forest. The grand-looking house, at the end of a long drive, amongst five acres of ancient woodland, looked more like the country pad of a wealthy person than a drama school. Hatfield House, as it was called, was a world away from the probation office. *I bet the furniture isn't bolted to the floor here!* I walked up the front steps of the building and gave my name to the lady sitting behind the desk, who smiled warmly and said, 'Just take a seat over there. Someone will come and call for you.' My heart was in my mouth. *Deep breaths, deep breaths, you can do this.* I remembered Mum. *You can and you will.*

'Alison Steadman,' a woman's voice called. I stood up and went into a large wood-panelled room and met Margaret Bury for the first time. Margaret, or Maggie as she was known, had founded East 15 a few years previously and was its first principal. All the training at the school was based on the methods and philosophy of the theatre director Joan Littlewood. Maggie had been a member of Joan's Theatre Workshop for fourteen years before leaving to set up East 15 in 1961. East 15 broke new ground both in the way that it trained its actors and what it offered them. The programme was designed to give students a complete immersion in all aspects of acting so that they'd head into the industry as versatile and prepared as possible. The sound of it enthralled me: classes in improvisation, ensemble work, a commitment to the classics as well as new writing and, most appealingly, a focus on being able to express the emotional truth of the character.

And now, here I was, only a few years since it had opened its doors, doing my first ever audition, to attempt to join the ranks of their alumni. There were only the two of us in the room – Maggie didn't have a board of people interrogating terrified prospective students. She must have seen my legs shake and sensed how uncomfortable I felt standing in front of her. As requested, I had prepared a poem and a bit of Shakespeare. Neither brought the house down. 'Why don't you come down here and begin again? Don't bother with all that text stuff,' she said. 'Let's do something else. Can you improvise?' That question was like liquid gold being poured into my ears. *Can I improvise? It's what I've been doing most of my life.* 'Yes, yes, I can. What would you like me to do?'

There was a bit of pause before I heard, 'Okay, so, you're Muhammad Ali, you've just won the world heavyweight title and all the press are around you with their cameras and microphones. Go!' It couldn't have been further away from me as a character, but I just jumped into the space, hunched my shoulders a bit, added some swagger and began to dance around on my feet doing my best to float like a butterfly and sting like a bee. It felt comfortable pretending like that.

Then she said, 'Okay, now you're a guide in a stately home. Go over there and come in that door. You've got a group of people with you. Go!' I breezed into the room as the know-it-all tour guide.

'Ladies and gentlemen, this is one of the most unique and renowned rooms in the house and over here, above the grand fireplace, we have a painting by the famed artist of the era— Eh, don't touch that please,' I said raising my voice. 'Please don't touch that! Can you tell him not to touch that and don't sit on the furniture. There can be no sitting on the furniture.' I wasn't in my comfort zone but being allowed to play freed me up and I went with the flow of it. For a moment, time collided as my childhood make-believe, youth theatre and a bit of life experience all melded together to enable me to let myself go and find my feet with it all.

'Well done, well done. That's great, Alison, Thank you. We'll let you know.' And off I went. As I left the building I could hardly breathe as my nerves suddenly caught up with me. Walking down the drive, I looked back at Hatfield House, which held my future in its hands, and the smiley lady opened the window and shouted, 'How did it go?'

How nice of her. 'I think it was okay,' I replied. 'I'm not sure, I hope so though.' She gave me a smile and said, 'I hope so too.'

It was the moment of support that I needed, and I turned back towards the driveway and headed towards the tube to make my way back home. The train journey was agonising as I replayed the day in my head. *Would Maggie have said that if she hadn't meant it? Why did the lady lean out the window? Did she know something? When will I know something?* Torture. It all felt so near, yet still so far away.

The next day at work it was tough not to regale Walton Probation Office with tales of my time at East 15 so I distracted myself by playing out the voices that were in various court reports that I had to type out, including a neighbourly dispute over a carton of eggs and the removal of some garden gnomes! The days went on and on and it felt like forever since I'd had my audition. Each morning, as I headed out of the house to work, the postman would pass by but never stop me. Then, about ten days after my return, he did. 'There's a letter here for you', handing me a brown foolscap envelope, my name and address handwritten on the front and a London postmark stamped across the right-hand side. This was it. This was the letter that I'd been waiting on. This was the letter that would reveal my future. Peeling back the lip of the envelope I slowly pulled out the paper inside. The letter heading was East 15. My eyes quickly darted down the page. 'Dear Alison, Thank you for coming to see us and auditioning for a place on our Drama course. We're pleased to inform you,' that was the phrase I was looking for, 'that we think that you have promise and would benefit from a training at East 15.' I let out a huge sigh. *Thank you, Maggie. Thank you, Jim. Thank you, Mum and Dad.* I turned on my heels and ran as fast as I could back to 22 Sherwyn Road, rushed up the stairs and into my parents' bedroom. 'I've got in, I've got in, I've got in,' I sang out, waving the letter in the air and hardly able to contain my excitement as my sleeping parents came to and began to realise what all the commotion was about. 'She's got in. You've got in. I've got in,' was the cacophony of sound that filled the room. Everyone was delighted. It wasn't only a big step for me, but one for my mum and dad too. They had sacrificed so many of their own dreams over the years and had been determined that things would be different for me. They couldn't have been happier. 'See,' Mum said. 'Never say you can't. Now off you go and remember to hand in your notice.'

CHAPTER 9

Blank Canvas

So it was that in September 1966 I was sitting on the 11.30 a.m. train from Liverpool Lime Street to London Euston waving goodbye to Mum and Dad.

The weeks before had been a hectic and emotional time, full of preparation and lots of repeated farewells. This was the first big moment of change in my life and I felt it in my core. It was like jumping out a plane. Not that I've ever done that, but the enormity felt the same for me. Liverpool was my home. It was what I knew. I hadn't really been anywhere before, or done anything, and certainly not on my own. For twenty years, all I had known was consistency and there I was on a train about to try for a life as an actress, one that might be full of inconsistency and change. *What was I doing? Perhaps my dad had been right? Oh well, at least I've got shorthand typing to fall back on if I need it. I hope I don't need it. There's always the shipping office. Pull yourself together. You're on your own. No turning back.* Is there a word that represents how a mixture of terror and excitement feels? If there is, then that's what I felt sitting on that train. I was overwhelmed by a sense of unknowingness and suspense mixed up with fear and anticipation.

There had been such a lot to gather up and organise. I'd got the place but then I had to get all the kit, which isn't something I'd factored in at all. The list was ten miles long and full of things that sounded dead theatrical. There was nothing on it that I could buy in C&A Modes or from any of the big stores in town, and even if they did sell the required items, I didn't have the money for them. If Grandma Evans had still been alive, she'd have run everything up for me, but that wasn't an option, and I couldn't ask my mum as she hadn't inherited the sewing gene at all. Luckily the mother of a friend of mine was able to make me the drop-to-the-floor practice skirt that I needed, and altered a one-piece swimming costume to fashion it into the black leotard that was required for movement classes. Fencing jackets and masks weren't to be found in Anfield, at least not of the sort that would be permitted, but luckily I was told that I could pick up some second-hand stuff left by final-year students when I arrived at East 15. It was very much a case of make do and mend, as I'm sure it was for all students from a similar background to mine. Despite there being a grant to cover all the tuition, accommodation and living costs, which made it possible for me to take up the offer in the first place, there were still many things that I needed to buy that put a pressure on the family's purse strings. And then there were the books! The library list of books by people I'd never heard of, rarely heard of and only slightly heard of was extensive and there was no way I could afford *The Complete Works of Shakespeare* and the collection of books by Konstantin Stanislavski: *Building a Character*, *Creating a Role* and *An Actor Prepares*. There would be no preparing anything if I didn't get these books and I began to despair as the hidden cost of trying to pursue my dream became a reality. Unbeknownst to me, as I was working my notice at Walton Probation Office, my colleagues, who weren't exactly rolling in money themselves, were clubbing together to buy the books that I needed. It's a gesture that I've never forgotten.

The journey to London felt like it was never going to end; in many ways, I didn't want it to as the thought of heading off across the city to Loughton and my first ever set of digs daunted me. *It's all going to be okay and nothing bad will happen to me*, I told myself as I firmly locked away my untold worries and focused on my bright new future. I'd had no idea of how to find a place to stay, in a place that I didn't know and had only visited once. It would all be relatively easy now, but back in 1966 it was much more of a slog, unless you had people who knew people who knew people, which very luckily I did. It was a bit like that scene from *The 101 Dalmatians*, when one dog barks across to another who barks across to another in the search for the pups. In my case, it was a search for somewhere to live. Jack Cogley from the probation office knew someone who knew someone in the southern division of the service and that person put me in touch with Mrs Wright who had a room in a flat that was a bus ride and a short walk away from East 15.

Mrs Wright, who should really have been called Mrs Wrong, was elderly, with short grey hair and glasses. She had agreed to take me in, but it felt that she done so reluctantly, and it soon became quite apparent that she really didn't want me there at all. There wasn't a Mr Wright and Mrs Wright was constantly preoccupied with my schedule. 'What time will you be back?' she'd chirrup. 'Make sure you lock the door after you. Don't make a noise if you get back late.' Living with Mrs Wright was like being a teenager with an overly restrictive parent and I walked on eggshells doing my utmost not to displease her. It wasn't easy for either of us, but it was a place to sleep as I got used to my new way of life.

Several weeks into our first term a crowd of us went into the West End together to see a show. I had dreamed of doing this sort of thing for so many years and it felt exhilarating to be part of a group of trainee actors going out to see a group of professional actors on stage. The evening had been full of laughter and great chat as we all brought our A game to the night out in an endeavour to begin to play the role of *being an actor*. There was a skip in my step when I got out of the tube and happily began to make my way up Loughton High Road. It was quite late and as I was walking along a car slowly pulled up beside me. The window rolled down and then a perfectly nice-sounding man said, 'Would you like a lift?'

A slight chill swept over me and I replied, 'No, I'm fine thanks, I've only got to go down—'

Before I could finish, he said, 'Are you sure that you know where you're going? Is it far?'

Needing him to drive on and get lost I said, 'No, it's fine, it's just down that alleyway down there, not far at all, just down there,' as firmly as I could muster.

He drove off but something inside me, call it instinct or survival, told me to keep my eye on the car. It turned down the alleyway that I'd mentioned that I'd be heading down. As it was the only route back to Mrs Wright's flat, I had no choice but to go down the alleyway too. The car was parked up a little further down. Nothing about this felt right and, to add to my concern, I noticed that the man was no longer inside the vehicle, but was hiding, not very well, at the side of it, crouching as if he was getting ready to pounce. *Just walk straight by and then make a run for it. You can do this.* As I walked by, he peeped out and then hid again. It looked pathetic and very weird. *He could jump on me*, was the thought that slapped me in the face as I realised this wasn't an ideal situation to be in. *Run.* And I bolted to the bottom of the lane, up the flight of steps that led to the door of the flat, ran in and slammed the door! I was too scared to bother to be quiet this time and too afraid to tell Mrs Wright because I thought she'd say, 'Oh, here we go, she's causing trouble now by bringing back men.' I closed the door to my room behind me then stood with my back against it before flopping down onto my bed while trying to breathe more slowly and get my heart rate down. I was terrified. This man knew where I lived, and he might come back. *Who should I tell? Should I mention it at all?* My mind flipped to a memory that I'd been trying to push to the back of my mind, an incident that had happened a few years previously that I'd sworn to myself I'd never share with anyone.

I'd say that I'm a trusting person and that my parents brought me up to see the good in people and things, and not the worst. Did this make me naive and overly innocent, foolish even? All I know is that every Friday evening for most of my teenage years I spent time in the company of adults that I trusted and felt safe with. These were people, like Jim Wiggins, Tony Joy and Mildred Spencer, who did nothing but act in our best interests and gently guide us to take the steps that we needed to move ourselves forward in life. It was offered freely, and nothing was expected in return. The youth theatre felt like family, and it was all that I knew. From time to time though we'd have visiting tutors who would join to teach us something specific or to direct a play; this felt special, and we always enjoyed it. For a few weeks, a teacher from one of the local secondary schools came in to run workshops for us. He was an extremely funny man; he'd make us all laugh and we were all very fond of him. It was the end of our usual Friday-night class, although we were rehearsing in the city centre and not in our regular room in Anfield Road School. As we were packing up to leave, the visiting tutor came over to me and said, 'You live near me, don't you?'

I didn't know where he lived and said, 'I live in Anfield,' to which he replied, 'Oh, I live in Bootle, it's not far from you, I'll give you a lift if you like?'

I'd already arranged something and replied, 'No, it's okay thanks, I'm going to get the bus with my friend.'

The funny teacher didn't take my no for an answer and went on, 'Come on, I'll drop you off, you'll be back home much sooner if I do.' Perhaps it was because he was being so friendly that I agreed to go with him, or maybe because he'd always been so lovely to us and made us laugh, or maybe it was because my sixteen-year-old self felt too embarrassed to continue to say no. We stepped outside, and he guided me to where his car was parked. I'd never seen a vehicle like it. It was one of the new minuscule bubble cars, with no doors and a roof that lifted up and down to let people in and out. It could be described as cosy if you wanted to squash up next to someone, or awkward if you didn't. My instinct was screaming at me not to get in the car, but the roof lifted, and I stepped in and sat down. It makes me shudder to think about how compliant I was. The workshop leader got in beside me and pulled the roof down. It was like being trapped inside a small cave and a feeling of claustrophobia washed over me. There was no way out. *It'll be fine. It'll be fine*, I said to myself as we drove off. *He's a teacher.* And then the thing that you think only happens in scary films began to happen to me. Instead of heading in the direction of Anfield and driving me home, the teacher, the man who made us laugh and made us like him, drove out to Sefton Park. The park is huge with multiple entrances and driveways and large areas of woodland. The indicator light ticked over very deliberately, sounding like a countdown, and the car curved into the park. *Counting down to what? Why are we in Sefton Park?* It wasn't somewhere that I knew very well or went very often, and my mind raced trying to think of which way to run if I ever got out of the car.

It was 9.30 p.m. and darkness had descended. I knew Liverpool well enough to know that driving through the park wasn't a short cut to Anfield and the safety of 22 Sherwyn Road. 'Which way are we going?' I asked, trying not to sound too anxious. 'This isn't the way home.' He turned and looked at me but said nothing and carried on driving. It was becoming darker and darker as we headed deeper into the wooded area of park until, finally, we were surrounded by tall, dense groupings of trees and undergrowth. The car slowed down and he pulled up into the blackness of an isolated spot. There was no traffic, no other people, just us. *What do I do? What can I do? I'm stuck.* He turned, looked at me and then took my hand in one of his, and with the other began to trace patterns on my palm with the tips of his fingers as he stared at me with an ominous look in his eyes. The feeling of his nails crawling on my skin made me feel sick but any time I flinched he'd take a more insistent, firmer hold. So many terrible images flashed through my mind at that moment. *What did he want? This isn't normal. This feels far from normal.* It became stranger and stranger. 'Recite a poem,' he demanded, and I frantically tried to remember something. 'Recite a poem!' He reached across, touched my knee and tauntingly walked his fingers up and down my thigh talking about all the things that he'd like to do to me. My heart was pounding in my chest like a drum solo and I took careful slow breaths in an attempt to keep quiet and not react to the proximity of his sinister presence, but inside all my alarms bells were going off and I was shrieking. 'I'm going to tell them all about you at the youth theatre,' he sneered. It was as if I'd initiated whatever game was being played out and was enjoying it. I wasn't. 'Who do you think they'd believe? A schoolgirl or me?' He was enjoying this.

'I was a monk and then in the Army and now I'm a schoolteacher. They'd believe me over you, and don't forget that.' What a thought to put into my young, vulnerable mind. 'I could do whatever I want with you now. I could murder you and dump your body in the park. No one would know it was me. No one knows we're here together. No one knows that you're here with me.' He was right about that. I suddenly realised that no one else had been around when we'd left the building together and driven off in his car. It had all been planned.

An hour must have passed with this man, who, over the last five weeks had gained our trust, who'd given us no reason to doubt him, and who was now sleazily stroking my palm, then rubbing his hands up and down my legs, and worst of all whispering the most horrendous graphic details of what he could do to me, what he'd like to do to me, as he breathed all over me. And then he stopped. Just like that. He put the key into the ignition, the car started up, and he drove out of the park and dropped me on Sherwyn Road as if none of it had happened and that everything was completely normal. It was nearly 11.00 p.m. I knew that my parents would be worried as I was coming from the city centre, and this was a far later return than usual. I jumped out the car and ran as fast as I could into the house. 'Where've you been, we've been so worried,' said my mum. My impulse was to run into her arms and cry but instead I said, 'It's all fine, youth theatre went on a bit longer than it should have done and I missed the bus. I'm fine, nothing to worry about.' Excuse after excuse because I didn't have the words to tell her about what had just happened. I was sixteen and this man's threats had robbed me of telling the truth to my mum. *If I tell her she won't let me go back to youth theatre again and then that will be that.* I was so muddled by it all and quickly said my goodnights, rushed upstairs to my room and got into the safety of my bed, pulling the covers over me in an act of self-protection. His mocking, 'Who'd you think they'd believe?' kept going around in my head and flashes of his circling fingers on my palms and his hands making an impression on my legs appeared every time I closed my eyes. *Why me? Why had he picked on me? He's about to get married. How could he do that?*

The following Friday night I headed into the youth theatre hoping that he wouldn't be there. I was determined that he wasn't going to soil the love that I had for the Friday-night classes and make me buckle under the emotional pressure that I was feeling from the experience in Sefton Park. However, when I entered the room there he was looking like a full-blooded predator who'd come back to put his yet uncaught prey in its place. He stood in the middle of the room with his hands on his hips, 'Right, here's the improvisation for tonight. I want you all to get ready for bed and then to get into bed. Is that clear? So, off you go.' We all began to set the scene for ourselves and build our improvisations. I was aware that he was staring at me steadfastly with a gleam in his eye and didn't avert his gaze once. 'Stop, stop,' he said, 'this is silly, none of you are taking your clothes off. We all take our clothes off before going to bed, don't we? So, begin again and this time remember to take all your clothes off.' There was no choice but to do as he told us to, and we all began to mime taking our clothes off. It was an excruciating five minutes and he didn't take his eyes off me for a moment. It was as if he was laying down a gauntlet, 'Don't you dare tell anyone, or else.'

The Loughton peeping Tom in the car earlier had been bad enough but nothing compared to what had happened in the bubble car in Sefton Park four years previously. *Nothing like this must ever happen again*, I thought, as I turned over on my bed and tried to push all the fearful images far away, *It mustn't*. I resolved to move out of Mrs Wright's flat at the end of term and to keep storing the dreadful memory of my encounter with the man who had groomed us all to trust him deep within the back of my mind. *I can't allow this to hurt me anymore. It's time to move on and continue with a clean slate, a blank canvas.*

A blank canvas has limitless possibilities. It's about what might happen next, what story might be told. For as long as I can remember, the notion of a blank canvas has always captured my imagination and excited me, especially if it was linked to an open space or an empty stage where I could paint a picture out of my make-believe. It was never *No it's not possible* or *I can't do that*. The blank canvas was always about possibility and daring to take up the chance to create something new.

East 15 was my blank canvas. This was the place where I was going to discover how to use all aspects of my being to tell stories and it felt daunting. Maggie Bury had seen something in me as I'd boxed and tour-guided my way through my audition several months earlier, but that was then, and this was now. It was going to be far more testing than creating the couple of improvisations that had been thrown at me. Sitting on the floor of the large drawing room, in the big house that was to be where I threw colour onto my own blank canvas, I reminded myself that this wasn't just about me. Acting is a team sport, and it was about everyone else too, their energy, their imagination. It was my responsibility to collaborate, to be a positive part of the team, not to block but to listen carefully and absorb before adding and building to what was going on. *Thank goodness for all those years at the youth theatre.* I might not have had posh elocution lessons or seen many professional plays on the stage, but I had been immersed in the telling of stories for years, and now, here at East 15, some brilliant teachers were going to help me discover how to get better and better at doing it.

The smell of cigarette smoke wafted over our newly formed seated floor circle as one of my fellow first-year students lit up a cigarette. It felt a bit daring to me. *Perhaps it's that sort of place where anything goes*, is what I thought, before the idea was very quickly stubbed out by Maggie Bury entering the room, long hair flowing, wearing an Afghan coat and saying, 'There is to be no smoking in the house.' There were rules and we were here to learn them. During that first year, it was like preparing to create an amazing piece of art as we scraped off the paint from the canvas that we'd each brought into East 15 and took everything back to basics. It was a strict routine of voice and movement and improvisation, before we began to tackle any scenes, let alone a full-length play.

There was so much learning to be done. Maria Santa Vani, our movement teacher, was tiny but she had the biggest impact on me during my time at college, as everything that she did was designed to help us try to understand another human being by beginning from a physical point of view, and this really resonated with me. She took us right back to our so-called blank canvas and we spent weeks learning how to do a neutral walk. Chalking a large square on the floor, Maria would say, 'Right, one at a time, I'd like you to walk on the line and go from edge to edge of the square without bringing your own way of walking into the exercise or putting on anyone else's.' It's easier said than done, so we'd spend hours and hours trying to perfect our neutral walks along the fine line. There was a great deal of starting again in our attempts to walk neutrally! It was hilarious too, as week after week, no matter how often she tried, one of the girls would continually thrust out her bust, swing her hips from side to side and grace the square as if it were a catwalk. 'Right,' Maria would say, 'put your hands by your side,' which the girl did. 'Straighten your back and keep it straight,' which the girl did. 'Keep your head and eyes up and look forward,' which the girl did. 'Now off you go.' And without fail, time after time, the hips would swing and sway as the ample bust led the way and the girl sashayed around the square. It was character-building stuff.

'Look around the room and look at each other's shapes. Stare, it's not rude. You're honing your observational skills and beginning to read people by how they hold themselves.' The body speaks and you can tell a lot from another person's walk, posture and gesture. 'Now find a partner, someone who you think is a similar size to you.' We all looked around the room and slowly began to get ourselves into couples without offending anyone who might be mistaken about what size they thought they were. Maria's next instruction came as a bit of a surprise. 'Right, now I want you to swap clothes with your partner and come back into the room wearing them.' I looked down at my scruffy jeans and the big, brown woolly jumper that I'd flung on without much thought earlier in the day. It was winter and I'd dressed for warmth and ease of movement, not style. My partner's clothes were tight, mostly pink and very bust revealing – the polar opposite to mine. We trusted Maria implicitly, and spent the rest of the class inhabiting our partner's clothes and their physicality. It was one of the most memorable days for me and hugely insightful. In that one simple task of inviting us to swap clothes, Maria had quietly taught us so much about how the choices we make about our exterior self can have an impact on how we're perceived by others, as well as seep into the subconscious narrative that we tell ourselves. It's obvious to say, clothes change us, they do, but to discover why, in what way and how much, was the beginning of an exploration into detail that I'd call upon forever. A little later in the session, as we were swapping back into our own clothes, my busty partner boldly gave me some advice, possibly brought on by the fact that she'd had to slop about in my sack-like jumper all afternoon. 'Alison,' she said, 'when you buy a bra, you should always buy a smaller size, it helps to make your boobs look bigger.' Ouch! It's not something that I ever acted upon.

Alongside our daily movement classes, we had voice sessions to strengthen our vocal cords and support our delivery of language, as well as to give us an insight into how the way that they speak and use words can tell us so much about a person. It's not just the sound that comes from the mouth that reveals us, but speed, articulation, emphasis and enunciation. Jess, our brilliant voice teacher, was so encouraging and helpful as I began to explore tuning the sound of my own voice into another person's. 'You're Scouse, Alison,' she said, which I didn't think was as obvious as she was suggesting, as my accent wasn't as strong as some, 'and most people from Liverpool speak in the minor key, even if they're quite posh,' which I wasn't, 'and it's difficult to get out of the habit, Alison.' *Is it?* 'You need to be able to lift and drop your vocal range and go in and out of it like you're going up and down scales if you want to play all sorts of characters,' which I did. 'One of the best things you can do is listen to the news on the radio and repeat everything that you hear. That'll train you to use all the different registers that your voice has.' I began the next day and still consider it some of the best advice that I was ever given. I prepared to take to the stage without a trace of an Anfield accent, if need be, to ensure that the repertoire of roles that I could play was as rich as possible.

As first-year students we'd be invited to support our friends who were in the years above us by attending the plays that they put on in the main drawing room of the house. These were great occasions, and an opportunity to learn through watching and listening. It always felt like a special moment as we sat in a circle on the hard-backed wooden chairs and waited for the show to begin. It felt like a *family* affair and everyone who worked in the building would come along, including the lovely lady who worked in the school canteen and had the job of making sure that we were all fed and watered each day. At one such production a solitary empty seat in the front row remained free until just before it was about to begin when this rather large Welsh lady, who served us lunch, squeezed into it. She was due to be making the drinks at the interval so had planned to see the first half and then nip out, unnoticed, to get the tea urn all set up. I was sitting directly behind her and as the interval was getting closer, I became aware that she was getting a bit twitchy. *How was she going to get up and out to the canteen without disturbing things?* was the thought in my mind as she began to writhe and twist in the seat due to her body being rather tightly compressed into the chair. It was a Chekhov play and there was a boy standing within touching distance of the front row, wearing a shirt and braces. Little did he know how essential his costume was going to become. Mrs Stuck-in-her-Chair looked down at her watch and realised that she was leaving it a bit tight if she wanted to get the teas out on time. To make matter worse, she was worryingly wedged into her seat and no amount of twisting and turning was helping to release her. What happened next was the stuff of comedy-sketch dreams and one of the funniest things I've witnessed during a performance. Not being able to get herself out of the chair, and with the tea urn whistling through the hatch, she reached over to the boy, grabbed a hold of his braces to haul herself out of her compromising position and with a quick, 'Yaki dah,' to the actor, who was looking far less Chekhovian than five minutes earlier, straightened her pinny and headed off to make the tea. Who ever said that the drama was all on stage?!

Stanislavski's book *An Actor Prepares* was one of my most treasured possessions during my time at East 15. There is so much learning in every chapter and I devoured it. Better still was the practical work that we did with Maggie Bury that enabled us to put into practice the techniques in the different areas of acting that were covered in the book. Stanislavski tells the story of a young actress called Maria who, during an emotional scene, became so overwrought that she crushed her character's wine glass in her palm shredding her soft flesh to pieces. Stanislavski used this to remind actors that they must never get so caught up within their acting that they become unaware of their reality and how essential it was to have a third eye on things. Cut to our class with Maggie, excuse the pun, and a girl in a scene from *The Crucible* by Arthur Miller. When her character had to wake up and get out of bed saying, 'I'm going to fly to Mamma,' our classmate ran across the room as fast as if she was just out of the starting blocks for a 100-metre sprint and straight into a pane of glass which shattered, leaving her also with cuts on her hands. The next day, Maggie, who was never one to cosset us, said to the bandaged girl, 'You didn't have your third eye switched on.' She then turned to us all saying, 'Remember Maria with the wine glass?' Class over. Stanislavski was in the room.

That first year of laying down foundations and learning to let go was an essential step in beginning to build and secure my shaky confidence so that I felt more robust and able to take on everything that was thrown at us. It was a completely different world for me and even though I'd muck in with everything that I was tasked with, I wasn't always as sure footed as I might have appeared. Perhaps my assessment of myself was overly harsh but during that first year I didn't always feel adequate and that same feeling of dread that I got when teachers would ask me to read aloud at school often simmered very close to the surface at East 15. It felt like everyone else knew so much more than me, that they'd all read *The Complete Works of Shakespeare*, at least twice, as well as the Greeks. I'd never even read a whole play. It wasn't just me though, there were lots of us who needed to play catch up. 'You're not knowledgeable enough,' Maggie Bury said to the year group during our final session. 'If you want to be actors then you need to read plays,' and with that she packed us all off for the summer holidays with what she considered was an essential reading list. Our first three terms at East 15 had begun to stir a change in us: we were growing up and becoming more adventurous. We were beginning to mix colours on our individual blank canvasses, and as my train headed out of Euston to Liverpool Lime Street, I knew that returning to my roots would add to the picture too.

CHAPTER 10

My Name Is Alison Steadman

T he final term! *How has that happened? Where has the time gone? Am I ready to leave the security of East 15 and all my classmates and friends?* The thought of leaving wasn't one that I wanted to countenance. *There's still a term to go. Hang on to it. Have fun.*

I'd returned from Lincoln and *The Prime of Jean Brodie*, with no plan. Luckily my brazen and enthusiastic declaration of 'This is the real me!' to a theatre bar packed with press-night guests had gone largely unnoticed, although Martin Duncan, our stage manager, and his parents did turn around for a moment and give watery smiles. I wanted the ground to swallow me up. The run of the show, which was only a couple of weeks, had been the continuation of training that I needed before heading back to East 15 for the final term and to the gentle teasing from my classmates about the fact that I'd taken my clothes off on stage. 'Why don't you audition for the revival of *Hair*? Perhaps you should create a naked monologue called *Revealing All*! Or even better, *Revealing Alison*!' This was all water off a duck's back to me. It hadn't been gratuitous, the scene was in the script and Richard Wherrett, the director and our tutor, had ensured that it was all done extremely professionally and with care. There were more important things to be concerned about. This was our final term.

By this stage in our training, we were staging full-length productions, and our repertoire was brimming with some of the *greats* in terms of plays. It was only natural to want a bite at all of the leading roles, but we'd had it drummed into us that, 'There's no such thing as a small part, only small actors!' Having taken smaller roles in other productions, in Shakespeare's *King Lear* I had a larger role playing Regan, Lear's middle daughter. Regan is devious, dangerous, selfish and ambitious for power, and I adored playing her. It's a huge play with epic themes and we needed to get this into our bodies as well as our heads. During our rehearsals, Maggie, who was directing us, said, 'Okay, get your coats on everyone, we're going outside.' It was wintery and snow was falling as she began to march vigorously around the grounds with her arms gesturing wildly, repeating from the play: 'Blow winds and crack your cheeks, blow you cataracts and hurricanoes.' We all followed suit. There was a chill wind that was blowing the snow all around us as we called to the elements over and over until we understood at a visceral level the meaning of what was being said. I thought back to my early experiences of speaking Shakespeare aloud, how I'd felt the sounds within the words and how the emotions had stirred within me.

There was a lot of fun to be had, but I struggled too. A voice in my head would be saying, *You need to do better, stop showing yourself up, you're not good enough, they think that you're rubbish.* It's called imposter syndrome these days. *Get a hold of yourself, Alison. You can do this*, was a regular mantra. I was definitely over-complicating matters and needed to find a way to take it back to basics. During that final year at East 15 one piece of work really got me down and panic was beginning to set in as time was running out before the show opened to an audience. Sitting in front of the television one evening, in a bit of a fog, I began to pay particular attention to one character. There was something about them that struck a chord with me, and I thought that I'd experiment with taking aspects of what I had seen and try to build it into how I played my role. It worked! Something had clicked. It was a wonderful feeling. I'd found the character, it was mine, and now I could do what I wanted with it and begin to play. It was a very clear moment of understanding how I needed to work, as well as a reassuring reminder that I'd been doing this since my first impressions of Hylda Baker. Sometimes we need to go back to go forward.

There's no business like show business took on a very different meaning during those last weeks as the realisation that we were about to leave took hold. It was one thing play acting at drama school but if we wanted to work and have a career then we needed to think of ourselves as business propositions. It felt ugly and wrong and all the fibres in my body wanted to resist it. *Oh God! Who do I write to? What do I say? Do I write to agents first or to directors? Perhaps I should write to the theatres? Should I get back in touch with Walton Probation Office? I'm not going to work in a shipping office!* The prospect of walking down the steps and leaving the building that had given me so much and had offered such happiness and security for three years made me so incredibly nervous. But despite my internal resistance I wrote letter after letter to try to avoid being jobless and penniless. It was all so labour intensive back then, paper and pen, envelopes and stamps, as well as trying to get to the post on time. It felt like begging. 'To whom it may concern, My name is Alison Steadman and I'd be very grateful if you'd consider auditioning me for your forthcoming season.' Goodness knows how many letters must have gone straight into the bin without even being read. It wasn't easy to launch yourself. On top of all of that most of the agents wouldn't consider you until they could see you in a job and it was impossible to get a job without an Equity card, which you could only be given by certain accredited theatres. Trapped! As our last day loomed, the pressure mounted and mounted, and the feeling of standing on the edge of a precipice felt very real.

The school lined up in-house auditions with some of the freelance directors that we'd worked with over our time there and gave us a showcase as an opportunity to invite key people as well as family and friends. My parents made the trip from Liverpool; it was the first time that they'd seen where I'd been studying. Mum was all dressed up in her best attire for the occasion, including wearing a hat, and the astonished look that she gave me when Maggie came wafting in wearing an Afghan coat with her hair loose over her shoulders, and introduced herself, translated as, 'Is *she* the principal?' It was the first time that my two very different worlds had collided. It was a necessary combustion that indicated that from now on I'd be spending more time in one of them than the other.

I got lucky having the parents that I did. It would have been so much easier for them for dissuade me from following my passion to become an actress, and instead encourage me to stay closer to home and get a *proper job*. It wasn't until this end-of-year show that I began to realise just how lucky I was, when only a few of the parents turned up. I can remember during my first term there, as we were all getting to know each other, being astonished by how many parents had stopped talking to their children, mostly the boys, due to their decision to try to make it as an actor and begin by training at East 15. It wasn't deemed a suitable job for the likes of *us*. This wasn't a thought that crossed my own mind, however. I'd had such a great deal of support and encouragement that when I arrived at East 15, it felt like I was meant to be there. No one else in my family had done anything other than go to school, then leave formal education by the time they were sixteen and go to work. Going on to further education, as I did, plus to train in something that was regarded as radical and a risk, was a huge first for my family and it says a great deal about who my parents were as people that they did all that they could to make it possible for me.

It was a family affair and although my Grandma Evans had died by the time I went to drama school, my Grandma Steadman was still alive and completely behind it all. When I returned home after my first term away, I had decided to show my parents some of my newly learnt skills and got dressed up as our lovely Scottish neighbour, Mrs Grey, and began to have a chat with my mum, much in the same way I'd heard them talking during their garden meetings when they were pegging out the washing. There was a knock at the door and, my grandma came in. I kept on chatting in the guise of Mrs Grey. She had no idea that it was me and it took her some time before she realised that it couldn't be Mrs Grey. As I revealed myself, she said, 'You're very good you know. You should be an actress.'

Thank goodness for Philip Hedley is all I can say. Philip had been one of the first students at East 15 back in 1961. He wasn't much older than us so we always felt a great connection with him and how he worked. Philip was a risk taker. Having been given the opportunity to return to East 15 after graduation so that he could hone his skills as a director, he returned the kindness by encouraging new talent and always tried to find ways of supporting graduates through the tricky waters of their early days in the business. As well as teaching at East 15, Philip had been made Artistic Director at Lincoln Theatre Royal and although he hadn't directed *The Prime of Miss Jean Brodie*, he had seen me in it as well as in several of our final shows. Thank goodness for Philip Hedley. I can't say it enough. I'll always be grateful to him for giving me an audition at Lincoln towards the end of my time at East 15 and before I wandered into the unknown wilderness of trying to be a professional actress. The audition at Lincoln went well but, as with all auditions, you never did know really. That feeling of impending doom and how to manage the sense of rejection wasn't something that had been talked about so I just hoped for the best.

The last day arrived. To celebrate the achievements of the past three years we'd decided to organise a farewell party and go out with a bang. 'Hey, Alison,' someone shouted over the music from the far end of the room, 'there's a letter for you in the hall.' The last time someone had said there was a letter for me was when our local postie at Sherwyn Road had stopped me on my way to work, to hand me the envelope that had then transported me from Liverpool L4 to London E15. 'Steadman, did you get that? There's a letter for you on the hall table.' I'd written loads of letters; it was probably yet another thanks-but-no-thanks note, so I didn't rush across to the door that led into the hall. But then again … Ever the optimist, something that my mum had handed down to me, the feeling of *What if?* began to rise in me. 'There's a letter for you' was a sign. The large oak table in the hall was usually strewn with letters, theatre programmes and other paraphernalia; however, possibly because it was the last day of term and everyone was about to leave, it looked quite bare and so the slimline envelope with my name on it stood out immediately. There was also one for my friend Howard Lloyd Lewis. They looked identical and both had a Lincoln stamp mark on them. There's always a moment with letters isn't there, when the thought of leaving it unopened is preferable to opening it up to reveal the communication that's inside? *Perhaps I should wait 'til later? Should I go and get Howard and get him to open his first?* I looked down at my letter and feeling a surge of hopefulness opened it where I stood. 'Dear Alison,

Thank you for auditioning for me. I'm pleased to be able to offer you a position as Acting ASM at the Theatre Royal Lincoln. If you could let me know if this is something that appeals or not, then we'll take it from there.' Howard and I had both been offered Acting ASM roles, which back in those days stood for Acting Assistant Stage Manager and meant that we'd have roles, but not in every show, and when we weren't in costume we'd cover backstage jobs. So Howard and I ended our time at East 15 with a sprinkle of serendipity and a good reason to get back to the party and celebrate.

In 1969, the regional repertory system was still very robust and there were theatres, grand and small, dotted all over the regions, that programmed annual seasons of work, some that only covered the summer months and other larger theatres that offered a year-round series of plays. For young actors, being offered a role in a repertory theatre was a brilliant way to keep learning your craft as it was usually a case of twice-nightly shows and a new show to learn every fourteen days. This kept us all on our toes and the fortnightly routine of rehearsing a play whilst another was on stage was exhausting but we weren't complaining. Being busy and in work, and having the opportunity to play roles that we'd never get to play in the West End at this stage of our careers was a gift.

Once again, it was a case of packing up and finding digs, which was a bit easier than my first attempt as the theatre had a list of places that they recommended in Lincoln. There was quite a formal process for securing a room and usually there was an interview with the prospective landlady that included the loaded question, 'And do you have a boyfriend?' I soon learned that the correct answer was, 'No, but I do have a husband.' I'd go along to the interview with a fake wedding band that was fashioned from a curtain ring. It was the only way, if you did have a boyfriend (which I did), of being able to invite him to stay overnight at any time. It was utterly ridiculous really. My digs, a room in a huge, sprawling Victorian house owned by a retired couple, were close to the theatre and it felt safe enough to walk home in the evening. The husband, a retired rugby player, with swollen cauliflower ears, was completely deaf but his wife was one of the fussiest people that I'd ever met. They lived downstairs and rented the four upstairs rooms to actors. Mrs Fusspot was always hoovering and finding something to grumble about. She was constantly saying to me, 'Jean Boht's husband is coming next week, and she *is* married,' as if to say, 'I'm on to you, young lady.' But it was a lovely house to stay in, safe and comfortable, and we had our own bathroom upstairs which meant that we didn't have to be more involved with the couple downstairs than we wanted to be.

Even though I'd announced my marital status and made sure to wear my curtain ring on my wedding finger, permission had to be requested before inviting anyone to stay over. I explained that my husband would be arriving late one Friday night and that he'd be sleeping in late on Saturday morning, while I went into the theatre to rehearse and then do a matinee. 'Well,' came an indignant huffy sound, 'how am I supposed to hoover the room then?' I reined in my sweary response and said, 'Can't you leave it until later?' She puffed herself up like a squawking parakeet and said, 'No. No, I can't leave it until later. I always hoover at eleven o'clock on a Saturday and this Saturday will be exactly the same!' That was me told.

Each week when we knocked on her living-room door to hand in the little rent books that she'd given us, she'd open the door, leaving it slightly ajar, and go over to her desk to get a pen to sign the book. It was the same every week. She was always dressed up as if she was about to go to a dance, she'd hoover the carpet and collect the rent dressed up to the nines in this sticky-out skirt and her hair all set even though the 1950s had faded into the distance. Several weeks into my stay, I knocked at the door, and she answered with her typical curt, 'Oh hello,' before heading to her desk. She'd left the door open wider than usual so I could see her husband sitting in his chair with his back to the door. He'd no idea that I was there and when his wife walked past, he put his hand up her skirt and she squealed, 'Oh get off, get off!' She signed the rent book, came back to the door a little flustered and blushy, looked at me coyly and said, 'Oh, you'll have to excuse him, he's just had a bath!' It was a much as I could do to say thank you before she shut the door and I burst into fits of laughter.

We'd never had to do backstage jobs at East 15 and I hadn't a clue at first. But I took the responsibility of being an Acting ASM in this beautiful theatre, with its luscious red velvet curtains and proper stage lighting, very seriously. It was an education, as I moved from prop making to costume maintenance to cooking, as well as actual rehearsals for any play that I was in.

The first time I was working with the prop master he said, 'Your job, Alison, is to make the ice cream for tonight. It's got to be coloured ice cream, you know the sort? It's in a block, you know the one.' I didn't know the one. *Oh no! Not on my first job. I've no idea how to make ice cream let alone the multicoloured variety.* Plucking up my courage and going back to the prop master I said, 'Excuse me, I've got a problem. I've got to make a block of coloured ice cream and I've no idea, even if I can make the ice cream, how to stop it melting.' He looked at me and said, 'Right, here's some money. Go to the shops and buy a packet of Smash and some raspberry- and chocolate-flavoured food colouring. When you make the Smash divide it into three then add the colours to two parts, and that's that, you'll have Neapolitan ice cream.' It was that simple and I graduated from making ice cream to making whisky and wine from watered-down tea and as the weeks went on relaxed into it all.

Perhaps I relaxed too much. Once I was standing in the wings watching one of the shows from the side when I realised that I'd forgotten to set a particular food prop on stage. *Oh no! What can I do?* I grabbed the edible prop from the table and began to frantically wave to the actress on stage until she caught my eye. She walked straight into the wings, took it from me, then marched back on but came out through the bedroom with the food and not the kitchen, as she was meant to in the script. I don't know if anyone noticed but I was mortified.

The production team were great to work with and naughty too, which was dangerous territory for me given my inclination to laugh when I wasn't supposed to. In Arnold Wesker's kitchen-sink drama *Roots*, my small role required me to sit at a table towards the back of the stage, but still in view. The table was laid out for full afternoon tea with cake that had been made from yellow foam bath sponges. It definitely wasn't edible. A few of the other actors sitting at the table kept offering me bits of cake to eat, which of course I couldn't, but they kept on and on until I couldn't stop laughing and the director really told me off for that. It's hazardous, laughter like that.

So, by day I was sweeping the stage and making ice cream and the like while by night, if it was one of my shows, I was on stage in some great roles. We'd tackled Shakespeare at college, but the Theatre Royal Lincoln surprised me by giving me my first opportunity of doing it professionally when they cast me as Ophelia to Brian Prothero's Hamlet. Ophelia was a much bigger role than I'd had before and the character captivated me. She is a young girl, madly in love and totally confused by the contrary nature of her boyfriend.

That, combined with the tragic death of her beloved father, Polonius, at the hands of her boyfriend, spirals her, understandably, into an unbalanced place. Ophelia's text is delicate and real, and she expresses exactly what a young woman would express if these things had happened to her. It was important to me to get it right. I was moved by it, and I wanted the audience to be moved by it too. As we were heading into our technical rehearsals just before opening, I was handed the headdress that the designer had created for Ophelia's death scene. *No, I'm not wearing that*, I thought, not for the first time at the Theatre Royal. *I look ridiculous*, and I took myself to the wardrobe team and asked if it could be swapped? They gave me a few plastic flowers which didn't really help me to feel the moment, so I went back to the ridiculous one. One evening after the show, I was in the theatre bar when an elderly lady came up to me and said, 'I hope you don't mind me interrupting you, but I just wanted to say that the headdress that you wore was wonderful. It was just so appropriate because it has honesty woven through it.' I wasn't sure what she meant. 'Honesty?' 'Yes, that's the name of the flower. Honesty.' I loved it after that. Ophelia is a true and honest person, and the headdress was perfect for her.

My first season in Lincoln was a stepping stone; I felt lucky to be there and grateful for it. Being an Acting ASM gave me an understanding and respect for the complete world of the theatre and everyone that works in one. 'The play's the thing,' as Hamlet says, but it's not the only thing. Everything that happens around the action on stage is what makes theatre, and the audience is a huge part of that too.

Towards the end of my time there, at the end of the evening performance of *The Plough and the Stars* by Sean O'Casey, one of the team said, 'Someone's at the stage door for you, Alison.' This was a bit odd as I hadn't any guests in, mainly because all I did was run on stage with a suitcase, do a scene in a shop, then run off again. I know, I know, there's no such thing as a small part! It was a small part though and one that I really enjoyed. 'Alison Steadman to the stage door' came over the tannoy. I was still in the dressing room taking my time to get changed back into myself, so I quickly swept up all my stuff and headed down.

There, standing just outside in the dank, cold, miserable evening, was Joan Littlewood. Joan Littlewood, my theatre heroine, standing there waiting for me. I could hardly believe it. 'Hello,' I said without wanting to look and sound too starstruck. This was Joan Littlewood after all. Joan Littlewood, the giant who had changed how theatre in the UK was being performed forever. Joan Littlewood who had given Maggie Bury and Philip Hedley such inspiration and who in turn had handed it on to me. *This is a moment. This is like meeting the Queen.* We shook hands and she said, 'I just wanted to say well done on that scene, beautiful. You did it really well.' I couldn't believe it, *Oh my God*, I thought, *Joan Littlewood liked my work*, and replied, 'Thank you, thank you very much,' and then she gave a nod, smiled and off she went. *Did that just happen? Who would have thought.*

I headed back in through the stage door to collect my bits and pieces. Martin Duncan, our stage manager, was there and he threw one of my lines from another play at me, something that we always did when we saw each other.

'Well, I aren't grumbling,' he said. How true. I certainly wasn't.

TOP LEFT: No cozzie, but vest and knickers will do. Me (right) and my oldest friend, Hilary, on New Brighton beach.

TOP CENTRE: Kilted. Well, I am a Campbell after all.

TOP RIGHT: My fourth birthday party, completed as always by a cake made with love by my mum.

MIDDLE LEFT: Just after pulling Father Christmas's beard. It wasn't real!

MIDDLE CENTRE: Whisky: the love of my life.

BELOW: 'Say cheese!' So I did, but I'm not sure what the others said!

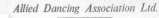

Allied Dancing Association Ltd.

'MEDAL' & 'DIPLOMA'
AMATEUR BALLROOM TESTS

No. 31 · Name of Candidate...... Alison Steadman......

GRADE...... Jnr.Silver (Dip).

DANCES	Marks Awarded	REMARKS
WALTZ —	20	
FOX TROT —	20	
TANGO —	20	Hip contact needed.
QUICKSTEP —	20	
Additional Dances		

COMMENDED

MARKINGS

Maximum Marks in all Grades ..	25
Pass Marks in Bronze Medal Test	15
Pass Marks in Silver Medal Test	18
Pass Marks in Gold Medal Test	21
Pass Marks in Allied Emblem	23

in each Dance

This Result Form is for the use of the Teachers only

TOP LEFT: My lovely mum, looking so elegant in poor Mr Fox. Her fur was to become the prefect prop for my Hylda Baker impression.

TOP MIDDLE: A magical moment for my grandparents Maurice Evans and Mary Campbell.

TOP RIGHT: More hip action needed? I don't think so.

MIDDLE: Sent for a reason. Four-year-old George Percival Steadman, surrounded by love.

BELOW: Childwall Valley High School production of *The Gypsy Baron*. In the back row behind the lead, but with my eyes on centre stage.

TOP: Taking it all terribly seriously as a serving girl in a youth theatre production of *Doctor and the Devils* in 1963.

MIDDLE LEFT: With friends Millie and Judy, practising commedia dell'arte at my pioneering drama school, East 15.

MIDDLE RIGHT: And they all lived happily ever after! Student production of *Ali Baba*, 1968.

BOTTOM RIGHT: *The Prime of Miss Jean Brodie*. Still with my clothes on!

TOP LEFT: The look of love. Howard Lloyd Lewis and I acting it up in our first season.

TOP RIGHT: *Black Comedy*, blonde wig. Not my best look.

MIDDLE: Aging up (and looking like I've got a bag of flour on my head) at the Bolton Octagon.

BOTTOM LEFT: Won't you Charleston with me? *The Boy Friend*, Worcester Theatre, 1972.

BOTTOM RIGHT: My first professional Shakespeare.

Lincoln Theatre Company

LINCOLN THEATRE COMPANY

HAMLET
by WILLIAM SHAKESPEARE

CAST :

Claudius, King of Denmark	JOHN LIVESEY
Hamlet, Prince of Denmark, son to the late, and nephew to the present King	BRIAN PROTHEROE
Polonius, Principal Secretary of State	RON HACKETT
Horatio, friend to Hamlet	HOWARD LLOYD-LEWIS
Laertes, son to Polonius	NEIL McLAUCHLAN
Valtemand	JOHN PRICE
Cornelius } Ambassadors to Norway	DAVID BRADFORD
Rosencrantz } formerly fellow students	MARTIN DUNCAN
Guildenstern } with Hamlet	DAVID HILL
Osric	DAVID PEART
A Gentleman	JOHN PRICE
A Doctor of Divinity	MARTIN DUNCAN
Marcellus	DAVID PEART
Barnardo } Gentlemen of the Guard	DAVID HILL
Francisco }	MARTIN DUNCAN
Revaldo, servant to Polonius	JOHN HALSTEAD
First Player	JOHN HALSTEAD
Player Queen	DAVID BRADFORD
Player Poisoner	JOHN PRICE
Players	NEIL McLAUCHLAN, ANDREW ATTWELL
1st Gravedigger	DEREK FUKE
2nd Gravedigger	JOHN HALSTEAD
Fortinbras, Prince of Norway	JOHN PRICE
Captain	RON HACKETT
Sailor	DAVID BRADFORD
Gertrude, Queen of Denmark, mother to Hamlet	JEAN BOHT
Ophelia, daughter to Polonius	ALISON STEADMAN
The Ghost of Hamlet's Father	DEREK FUKE
Followers of Laertes	Nigel Thomas, Ian Mansell, Gareth Thompson, N. J. Waring, P. Cheseldine, Colin Branwer, Raymond Law, Terence Goodacre, Richard Simpson, Ian Millsop, Neil Robins, Neil Fuller, Larry Bristin

There will be one interval of fifteen minutes

TOP LEFT: Rachel Davies and I having Two Hoots on Paradise Street.

TOP RIGHT: Top hats and tails.

MIDDLE LEFT: *Billy Liar* putting years on Rachel in Rhyl.

MIDDLE RIGHT: Uncle Play was a gift from my niece when she discovered I hadn't had a teddy. He toured the rep theatres too!

BOTTOM RIGHT: Our Bond girls audition. Look out, Ursula Andress!

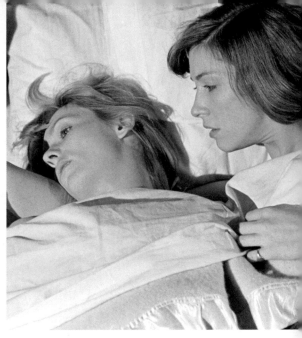

TOP LEFT: One of my first professional headshots.

TOP RIGHT: Myra Frances and I leading the way in *Girl*.

LEFT: *Through the Night*. Groundbreaking. Heart aching. Based on a true story.

BELOW: Guilty or not guilty: ITV's *Crown Court*.

TOP: *Nuts in May*. Lumpy legs. Not my own.

ABOVE: More like chilly in May! Me, Mike Leigh and Roger Sloman.

RIGHT: Are we nearly there, Keith?

TOP: You don't mind do you, Ange? First run of *Abigail's Party* at the Hampstead Theatre.

ABOVE: You can't see my bump can you, Ange?

CHAPTER 11

Route Map

Do any of us really know where we're going? Is there a map that we follow? Even if there is, I'd be useless at following it, although my inner sat nav, my natural instinct, might just point me in the right direction. I'd have done better back in the day when all that people had to rely on was what was around them. Trust the trees to tell you north from south, east and west. The side with more leaves, the sunny side, is south. If one side of the tree has more moss than the other, then that's north, because when it rains the water dries quicker on the side with sun and moss will grow anywhere the water lingers. Similarly, if you see a puddle on one side of a road, it's because that's the north side. The bend of tree branches can tell us how the wind blows. If you get totally lost then you can always head into the nearest church, as the altar is east and the entrance is west. And then there are clouds. Have I got my head in the clouds? I don't think so. But I do know that, apart from being sure about wanting to go to drama school and then giving it my best shot at earning a living performing, I've always followed my instinct. There wasn't a traveller's guide to working as an actress back then, so I'd go where the wind blew me, which was where the work was.

I'm not sure if there was more work around for young actors in the late 1960s and early 1970s than there is now, but with the opening of new theatres, designed to bring in new audiences and be the heart of the community, and the thriving rep system, there was usually somewhere to get a season of work and carve out the early stages of a career. The regional theatres were a godsend to us all, especially for actors, like me, who hadn't been plucked from Oxford or Cambridge or weren't able to waltz out of RADA, received pronunciation intact, and straight into a season of Noël Coward in the West End. It was a huge relief not to have to worry about money and an even bigger one that I didn't have to make use of my shorthand typing or go back to Walton Probation Office.

Not once during these tougher years of my early career did my parents make any comment other than a supportive one. There was nothing but endorsement and interest, which continued over the years. Right from the beginning, whenever I was in a show, my mum would look at her watch at 7.30 p.m. and say, 'That's our Alison about to go on stage tonight,' and she'd check in with me to see how it had gone afterwards. Both of my parents had a real enthusiasm for my work, but my mum especially so. Marjorie, like the rest of her family, had left school at fourteen and walked out of the gates and on to the end of the queue of people who stood outside the Meccano factory in the hope of getting a job. There wasn't even a flicker of choice for her; it was as if her future was mapped out from that moment. This wasn't something that I'd ever really had to contemplate and, apart from being aghast at my shipping office outburst, Mum was behind my choices all the way. She must have got the taste for my itinerant lifestyle through all the stories I shared with her as, once, and it was only once, she said to me, 'Oh, Alison, wouldn't it be fun if we could share a little flat in London together and I could learn something new.' I must have been about twenty-six, as it was before I was married, and I couldn't think of anything less fun at the time. When I think about what that statement truly represents, and her desire to keep living with hope and positivity, I wish that time had allowed her to have had that moment.

After Lincoln, my route map took me to the Bolton Octagon in Lancashire, which is where I first met my friend Rachel Davies, with whom I went on to share digs, holidays and lots of laugher. The Octagon had only opened a few years earlier in 1967 and was the first theatre in Britain to have a flexible space that meant the auditorium could be configured to what suited the show best. It was intimate and inclusive – a perfect space to encourage more tentative theatre-goers. The radical design of the building was also reflected in the ambition of the work. As well as the weekly theatre rep there was music, education work and small-scale tours. At the end of our three months in Bolton Rachel and I were contracted to a troupe taking three shows to the Little Theatre in Rhyl in North Wales so off we went on our first ever tour together.

Rachel and I had decided to find digs to share whilst we were away and we ended up in a small Victorian terraced house that only had a low front wall to distance it from the inaptly named Paradise Street. There was a house sign with 'Two Hoots' written on it and an image of two owls, so we called the couple who lived in the house Mr and Mrs Two Hoots. They were in their early sixties, or so we guessed. Everyone looked much older than they actually were in those days. Mrs Two Hoots would say, 'Oh girls, excuse the state of me, I never dress up, see,' and Mr Two Hoots, who had a glass eye, would say very little. They were seasoned renters of their rooms, and it was clear that they were trying to make some money, as the house was bursting at the seams. Rachel and I shared a room on the first floor, which had a bed and a couch. I was on the couch. There was a room right at the top of the house shared by a rock band, who were working for the summer season on Rhyl Pier. The Two Hoots had a double bed in the living room and the only bathroom was on the ground floor too. The bathroom door had a tiny little hole in it. Rachel would say, 'You know how he lost his eye, don't you? He was peeping at someone in the bath and when they found out they poked his eye with a stick.' The door to the living room was usually closed firmly shut when we got back after an evening show, but one night it was wide open, so we could see inside. The Two Hoots were lying in their bed under a baby-pink eiderdown, and there were frilly, pink-shaded table lamps on each side. Everything was pink and the room had the air of a lovers' boudoir. Mr Two Hoots was asleep, his glass eye open and the other shut, while Mrs Two Hoots was sitting up, dozing, but obviously waiting for us. 'Alison! Rachel!' she called out as she heard us in the hallway. 'Your comp-an-nee director rang and left you a message. Did you get that?' Her accent, which was a wonderful North Walian mash-up of Liverpudlian, Welsh and the Midlands, would reduce us to fits of the giggles and we loved to hear her talk. Mrs Two Hoots was a fabulous woman, and even though she didn't come to any of our shows she always took an interest. One evening there was a knock on our bedroom door. I opened it to Mrs Two Hoots standing holding a bra by its strap and saying, 'I spent 23 and 11 and it crucifies me.' Then, pressing it onto my chest. 'Is it any good now for you or Rachel?' It felt rude to refuse her.

Our time on Paradise Street was packed full of funny and poignant moments including the day the dog had run off and we walked into the house to, 'We've lost the dog,' from Mr Two Hoots, 'I'm really upset, see. She's not, she doesn't care about the dog.'

We'd walked into a domestic. 'That's not true, Wally, I love that dog, I do. I love that dog.' And she did. Her reaction was completely understandable as their daughter had run away from home and was missing – she must have been sick with worry most of the time and so the dog's absence was nothing by comparison. I often wondered if the reason that she didn't dress up was because she was too emotionally exhausted to bother with any of that. One day, on hearing us return, she opened the door of the Barbie-coloured living room and said, 'Rachel, Alison, I'm on air, I'm on air, love, I'm on air. She rang me. She rang me and she's alright.' All she kept on saying was, 'I'm on air, I'm on air.'

I felt a bit like that too, as directly after my contract at Bolton, my work compass took me to the Swan Theatre in Worcester, where I joined their rep company for a season. By this time, I was getting used to looking through the digs list that all the theatres provided and picking out a place that might suit me. Being within walking distance of the theatre was always important so I breathed a sigh of relief when I managed to secure a room and breakfast in a house that was close to the Swan. Once again, and I'll never know why, the landlady was stern and unfriendly – my welcome from her, the evening before our first read-through, was even colder than the weather we were having. It didn't really bother me though, but what did bother me was the sound that began almost as soon as my head hit the pillow that first night. A deep, gravelly moan seeped through the walls of the room and my heart began to thump. It sounded like someone was in some sort of pain. I'd no idea what it was or where it was coming from and decided that the safest thing to do was to stay in my room and wait it out. It was a long night, and I hardly slept a wink. Breakfast was an equally worrying affair as the landlady's dog insisted on licking my toes for the duration that I was sat at the table trying to eat a bowl of cornflakes. The moaning from the night before was still perturbing me so I ventured to ask, 'What was that noise in the house last night?'

The landlady turned and in an offhand way said, 'Oh that'll be the lions.' *She must be joking – lions?* But she wasn't. I'd arrived in the dark and hadn't realised that the house backed onto the racecourse where the circus was in town, nor had my landlady told me. The handlers had placed the lion cage away from the main tent and in a quieter spot. That spot just happened to be underneath my bedroom window and the noise that I'd heard was the lions snoring. They were very noisy bedfellows indeed.

Working in weekly or fortnightly rep wasn't a walk in the park. A bit like the football players of my childhood home ground at Anfield Road, we had to keep match fit to ensure that no one became unwell, leaving someone to take on their role or, worse still, the theatre having to cancel the show. The theatres were always strict about what we could and couldn't do, to avoid any mishaps, and so far nothing untoward had occurred on any of the shows that I'd been in. The first production in the season at the Swan was *The Boy Friend*, a full-on song-and-dance musical. On the first day of rehearsals the comp-an-nee manager said quite formally, 'In accordance with Equity rules, you must not engage in any activity that will put risk to the show or to your life.' It seemed a little dramatic to me. *What a daft thing to say*, I thought, *Why would any of us do anything that might risk our lives?* The show, set in Villa Caprice, home to Mme Dubonnet's School for Young Ladies, was a dream chance to stretch myself and get more experience of musical theatre, which I'd not done very much of – apart from *Ali Baba* at East 15, but that was a panto and didn't really count. *The Boy Friend* was Billy Martin's Saturday Dance Club meets the roaring twenties and there was no way that I'd risk being absent for a show. One of the big fast-paced dance numbers, 'Won't You Charleston with Me', involved me having to jump into the air and then swing my legs around my partner's, so I was thankful for all of those Saturday mornings of being put through my paces at Billy Martin's. I made sure that my commitment to the dance and any necessary hip-to-hip contact merited perfection, unlike my teenage tango.

Maybe we were all enjoying ourselves just a bit too much or had become laissez-faire with the need to be vigilant, but once the show was up and running and there was a bit of free time, the note of caution that we'd been given on our first day was a distant memory and a gang of us decided to go horse riding. Horse riding was most certainly on the list of things, with skiing, jumping out of a plane and acrobatics, that we weren't allowed to do. This didn't deter us. I hadn't done much horse riding, apart from on the wooden one in Blacklers store, and so needed to muster some courage. *Just impersonate the show jumpers that you've seen on the telly, it'll all be fine.* I sat up straight on the back of my horse, put my feet in the stirrups and held on firmly to the reins. 'Walk on,' I said gently, trying not to appear too worried. Who was I trying to kid? Horses can cut through any deception: this horse knew that I was dead scared and moved up a gear from a pleasant trot to a full-on gallop, before stopping abruptly and catapulting me over his head where I landed on uncushioned ground. I could say, 'It was the horse's fault, m'lud,' but that wouldn't be fair on the horse. It happened so quickly that there hadn't been time to release one of my legs from the stirrup and there I was, flat on my back, beside my sturdy steed, screeching in agony having torn a muscle in my still-attached limb. *I can't be off tonight. I can't be off tonight. Oh God. I'll be killed. Get me out of this.* The theatre gods must have been beaming down on me as I managed to walk away from the horse and have, obviously, lived to tell the tale!

Cut to that night and 'Won't You Charleston with Me'. My inner scream was *NO, I won't dance with you,* but I had no choice but to jump in the air and fling my legs around my dance partner as there was no way that I could own up to my pain (a bit of a recurring habit of mine) when I'd broken the rule. So, for days, during each performance, I smiled, put a lid on my scream and was the epitome of 'the show must go on'.

Who could have known that the horse would throw me? Who would have thought that the paths that crossed when Rachel and I met would lead to a lifelong friendship? And did I ever think that my route planner would take me all the way back to Liverpool so early in my career?

CHAPTER 12

Expanding Horizons

'If you just put away a little bit of money each week, it'll soon add up and we can go on holiday!'

Rachel was always so much better when it came to thinking about money than me. It wasn't as if I was spending excessively or anything like that, more like it was almost impossible to get to the end of the week, let alone put any money aside. 'Oh, I don't know, I want to but—'

'No buts,' said Rachel. 'You'll be living at home with your mum and dad during your next job. It's a year's contract, and if you're careful, you might be able to save enough to go abroad.'

She was right of course. Although the Octagon tour was continuing to Birmingham, taking Rachel with it, I had been offered a season at the pioneering Everyman Theatre on Hope Street in Liverpool. I'd be living back at 22 Sherwyn Road for the first time since leaving it four years earlier and, although I'd need to give my parents some money for board and lodging, I'd not be spending as much as I would have been staying in digs. 'Come on, Alison, think about it.'

I didn't need to think about it for long, as a foreign holiday with my best friend sounded too enticing. Going abroad wasn't something that was familiar to me or my family. We'd take weekend trips to New Brighton and Southport, while for longer breaks we'd pack out suitcases and take ferries to Llandudno or the Isle of Man. I'd once taken a bus to visit a boyfriend who was working in Germany, but this didn't really feel like 'going abroad' to me. Abroad in my mind meant going far away, travelling without a plan through countries that I'd only read about in books or seen in the holiday magazines that were newly appearing on the shelves as the opportunity to get away to places beyond the UK border became easier and easier. It was the early 1970s, our currency had changed, there was soaring inflation and unemployment, and Britain was on the cusp of joining the EEC, with the hope that the support of its closest neighbours and allies would help to get the country out of the doldrums. There was a glimmer of hope on the horizon, and I wanted to expand my own view of the world. 'You're on. I'll begin to save up. Let's go on holiday!'

Being back at Sherwyn Road felt simultaneously comforting and strange. It was wonderful to be surrounded by the familiarity of my growing-up years but there was a dawning realisation that I had continued to grow up and that this was an ongoing process that I didn't want to stop. My mum had worried that I might not come home when they waved me off at Lime Street Station way back in 1966, but she needn't have as I'd made short trips back at every opportunity, But this felt different. This wasn't a visit for Christmas, Easter or the summer break, it was for work, and I had to give it my full attention. This job felt like it carried a heavier weight of responsibility. I was on home ground again, in more ways than one.

The Everyman had opened a couple of years before I headed off to East 15 and had quickly gained a reputation for being edgy and political. Prior to becoming a theatre, it had been a cinema space and the meeting place for local musicians, poets and artists who formed a group called the Liverpool Scene. These maverick creatives thought that it was the perfect place for a theatre and so, after going through a bit of redevelopment, it opened its doors to audiences in 1964. In the few short years since it had attracted an exciting line-up of visionary directors, writers and actors all of whom wanted to take risks. Now I wanted to be bold and become part of it too.

'Go on then, tell me a joke,' was the first thing that the director, Alan Dossor, who'd auditioned me for the job at the Everyman, said to me. 'Tell me a joke,' he said, which wasn't what I was expecting. *Tell you a joke? You're not serious, Alan?* I was trying to buy myself time as I flicked through the deeply buried line-up of paltry jokes that were floating somewhere in my mind. I'm rubbish at telling jokes. I know how to make people laugh with the tone of my voice, the turn of my head, the look in my eye, but telling jokes has always made me feel awkward and put on the spot. It still does. 'Yeah, just tell us a joke, any joke, your favourite joke.' I didn't have a favourite joke, and this didn't feel very funny at all. 'I'm not great at telling jokes. I'm afraid,' and with that he let me off having to do any ill-prepared stand-up. We had a great chat, and I got the job. The two plays that I was cast in – *The Foursome* and *Soft or a Girl* – were plays for Liverpool and there was such a buzz around them both. We nicknamed Alan 'James Dean', as he was very good looking and had a bit of a mean, determined look about him. He was straight talking, took no nonsense and was inspirational. Alan knew that if the Everyman was to take off and succeed then it had to make deep-rooted connections with its community so right at the beginning of rehearsals he sat us all down and said very seriously and without any hint of a joke, 'Right, you're in Liverpool, you're doing plays for Liverpool people, they are your audience so you need to get to know them and this city.' It was a brilliant idea, and although I was from Liverpool many of the company weren't. He hired a bus and off we went to the Ford car factory in Speke, which was a huge employer in the city, where we were given a tour of the plant and the chance to chat to some of the people that worked there. Alan was determined that the plays that were put on served the community and that the company of actors that were in them were able to look outwards and not inwards, which can be a tendency for some.

Soft or a Girl by John McGrath had people queuing around the block for tickets and there was a moment in the script that brought the house down every night as it resonated with the audience so much. One character says, 'What Hitler and the Luftwaffe didn't do in the 1940s, Liverpool City Council have just done now.' This rang true for everyone, as the city seemed to be in a constant state of rebuilding and modernisation. *The Foursome* by Ted Whitehead caused even more of a stir as it advertised that it had nudity in it and the expectation was that the two girls, of which I was one and Polly Hemingway the other, would be taking their clothes off. In fact it was the boys! Even before we opened the show, it broke box-office records for selling more single seats than ever before. The play, which is also set in Liverpool, is the story of two young men who pick up two teenage girls on the beach at Freshfields and persuade them to hang out with them. It doesn't hold back and is funny as well as brutal. If it were put on today it might be described as a study of toxic masculinity but back in 1972 it was digested as an honest portrayal of teenage trauma. Well, as you can imagine, it wasn't the thought of a genteel picnic in the sand dunes that had the theatre packed to the rafters, it was the rude language, simulated sex and nudity. It was a raunchy piece so I needed to be upfront about the full frontal that my modest parents would see when they attended the show. 'Mum, you're going to see Jonathan Pryce walking around with no clothes on. Are you okay with that?' I'm not sure if she was but my parents took it all in their stride as their main purpose was to support me, as they always had done.

It was great to be back in the city and playing in front of a home crowd. *This must be what it feels like to be kicking off at the Kop end at Anfield*, I thought. I loved that I could speak in the minor key of my native soft Scouse. I had a line in the play, in response to another character saying to mine, 'What do you want? What do you want out of life?' that regularly caused so much laughter that we had to take a beat before continuing the dialogue. My character, who had her hair all done up and was wearing a thigh-skimming, pink fluffy dress, thinks for a while before saying earnestly, 'A house on the Wirral.' The volume of the laughter could have lifted the roof and left me feeling on air as Mrs Two Hoots would have said. Being back home was very special. Even though the backstage conditions of the Everyman weren't great, and the dressing rooms were dark and poky, we didn't care. Being on that stage at that time was like being in a rock band trying to woo the toughest crowd and if, or when, we did it was magical. It was where so many of us really began to under-stand how to work with a live audience, to gauge the temperature of the room and be brave about the choices we made. Our onstage conversations became after-show chats as we'd all gather in the bistro and socialise into the small hours. It was a seductive schedule as we'd rehearse by day, perform by night, and then enjoy affordable food and drinks as we chatted over the evening's show in the equivalent of a post-match debrief.

It was during one of these nights that the director Mike Leigh walked in with a couple of people, including someone who had been a few years ahead of me at Childwall Valley High School for Girls.

Mike had been a visiting director at East 15, although I wasn't in any of his productions. There were a few of us from college, including Roger Sloman, who were in that Everyman season, and so Mike had come along to watch some of our work as he was also going to be directing a show there. I'd always been intrigued by his approach with the final-year students, as rather than focusing on scenes, Mike would create full-length pieces using improvisation and I wanted to know more about it. His parents lived in Manchester so, given that it was relatively close, he would come over quite often and meet us all in the bistro afterwards. The chat was always sparky, and he'd talk a lot about the method that he was developing. Improvisation was my comfort zone and I used to think, *It would be lovely to work with him*, because every time we spoke together about making theatre his sounded like the sort of creative process that I wanted to be involved with. It was during this time that we slowly got to know each other better and started to become close. Mike came to watch *The Foursome*, and on that night a note was dropped into the dressing room that Polly and I shared, asking us if we'd meet him afterwards. Mike was about to direct his first piece of television drama in Manchester, *Hard Labour*, and he asked Polly and me if we'd consider being in it. The prospect of this felt enormous, like crossing into a new unexplored land. It was exactly what I wanted to do. But first, the holiday with Rachel.

The year-long contract at the Everyman and staying with my parents had, as Rachel predicted, allowed me to put a bit aside each week and save, so by the end of the season there was enough money to go on holiday. 'Let's go to Greece,' said Rachel. 'We can go all the way on a bus.' I knew nothing about Greece, apart from it being a place where centuries ago amazing plays had been written with powerful parts for women, that it was very warm and that the sea, which I'd seen pictures of, looked far more tempting than the Irish Sea Rachel and I had dipped ourselves into during the previous summer season at Rhyl. Sometimes on our days off from the Little Theatre, we'd say, 'Let's go for a swim,' and even though the water was absolutely freezing we'd run in, splash about for a bit and then run out. We'd call our brief bathe 'the nip nip show', but didn't charge anyone for the pleasure! The translucent, turquoise luminescence of the Aegean was much more appealing, and so we booked our passage from Victoria Coach Station in London to Athens, and off we went.

Being on a bus for days on end wasn't my idea of a holiday but luckily on the way there, after crossing the Channel by ferry to Belgium, the travel was broken by stopping overnight at a couple of hotels. Our budget was tight, and we took every opportunity to make it go further. It was my first experience of many things, including a continental breakfast. Rachel and I would linger at the table once everyone had finished and scoop up the leftover bread, ham and cheese to save for our lunches. We travelled through Germany to Austria and then down through what was then Yugoslavia. As the miles passed by and the landscape changed, I looked out of the window on to what looked like fields of gold. It was the first time that I'd ever seen a sunflower and it reminded me of Van Gogh's paintings of women tending to their fields of sun-shaped flowers.

Finally there was Athens, the busiest city I'd ever been to and overlooked by the marbled majesty of the Acropolis. I have to say that most of this was lost on us as we were so exhausted from the bus journey that all we wanted to do was get to a beautiful beach and sleep. To save our money we had booked into the cheapest hotel in Athens that we could find. It was worse than the bus for comfort, the bed was rock hard, and the pillows were like lumpy porridge.

'We've come all this way for this!' We just laughed and laughed at our faux high standards. We'd experienced Two Hoots in Paradise Street, remember.

'Let's go as far as we can,' I had said, and so, after a hard night in Athens, we took the ferry from the main port of Piraeus and headed south to Crete. We slept on the deck and, looking up at the sky, with the smell of boat fuel, the sound of the engine and the rocking swell of the sea, it felt that, at last, I was travelling. Boy, it was hot though, and my fair skin, which had only been exposed to the cool of an English summer, came out in an itchy red rash. There was a chance to stop over in Mykonos for twelve hours before heading onwards so, as we docked before dawn, we hauled our rucksacks and our tired bodies off the ferry. 'You want to come fishing?' a voice said as we walked along the front. One of the local fishermen stepped out in front of us and said again, 'You want to come fishing and come out on my boat?' There was no hesitation in our response, 'Yes, we'd love that.' He smiled and said, 'Come back at six, you come back at six and I be here.' We went back as instructed – the cluster of white buildings were beginning to glisten in the early-morning sunshine – but he was nowhere to be seen. 'He's having us on,' I said. 'He's not going to take us out fishing.' Then from a little further on, a hatch on the deck of one of the boats popped open and our fisherman's head appeared. 'Sorry, I sleep long.' He hauled himself out of the hatch and said, 'You coming?' Off we sailed on our accidentally chartered fishing trip on the Aegean Sea. The fish were plentiful and unusual – they may even have been a leeetle beeta lika seeeeeebazzzz, who knows? All of them looked scary to me. Hooking onto this (sorry!) our captain would take them off the line and hold them close to our faces to shock us. Mooring up the boat later that morning, he said, 'You come back at twelve and we eat.' We weren't sure about eating our catch but turned up nevertheless and our lovely fisherman had cooked us the tastiest fish stew. It was a delicious stopover before we headed onwards to Crete.

Many years later I returned to Mykonos to film *Shirley Valentine* with Pauline Collins. It felt like a completely different island as there had been so much development in the intervening years and I felt lucky to have experienced it before its commercial expansion. We had an early-morning call so that we could film on the beach without being disturbed or being a disturbance to holiday-makers. The shot was to be of Shirley and her friend, Jane (me), alone together, walking along the beach. The location team had chosen one of the beaches on the far side of the island because it had a nudist section, so they thought that it would be much quieter and less distracting. Goodness knows why they thought that! Pauline and I were asked to stand side by side and walk by the water's edge in as straight a direction as possible. 'Action!' shouted the director of photography, and we began to walk. As we were walking and talking, I became aware that our gaze was increasingly fixated on a shape that lay ahead of us. Initially it looked like the remains of a sand sculpture that had been created the day before but with each step closer it became clear that we were in denial about the naked reality of what was being presented to us. There, in full view, was a completely naked guy lying face down in the sand with his tanned bottom half in shallow water and his buttocks popping up in true gluteus-maximus glory. And if that wasn't enough, he was doing press-ups. Press-ups! The look in his eye suggested that he had some other form of exercise in mind … The camera was rolling, and I knew that stopping wasn't an option. *Oh God, how will I remember my lines and keep a straight face when all I can see is this bloke going through his morning-glory routine.*

He saw the camera, he saw us and he knew full well that we could see him. It was a rude awakening.

It was early morning when the ferry docked in Heraklion and, not wanting to waste any time, we hopped on a bus that we hoped would take us to the little fishing village that we had decided to base ourselves in. I'm not so sure if we'd have taken the bus if we'd known just how reckless the man at the wheel was, or that the route that he would take us on would travel through the unlit mountain tunnels of the Samaria Gorge and twist and turn on single-lane roads without edges that skimmed a perilous drop into the sea below. It was a rickety old contraption, and banging on his horn time and again the driver would take blind corner after blind corner leaving us all feeling like we were about to meet our maker. Two-thirds of the way up one of the steep inclines, the bus suddenly halted, and a couple of elderly people stepped off. Glancing out the window I noticed that they were praying in front of a small roadside shrine dedicated to St Christopher and placing coins at his feet. Thank goodness for the patron saint of travel and his safe keeping of people who took the mountain route from Heraklion to Agios Nikolaos. We got there in one piece although my legs felt like jelly as I hoisted my rucksack onto my back and lowered myself, step by step, off our near-death trap.

Hot and exhausted we dumped ourselves at the first café we came to. 'I'm going for a swim and nothing's going to stop me.'

Totally shattered, Rachel looked at me and said, 'What?'

It wasn't up for discussion. 'I have to,' I said. 'I'm boiling up. Grabbing my swimsuit from the top of my rucksack I ran inside to the toilet, did a quick change and then dashed across the road and into the sea. My body felt sensations that were completely new to it, and as I turned over onto my back and lay floating on the surface it was like all the stresses of the journey were being washed away. The rippling of the water, the mild tang of salt and the dappled sunlight dancing on the surface combined to transport me into a state of complete relaxation. This was so unlike the other summers of my life; it was a world away from the open-air pool in New Brighton. Above was the bluest of skies and in front of me the mountains that were gradually turning pink as the sun shone on them and lit up the limestone within them. The peace that I felt at that moment is a memory that will never leave me.

We settled into the way of things, passing our time swimming and sightseeing, but never before breakfast. I fell in love with our Greek breakfasts of halloumi and yogurt with honey, which had no resemblance to the runny yoghurt that my mum had served as she began to embrace the convenience foods of the 1960s. I can remember my mum saying, 'We've got *yoghurt* for pudding tonight.' It was as if she had learned a foreign word and was introducing us to a new language. Anyway, the café owner would serve us the yoghurt and then bring over the hot grilled cheese in a little pan that kept it warm. Each day felt like being on our own film set and that we were the stars. On the trip that we made to the ancient Minoan settlement of Knossos, the bus stopped along the way and this vision of beauty appeared. He must have been about twenty, with golden curly hair that framed his face, exactly as I had always imagined a Greek god to look like. I was in heaven. It was probably the heat, the newness, the difference, but for the rest of the journey I couldn't take my eyes off this creature of Eros who was standing hanging on to the strap that dangled from the roof of the bus.

These times that we all have as young adults, when we think we're all grown-up but are still works in progress, leave such an impression upon us. That feeling of carefreeness and a sense of getting to know myself a bit better was such an invaluable cushion to rest upon before taking my first steps into television with *Hard Labour*. I was hoping that the title wouldn't reflect the experience. My three weeks of time away from all that I knew had fuelled me, opened my eyes and given me lots to think about as I looked towards my new horizon.

CHAPTER 13

You're on the Telly

I had expected *Hard Labour* to be my TV debut, but before I started work on that I was offered a small part in *Bel Ami*, a five-part costume drama for BBC2. Small part is a bit of an exaggeration. It was an unnamed role and my lofty responsibility, along with about ten other girls adorned in beautifully crafted nineteenth-century dresses, was to strike a range of fencing poses to entertain the courtesans of Parisian society. When East 15 had sent me the list of things that I would require for drama school, including fencing equipment, it wasn't something that I thought would take up any of my professional life. Our classes had taught us how to use the different swords and hold ourselves in strange high-lunge positions, while strapped into form-fitting protective jackets with netted masks over our faces. I hadn't found it particularly enjoyable, even though I was quite good at it. But our tutor was a lovely man, and he must have thought that I was capable enough with a rapier not to do damage to anyone, because when he got the job as fight captain on *Bel Ami* he kindly invited me to be one of the fencing girls.

My mum and dad were so excited and gathered everyone in front of the television a bit like Pam does in *Gavin and Stacey* to watch Mick's fifteen seconds of fame on BBC News. It was a lavish scene

– not quite a case of blink and you'll miss me like Mick's, but hardly a notable debut. 'Oh, Alison. You were wonderful. What a thing. You're on the telly. Who'd have thought?!' Mum and Dad were thrilled.

The role in *Bel Ami* was a useful first taste of being on a TV set as opposed to a stage. It was a completely new environment for me, and the familiar nervousness made its invasive presence known again as I prepared for my next role. *Hard Labour* was to be one of the dramas in the BBC's third series of *Play for Today* and I didn't want to let myself or anyone else down. Liz Smith played Mrs Thornley, her first leading role, Polly played her daughter, Ann, and I was Mrs Thornley's daughter-in-law, Veronica, married to her son, Edward, played by Bernard Hill. Even though I'd spent years improvising at the youth theatre, had trained at East 15 and been kept busy in repertory theatre, I still allowed the voice in my head to intrude and unnerve me a bit. *Oh God, this is telly. I need to get it right. I can't make any mistakes. What if I don't hit the mark?* It was a ridiculous state to get myself into. I was too much in my head and put far too much emphasis on the fact that this was TV. *Hard Labour* was filmed on location and not in a studio, so there was none of the 'Quiet, studio, VTR running' and so on that filled me with nerves later in my career. But it was still terrifying; my voice started to shake and become light and breathy as I delivered my first ever lines on camera. Playing an improvised character that would be watched by a television audience wasn't what rattled me. It was the camera that did it. It felt like it was spying on us; it took me some time before I understood that the camera was our friend and not the enemy. Veronica was a decent cameo role and a good first TV job, but looking back I don't think that I was ready for it. I needed a bit more time and experience behind me to do the role credit. Then again, this was exactly the experience I needed to prepare me for the roll-call of women that I created through improvisation working with Mike a few years later.

On another of my early TV jobs I was doing a single episode in a series, and I couldn't shake the fear of the camera off me. I was mortified when I fluffed my lines and asked, 'Can I do that again?' The answer was a firm 'no' and the camera moved on.

Not taking no for an answer, I asked one of the assistants if I could do it again and he said, 'Well, if there's any time, we might be able to squeeze it in at the very end.' Result.

'Okay. Thanks. I'll stay here until the end.'

The assistant looked perplexed and said, 'No, go back to your dressing room.' There was a bit of a stand-off when I said I'd rather stay there to do that scene again if there was time.

They got to the end of the take and someone said, 'Thank you, studio!' which meant that it was a wrap for everyone.

There was ten minutes of studio time left so I said, 'No. I want to do that scene again.' It was a bit like the 'Please, sir, can I have some more?' line in *Oliver!*

'Erm, Alison really wants to do that scene again as she fluffed her line,' said the assistant and they reluctantly agreed to use the leftover time to give me another go. I was determined that on the shaky 1970s set, the audience would not also be seeing a shaky Alison Steadman.

It's almost unbelievable to think that there were only three television channels at the time – BBC1, BBC2 and ITV – and that so much was being done for the first time, making all of us who were involved both on- and off-screen pioneers of sorts. We were at the forefront of significant development and change: the first generation of actors to have all of our screen work filmed in colour, as well as getting the opportunity to perform in programmes that offered a more diverse view of the time and more thought-provoking content. Yes, the budgets were low, the scenery was shaky and retakes were mainly unheard of, but what a time it was for learning our craft. If the repertory system sturdied our chops for theatre and developed our sense of how to understand and work with live audiences, then 1970s TV offered time for experimentation, getting to know and like the camera, as well as to blend our theatrical roots with the more technical form.

It's only on reflection that I can see how one thing led to another and how it all began to intertwine as time passed and can acknowledge that this vital combination massively contributed to the performer that I am. My unmapped life had steered me to East 15, which had guided me to Philip Hedley and Lincoln, which had taken me to the Everyman in Liverpool, which is where Mike Leigh had offered me my first TV role *Hard Labour*, which had introduced me to Tony Garnett, who was producing the show. These were all small yet significant steps along my untrodden road.

By 1972 my relationship with Mike had blossomed into something more personal and we were living together in a flat in London. Since leaving drama school three years earlier, I'd worked non-stop, getting jobs on my own accord. But doing TV with no one to look after the more complicated contract side of things made me say to Mike and Tony Garnett, 'I think that I need an agent now.' Tony stepped in to help, much in the way that Jack Cogley from Walton Probation Office had helped me find my first digs in Essex. He knew a person who knew a person and that's how I acquired my first agent. I thought back to the piles of letters that I'd written to agents during my final term at East 15, the total silence that had ensued after I'd posted them and the desolation I'd felt when no one had replied. The adage 'it's not what you know but who you know' felt very apt as Tony introduced me to the grumpy old man who was to represent me.

I'd no idea what an agent could do for me back then, but I did know what sort of work I wanted to do and how I wanted to do it, and this chap wasn't in line with it at all. It was a complete mismatch, so after a relatively short period of time I decided to pluck up the courage to tell him we were going to have to part ways.

His office in Soho was on the first floor of a rather run-down building on Greek Street, which had once been much grander than it now appeared. I felt a bit anxious about knocking on his door and giving him my it's-not-you-it's-me spiel, even though it was most definitely him. 'Come in!' he barked as I tapped on the door. *This isn't going to be pleasant*, I thought, not least because the room was filled with a haze of cigar smoke and the cramped, messy space, which was strewn with papers and books and photographs of other actors, was quite overwhelming. The agent was on the phone and indicated at me to sit down on the chair on the other side of the desk that he was sitting behind.

'No, no, no, no. I'm afraid not,' he was saying pompously. 'Absolutely not. As I said in my letter to you, my books are full!' And with that he slammed the phone down. I thought of all the letters that I'd sent to agents and felt for the person on the other end of the rude and abrupt call. *You've had a lucky escape* also crossed my mind.

Turning his attention to me, he puffed on the cigar and leant back in his chair saying, 'That happens all the time you know, Alison. I get hundreds of calls from people wanting me to be their agent but it's not possible for me to take them on as I'm very selective, you know. Very selective.'

He was so full of himself and so, quite unlike myself, I curtly said, 'Well, I'm just about to leave you so you'll have space for someone else then, won't you?'

He looked rather taken aback and spluttered, 'Oh, are you now? And where are you going?' He was being so superior but luckily I could lob back a response as a former drama school associate had already put me in touch with another far more suitable agent.

'I'm going to be taken on by Bill Horne Management,' I said.

'Horne? Horne?' he blustered. 'No. Never heard of him.' And then puffing his cigar smoke in my direction he opened the desk drawer, took out my headshots and other pictures, and put them firmly down in front of me. There was no further exchange. I picked up my career and walked out of his office and into Bill Horne Management, who went on to represent me for nearly twenty years. I'd made the right choice.

As an actress, choice has been a constant companion and I'm very lucky that it has. *Should I work with this director? Should I take this role?* There are times in life when we turn right when we should have turned left and vice-versa, and I've had my fair share of standing at the crossroads and making a choice to turn in a particular direction without knowing what I may encounter down the road. But sometimes a choice is taken out of our hands and circumstances prevail that can lead us to places that bring fulfilment and happiness.

This is what happened when I fell into working on the radio. Somewhere along the line I'd been told that you could audition for radio work on the BBC without needing to have an invitation to do so. It seemed very straightforward: all that was required was to apply for a recording slot, then you'd be given a time to head along to a sound booth at Broadcasting House to tape your audition pieces.

I'm not sure what I thought would or wouldn't happen when I finished the song and speech that I'd selected to record, but as I came out of the booth, the elderly man who had been coordinating the technical side of things called me over. 'Alison, can I tell you something?' I'd no idea what he was going to say and prepared myself for a bad review of the pieces I'd just recited. 'I just want to say,' he went on, 'I think that you should do radio, I really do.' I breathed a sigh of relief. 'I shouldn't be telling you this, but I'm going to as I'm about to retire and won't be doing this job for much longer.' It was becoming more intriguing by the minute. He continued, 'The tape that you've just recorded won't get listened to – no one ever listens to them, they can't be bothered.' My mind flashed back to the piles of unopened letters to agents and directors – and, even worse, the cursory uniform replies that remained unsigned by the person whose attention had been sought. 'I'm telling you this, Alison, as you need to make a phone call and say, will you listen to my tape. Here's the number.' He scribbled down a telephone number on a piece of paper and handed it to me.

'Thank you, that's kind of you,' I said.

'You really should do radio as you're rather good at it.'

The kind man in the booth hadn't needed to do that at all. It was another moment of the compass doing its own thing and all I had to do was trust that it was the right thing. And in this instance it was. Although I was never brave enough to call the number – it just wasn't something I'd feel comfortable doing – he had encouraged me to push myself forward, a bit like Jim Wiggins had encouraged me to audition for drama school. Having an endorsement from someone else who was saying that it was worth a shot really helped me.

Like so many other moments in my early career, the path led back, once again, to East 15. David Casey, one of the chaps in my year, would invite his dad, James, to our shows, as he was in the business and took an interest, which was quite a rare thing for the parents of drama students to do back then. As Head of Light Entertainment at BBC Manchester, it was James Casey who gave me my first break in radio.

James introduced me to Eddie Braben, who was writing a series called *The Worst Show on the Wireless*, which James was producing, and he asked me to be in it. Eddie was a successful TV comedy writer, having worked on *The Ken Dodd Show* and *The Morecambe & Wise Show* but his first love was radio comedy. He was a big fan of Arthur Askey's 1930s radio work – this was much earlier than *Before Your Very Eyes*, featuring the infamous Sabrina who I impersonated as a nine-year-old. He had taken some time off from writing as from the moment that he'd begun to write for Ken Dodd in the early 1960s, and then formed the collaboration with Morecambe and Wise, it had been non-stop and by 1972 he was burnt out. It's no wonder. Delivering script after script must be exhausting, especially having to make it funny and keep the surprises coming from series to series. It was when he was on his way to deliver the script for another Christmas Special for Eric and Ernie that he just fell apart. Eddie was on the train from Liverpool to London but didn't make it and got off at Watford instead. He just ran and ran, and didn't deliver the script or any others for some time after. It was James Casey who later said to him, 'Look, why don't you do a radio series, nothing heavy duty, lots of short sketches, funny stuff but no pressure,' and that persuaded him to dip his toe back into the water. It wasn't easy at all, as his breakdown had severely knocked his confidence, and the thought of writing and not being able to do himself justice was a painful one.

Eddie was a fellow Scouser. He had a native humour that was familiar and comfortable to me, and we got on immediately. He was such a down-to-earth kind of guy. Even though he'd had phenomenal TV success with *Morecambe & Wise*, there were no airs and graces to him – he was upfront and straightforward. 'Hello, Alison,' he'd say. 'Here are the scripts, I've added something that I think you'll enjoy.' He was always adding bits and pieces to get the characters spot on, so that we'd all have the confidence to perform them in front of a live studio audience each Sunday in Manchester. Eddie was brilliant at listening to what was going on around him and he must have overheard me mucking about in one of my silly voices one day. I sometimes slipped into pretending to be an elderly Scouse woman who'd taken her teeth out so when she spoke it sounded as though she had a lisp and was on twenty cigarettes a day. 'So, I said to our Sid, "Hey, Sid, give me the seeds, I wanna plant some flowers in the garden, see."' The next day the script included a whole sketch with this new character, who then appeared each week for the rest of the series. It was such a gift from Eddie to be able to work like this. Each week the cast, which included Bill Pertwee and my pal from East 15 James's son David, as well as Eddie himself, would get to perform the same set of brilliant characters in a different story. Being in front of a live audience and testing out how to time things so that the comedy lifted off the page was invaluable for me. Spending week upon week doing this was a real confidence boost. I loved, loved, loved it.

Radio is so liberating. It's a great form and from my first encounter with *Listen with Mother* when I was four, I've been smitten by it. The world is your oyster, as they say: you can be on the moon, you can be on the other side of the world or down a mine, you can travel across time or be transported to London where the buses are red and not green. There are no limits. You can play who you want, you can be who you want, in much the same way that, as a child, I could be Hylda Baker, the Queen or the Toothpaste Attacker. A bonus extra is that there are no costumes to worry about or the need to spend hours and hours trying to avoid staring at yourself in front of the mirror whilst being made up as the character that you're playing. And the bonus extra on top of the bonus extra is that there's no need to learn lines as you can have your script in hand! The opportunities are endless and, to coin that now well-worn phrase, the only limit is your imagination.

It was huge fun back in the day when everything was far less technical than it is today. We'd all have a set of props that were there to help us achieve the soundscape required. On one occasion, I had to take out a set of false teeth from my mouth and put them on a table. As my own real teeth were very firmly embedded, I'd no idea how we were going to achieve this. 'How am I going to do this?' I said to the young props guy. Quick as a flash he came back with two Scrabble pieces and said, 'Just put these in your mouth and rattle them around a bit, then take them out and put them on the table – it'll sound like false teeth.' *How had he worked that out?* What a great job it must have been, to come up with solutions for sound effects in that way. It might have been a bit homemade, but it did the trick, and I adored being part of it all. It leaned right into my sense of playfulness and knowing that the best way to explore possibilities was through trial and error – and improvisation. If there was a direction that said 'She gets out of the car' we'd have to make the appropriate sound. I'd be sitting on a normal seat, then the props team would bring over an unhinged car door which I'd open before getting out of my seat and closing the door. Simple yet effective, as well as hilarious to take part in. These days it's all done digitally after the voice recording has been laid down. It's so much easier but not as much fun.

Radio work has allowed me to keep exercising my character building and I've been fortunate to have had an almost constant flow of it throughout my career. I will be forever grateful to James Casey for taking me under his wing at BBC Manchester in the early days and giving me the chance to play and pull and stretch my performance muscles. Radio has introduced me to brilliant writers too, including Sue Limb. Over the years, I've developed a sense of the sort of writing that works for me; over and above all else, I need to be able to hear the voice of the character that I'm playing. Sue Limb is brilliant at this and she's one of my favourite writers to work with. If Sue has written it, then I'm happy to be in it.

Playing musician and farmer Cicely in her most recent series, *Mucking In*, in 2022 was right up my street. As a child I used to fantasise about living on a farm; our local recreation ground would be where I'd act out having a pony, and I'd quite literally get *mucked in*. The wonderful thing about Sue's writing is that it's so layered. Yes, there are jokes and the situations are funny, but, as in most great comedy writing, there is a great deal of pathos too. *Mucking In* was full of the meaty stuff of a family that lived together as well as worked together, so you can imagine the scope for misunderstanding, secrets and lies, break-ups and make-ups. It was also fabulous to be reunited with Morwenna Banks and Nigel Planer who I also worked with on Sue's radio series *Skeletons in the Cupboard* and *Gloomsbury*.

Ah, *Gloomsbury* – the high jinks and shenanigans of a bohemian literary set and their lives and loves. What a treat it was. I only needed to read six pages of the script to know that it was for me. I rang my agent and, with no doubt in my mind at all, said, 'Yes. Yes please. This is for me.' We made five series between 2012 and 2018, and I could very happily do many more as I adored it so much. Sometimes in life the stars align, and everything feels right. *Gloomsbury* felt very right. One of the most appealing things about radio is that you can be offered roles that are very different to how you are as a person, and this is what I've always wanted. *Gloomsbury* enabled me to do this. Most of us played several parts. I had the joy of playing Virginia Woolf – only on radio would I be cast as her – who was renamed as Ginny Fox. The incomparable Miriam Margolyes played Vita Sackville-West, the creator of Sissinghurst Castle Garden, renamed as Vera Sackcloth-Vest, creator of Sizzlinghurst Castle; I also played Vera's housekeeper, Mrs Gosling, as well as Lady Ottoline Morrell of Garsington Manor, renamed hysterically as Lady Utterline Immoral of Arsington Manor.

It was a wickedly funny spoof of the Bloomsbury Set and like most comedy work it needed to be tackled very seriously if it was to tickle an audience, so I went about getting under the skin of my characters in the same way that I would if I was performing on stage or screen. Even though all the names had been adjusted, the show reflected the real people the characters were based on and their complicated lives: men wanting to be women and women wanting to be men during a time when even to think like this was dangerous and prohibited. It would have been so easy to send them up cruelly, but Sue Limb writes so intelligently and found a way to capture them with warmth and wit. One of the first questions that I always ask is, *How does this person sound?* Sometimes, if the character is based on a real person, there might be access to sound and video recordings of them, which is always a huge help. But although there are lots of images of Virginia Woolf that are readily available there is far less audio material. However, I did manage to find a short extract from a lecture that she once gave, and spent hours and hours listening to it to try and capture the essence of how she sounded. The lecture was quite a dry listen and Ginny Fox, my character as written, was full of emotion, so I had to modify the sound and make it work for Ginny. Virginia Woolf sounded quite extraordinary, they all did in fact, so I'd concentrate on getting the sounds in the words right to add flavour to them and make sure to add an extra rrrrrrr-rolll to her rrrrrs.

I'm so glad that the kind man in the radio booth called me over and that I hadn't had to rush off and was able to stay on to hear what he had to say, 'You really should do radio, you're rather good at it.' He nudged me in a direction that led to many other rewarding creative encounters.

I wish that someone like him had been there to advise me when I was offered my first significant role on television and agreed to do something which felt, from the get-go, very wrong indeed.

CHAPTER 14

Turning Points

I t had such a distinctive opening, and even now I can hear the pipe-and-drum theme tune that accompanied the sequence of car lights flashing in the dark, which then honed into a fixed point on a map, to reveal a car speeding off into the distance. This unfolding montage marked the arrival of the first of a much grittier and true-to-life police procedural drama series on television. TV was changing. *Z Cars* exploded onto the small screen in the early 1960s. It was set in the imaginary urban conurbation of Newtown, which was based on Kirkby, an area of Liverpool, and it commanded a lot of attention in the north-west, as well as grabbing mine. The notion of giving it a go and trying to get a spot on it appealed to me. For one, it was set near my home patch, well almost, and for two, given that it was a continuing drama series, it felt like it might be a good next step into TV, after my non-speaking role in *Bel Ami* and my cameo in *Hard Labour*. At that point in my career, I'd had no real experience of working in a studio and it felt that I needed to get some.

The casting process is a bit of a blur, but if memory serves a friend had kindly recommended me so there wasn't any audition as such before I was offered the role of WC Baylis and went on to appear in two episodes: 'Suspicion' and 'Nuisance'. Taking the role turned out to be a wrong turn. But I wasn't to know that. I thought it was exciting to take this next step forward and learn a new skill. Like the other jobs that I'd had up until that point, I was looking forward to being part of the team and doing my best. I'd experienced such great kindness and generosity of spirit towards me from the moment that I auditioned for East 15, but this job gave me an unpleasant taste of police procedural that I'd rather have acquitted myself from.

It all began well. On day one, everyone involved in the episode was chatting and drinking coffee before beginning rehearsals, and I felt calm and ready. The atmosphere was friendly, and it felt good to be amongst such seasoned TV performers from whom I expected I could learn a great deal.

I'd made a careful choice of clothing for the day and turned up wearing a pair of beige dungarees, which were very fashionable at the time, and had kept my attire plain and simple. Whilst we were all engaged in the familiar small talk of a first-day meet-and-greet, a loud voice cut through us and said, looking me up and down at the same time, 'You know, Alison, it's very important the way one dresses.' The director made a very deliberate motion of eying me from top to toe and, still looking at me, she continued, 'I'm smart but casual, and that's the way one should dress on these occasions.' I've no idea what her intention was, but if it was to make me feel small, ridiculed and humiliated, then she had succeeded. That familiar inner voice intruded again: *I'm not sure if I'm going to be able to do this.* I had a great deal to learn as I'd only been in the profession for three years and this was my first time on an established drama series. My mistake was to think that, like on previous jobs, there would be someone at the helm who would kindly help me along my way. There wasn't.

The floor of the rehearsal room was marked out in tape. For a novice like me, it was quite difficult to get my bearings and differentiate between doors and rooms, and inside and out, due to the flatness of the map. There were no churches or trees or puddles on the ground to help me in a studio and the brightly coloured taped markings on the floor looked more like a child's game than the set of a police drama. On cue, I entered one of the taped spaces, 'Stop, stop, stop!' came the same sharp-edged voice.

'Sorry, I'm so sorry,' I said. I'd made a mistake and gone in through the wrong door.

'We'll have to all begin again because of Alison Steadman. And I'm going to be late for my appointment now.' I shrunk inside and possibly outside too. No one had spoken to me like this before and I wasn't sure why this director was being quite so aggressive. 'Come on, let's start again. In future can you make sure that you know the layout before coming to rehearsals and that you know where you're going?'

At that point my only thought was, *I know where I want to go and that's as far away from you as possible.* She went on and on. It had been a tiny mistake and she spent longer reprimanding and humiliating me that it took to go back and do it again. In fact, it was her who was wasting everyone's time, but I hadn't the nerve to say so.

Each day there was something or other that she was cross about and she'd get at me for the smallest thing. It became so bad that I dreaded getting off the tube and tears would sting in my eyes as I headed across the road to where filming was taking place. Recording in a TV studio is nerve wracking enough, but with her constant poking and prodding at me, it was hell. Everything is done on a continuous take and, 'Quiet, studio, just about to turn over, ten, nine, eight ...' was everyone's cue to stand by. There was added pressure if you had the first line and complete concentration was required. On one occasion the first line was mine. I was standing, full of trepidation, gearing myself up to be on cue and not make any mistakes, when I saw her walking towards me. *Oh God. What now?* I could feel my heart race, my breath become shallower and my confidence begin to falter. She really had got under my skin. 'Listen, Alison,' she whispered insistently into my ear. It was horrible having her so close to me. 'Listen to me. The producer doesn't like what you're doing. Right. Do you hear me? You've got to do better. Now come on. Speak up and get on with it.' And with that she walked off. 'Three, two, one. Action.' I had to walk on. My throat had tightened and there were tears in my eyes, surely she must have known that her last-minute intervention would cause this reaction in me after the weeks of bullying? I was totally confused, *Why is this happening to me? Why is she trying to make me buckle?* It was beyond me, so I asked a colleague when we were all in the bar later. The director was there too and had bought everyone a drink apart from me. 'It's because she fancies you,' was the knowing response. 'This is what she does.' It made no sense to me at all. *What? Well, if she does, why doesn't she ask me out for a drink or a coffee instead of bullying me?* If I could have walked out of the job, I would have but I was contracted.

If I could replay that time in my life, I'd have made some very different decisions. *If only* is such a hollow and wasted thought though, as none of us can turn back time, even though we might want to. We can only learn from the wrong turns and try to right ourselves again.

It was such a huge relief to get to the end of the shoot and I couldn't get out of there fast enough. I just longed to get home to the flat in Euston where Mike and I now lived so it was a bit frustrating that I couldn't just jump on the tube from the BBC studios on

Wood Lane as my last day of filming had been on location. However, there was a chap who was delivering some technical equipment to the studio, who I'd got chatting with and told excitedly that it was my last day and that I couldn't wait to get home. 'Do you fancy a lift?' he said. 'I could give you a lift if you want? I'm heading back to London in my van and there's plenty of room.'

My experience of men offering me lifts had left me cautious and so, 'No, it's okay, thanks, I can go and get the train,' is how I replied. Yet again, my no wasn't taken as an answer. This should have had my inner red light flashing on high alert.

'No, no, no, it's alright, I'll drop you off.'

And then came my momentary wrong turn, *He looks friendly enough, it'll be fine*, and I yielded and said, 'Are you able to drop me off in town?' It wasn't as if he was a stranger, we'd been chatting on set all day. It would save me a good amount of time to go back with him and would be much more comfortable.

'Are you going soon?' He nodded. 'Okay then, that's great.' It wasn't great though.

We were heading south towards the motorway and talking away in the usual light-hearted manner of people who don't know each other, when he took an unexpected detour down a side lane and pulled up on a verge beside a field. And so it began. Again. *Why hadn't I listened to my instinct? Why had I allowed this to happen again? How can I be so stupid!* My default position was to initially think that I was to blame. 'Come on, come on,' he said as he tried every which way to touch me up, putting his hand on my knee and grabbing at me. I could practically hear him say, 'You know you want it,' which I most certainly did not. It was terrifying. Once again there was no escape. This man was a stranger, and no one knew where I was. The worst thoughts attacked me. Mustering myself I shouted, 'Can you stop please. Just stop. I want to go home.' Images of being trapped in the bubble car in Sefton Park flooded back. 'Get lost. Stop it. I want to go home.' My protests must have unnerved him, thank goodness, as he put the key back in the ignition, pulled off back onto the road and whizzed off so speedily that I thought we'd have a crash. We drove in silence before he screeched recklessly onto the curb and came to an abrupt halt at the nearest train station. There was no goodbye – I couldn't bear to look at him – and I jumped out of the danger zone before he could inflict any more insult.

It was another lucky escape, but it was horrible and left its stain for some time. It's unforgivable for any person to try to take advantage of another and push them into situations that induce fear and cause lasting damage. The man with the van, like the owner of the bubble car, knew exactly what he was doing. He wasn't stupid. He had sensed my willingness to trust and had taken advantage of this.

Bullying a young and inexperienced person, as I was at the time, can never be justified. The woman on *Z Cars* had been given a position of responsibility and was there to direct us all, but to me her direction was always unkind, cruel, and deliberately so. In the early 1970s TV world, there wasn't a department that looked after people's welfare and so I chose to keep the experience to myself and move on. My silence hadn't been right. I should have spoken up and out, and helped to put a stop to it. But I was frightened to, as experiences like mine and those that were far worse were ignored and I was worried, at that stage, about causing trouble and my work being affected.

The great thing about life, though, is that it works in mysterious ways and often karma comes when you least expect it. A few years later, when I'd become better known due to the success of *Nuts in May* and *Abigail's Party*, I was in the restaurant at Television Centre on Wood Lane and this same woman saw me sitting there. She picked up her tray and walked over to me. 'Alison, hello, how lovely to see you,' she gushed. *Oh no you don't, don't you gush at me,* I thought and got up, said a brusque 'Hello' and moved to another table. I later discovered that she'd made the lives of many young actors and directors so miserable that they'd given up. Yet here she was able to move on and up through the world of TV and be feted and garlanded because no one at that time could be bothered to take what was going on behind the scenes seriously. The industry has become more watchful over the ensuing years, the duty of care towards people is far more rigorous and there are harsh penalties for transgressors, but it still does exist. We can only hope that no young person need experience the threats and bullying that I did from people who should have known better. She must have been a very unhappy and lonely person at heart, and I'm sure not even her BAFTA could alter that.

The closure that I needed for the hideous experience of getting into cars with men who had encouraged me to place my trust in them came decades later when I was older, wiser and braver, and in the familiar environment of the Liverpool-to-London train. 'This is the 11.00 a.m. train from Liverpool Lime Street to London Euston, with the expected arrival time of 2.00 p.m.,' came the announcement. I could recite the announcement by heart as I'd made so many trips on the route by then. We weren't long out of Lime Street and had just passed through the sandstone rockface that took the train on to open track where the carriages become much brighter as natural light floods in. I began my customary people watching and that was when I noticed him. He was sitting a few rows in front of me and facing forward, which was a relief as there was no way that he could see me. I recognised his shape in an instant and suppressed rage stirred within me. *So, there he is, after all this time, I'm going to say something to him right now.* But gut instinct prevented me from getting up and walking down the carriage to face him. *No. I won't. I'll be stuck on the train with him, and I don't want to be near to him any longer than I need to. I'll wait until we get to Euston.* The rest of the journey was unsettling and even though the incident in Sefton Park had taken place twenty years earlier, it was as clear to me as yesterday. 'The next stop is London Euston where this train will terminate.' I was careful to keep my head down and waited until he got off the train before gathering up my stuff and stepping out onto the platform. Seeing him walking ahead of me, I ran, calling out his name. He stopped, looked around and across the sea of faces, then noticed me. 'Hello,' I said as I walked towards him, my heart drumming powerfully in my chest. Standing straight in front of him I said, 'Do you remember me?'

And, with his head down, he went, 'Er, er, er.' I was furious.

'You should do. You threatened to rape and murder me in Sefton Park. I don't know how you could forget that. I haven't.' He turned red and began to tremble. 'You're a religious man, aren't you? Well, I hope that you've asked for God's forgiveness because I'll never forgive you.' He couldn't look at me.

'Oh, I have asked for his forgiveness, I have.' It wasn't enough.

'You've got daughters, haven't you?

'Er, yes, I have.' I could sense his growing unease.

'Well, I hope to God that they never meet a man like you. I'll never forget what you did, ever.'

And with that I just walked off. I couldn't say any more.

My youthful decision not to tell anyone had locked part of me away and I chose to remain quiet, haunted by, 'Who do you think they'd believe? A schoolgirl or me?' We can put in place as many safeguards as we like, but we can't change human nature and as long as that admired person, that trusted person, that successful person, that funny person yet that emotionally fraudulent person is able to subtly infiltrate and embed themselves before making their cleverly calculated strike, then there is risk.

I'm not one to speak ill of others and sharing these different experiences hasn't been easy. Despite the bubble-car incident being nearly sixty years ago, the shame and embarrassment that I've borne has been a constant weight. This and my time on *Z Cars* have remained clear memories that have disturbed my peace of mind. Like, the *Z Cars* director, bubble-car man went on to lead a successful and high-profile life and it had been troubling to have seen both of them move on without a care to the damage that they'd caused by their reprehensible behaviour. The man and woman, who tormented my inner life long after their actions affected my outer life, didn't have to face any consequences. In police procedural terms these are both unresolved cases, but I've made my peace with that now. The not naming of both of them is out of respect to their families, who played no part in the bad behaviour and aren't responsible in any way. As Lady Macbeth says, 'What's done is done.'

CHAPTER 15

Step by Step

L ife is what happens when you're busy making other plans, so they say, but as I've said planning wasn't really something in my repertoire. My approach, and it's still what I do, was to take things step by step, and this is what I tell young people who are training for a life in the business now. Step by step is all you can do and it's so important not to hear the applause or seek the credit before the hard work has been done. There is no shortcut, and it will always take the time that it takes. Looking back, I can see the golden threads of connection between me and other people that have led me to other people and so on. It's a relationship map that is constantly evolving.

By the mid-1970s my actual family tree had expanded to include Mike Leigh, after we married in 1973, and I now had a *professional* family tree taking root beside it. So many of the friends and colleagues from my East 15 and Everyman days were now stepping into radio and television. Often during my own work, which never ever felt like work, there was a face from the past or a link between me and someone else. Getting along with people is something that comes naturally to me. I like people and prefer to be with company than without, so this inclines me to enjoy being social and part of it all. We weren't given classes in being good company at college, but quite a bit of working in theatre, TV and radio is about having the ability to get along with others. During the 1970s one job led to another and, apart from the *Z Cars* interlude, a good time was had.

I wasn't going to allow my bump up against a bully deter me from making the best use of my opportunities and accepting jobs that would nourish me as a performer, while keeping my improvisation muscles stretched and my comedy bones strong. Eddie Braben had taken his writing back onto television and created *Frost's Weekly* as a satirical comedy vehicle for the TV host and journalist David Frost. Working with Eddie was always fun and after the hideous experience on *Z Cars* I was keen to return to much lighter entertainment. This wasn't to say that the schedule was light or the pressure less. It was a weekly programme – it's in the title – and it was non-stop from beginning to end. The premise of the show was that it was a sort of chat-show style of programme with David tightly scripted while the rest of us played characters that we'd developed for Eddie, which could be woven in and around the script. So David was the only one to have the script in front of him, whilst the rest of us didn't have anything but our wit and hutzpah. It was billed as a 'television magazine', with a blend of comedy, music, song and dance, and it was a forerunner for all those chat-show entertainments that followed.

Once again, I got to work with my old East 15 friend David Casey as well as Bill Pertwee of *Dad's Army* fame and the wonderful Julia McKenzie. The show was packed with at least seventy-five characters for us to play and have fun with, and the set-up was that we'd be David's guests and he'd interview us. As it had been for *The Worst Show on the Wireless*, *Frost's Weekly* was recorded in front of a live studio audience, which pumped up our adrenaline and, as the turn-around was tight, there was very little time for rehearsal. We had to be ready for all eventualities and take any changes on the chin. There wasn't the time for any diva-like behaviour nor did we expect to be afforded any special graces. The same didn't apply to our 'star' and once, as were going through the structure for the recording a chap came in and said, 'Excuse me, David, your car is here and waiting for you,' and with that David said, 'Sorry, I've got to go,' and off he went to be busy somewhere else.

We were constantly thrown in at the deep end but Eddie's framework and our willingness to improvise kept us all afloat. I loved it and it was yet another opportunity to learn. One of my fondest memories of the show is of creating a double act with Julia McKenzie that saw us transform into two sex-starved spinster sisters. They were prim and proper on the surface but underneath the tweed twinsets and pearls they were raging with hormones that needed to be unleashed. Our catch phrase was, 'Fond of men, always have been,' and this would stir up the lust in us so much so that we'd end up ripping David's shirt off each time the sister act appeared. *Frost's Weekly* was such a satisfying programme to make as it combined my love of improvisation and creating characters with giving me more experience of working on camera, and with a studio audience to boot. It felt far more comfortable to me than *Z Cars*, while the nature of the show and the live audience being there made me itch to get back to my first love, theatre.

Creating characters was my natural playground and at some point, in 1973, when I was larking about with Mike at home, I adopted a light wispy, lispy voice and startied to say things like, 'You know, Mike, I love white walls. I love white walls, but I don't like anything that is grey or brown. I like things to be bright and airy.' I was just having a laugh, but it was fun to muck about with this woman, whoever she was, and I thought that it might be interesting to try to explore her more. 'Well, you can,' Mike said. 'Let's develop the character further.' The Royal Court's Theatre Upstairs gave us a performance slot and Mike, Roger Sloman, Geoffrey Hutchings and I began the process of creating a short play that went on to be called *Wholesome Glory*, which then became the inspiration for our full-length TV drama, *Nuts in May* three years later.

I was twenty-seven and, a bit like my time at the Everyman in Liverpool, this felt like a pivotal moment for me. The Royal Court was a boundary-pushing building where anything could be possible; a writers' theatre where, in 1956, John Osborne's *Look Back in Anger* was first given life. The Theatre Upstairs was even smaller than the Little Theatre in Rhyl and with only sixty seats felt more like performing in someone's front room than in a theatre. I felt like the Royal Court suited me. The closeness of the space, and the intimacy that it demanded, was such a powerful and instructive environment for a performer, so ensuring that we played detail was of paramount importance for the three of us, as there was no room for generality. We were following in the footsteps of the likes of Caryl Churchill, Arnold Wesker and Joe Orton, and making it count mattered.

I've no idea if Candice Marie was inspired by anyone – maybe I met someone at a party who was pretty and very nice, who wanted everything to be good and perfect, who loved animals and was concerned for their welfare. 'No, I don't eat meat because it's not kind to the cows and it's not good for my health or the planet.' Roger Sloman, who played her husband Keith, had been the year below me at college and although we'd been at the Everyman at the same time, we'd never worked together. We clicked immediately, as there was a shared joy of creating a character from nowhere and we both enjoyed and trusted the process. *Wholesome Glory* was only a short run of two weeks, but we still immersed ourselves in as detailed a rehearsal process as if it was going on for much longer. What we didn't know then was that we were in fact sowing ideas for a much deeper adventure with two of the characters, Keith and Candice Marie. The characters emerged out of our rehearsal process with Mike who was guiding us in their development, as well as taking on the added duties of set designer and production manager. There was no budget as such, and Mike would go and hunt in second-hand furniture shops for things that might help us create a set. But we didn't really need much. You don't if the characters are strong and you believe in them as if you are them, so that the audience do too. From very early on in the process, Roger and I began to develop them as an eco-aware vegetarian couple with very particular views on life and how to live it. Geoffrey created a character that became Roger's brother who was extremely keen on eating meat: big meat, huge meat and lots of it, not just the occasional bacon sandwich. Keith and Candice Marie were offended by Geoffrey's character and Roger would say in Keith's deep, slow-speaking manner, 'No, no, no, no, you mustn't eat meat. We've got to save the planet.'

Developing a character that must be believable over a length of time, even if it's just a short play, is different from creating shorter sketch-show ones, although there must also be something within them too if the audience is to connect with them and for it to be funny. Developing a believable person who has relationships with other believable people isn't created out of sketch work. During our time on *Wholesome Glory*, Mike guided us in such a way that never felt onerous or fussy; there was an ease and naturalness that enabled us all to breathe life into these other people. It was my first experience of creating a fully formed character out of an improvised process. Improvisation can be misunderstood, and I think that I may have misunderstood what it was and what it could lead to. Looking back to my Hylda Baker moments and even my elderly lady from youth-theatre days, I realise that these were sketch-show characters rather than fully believable human beings. Working with Mike on *Wholesome Glory* was very different indeed.

In all the work I did with Mike he took a very precise route and was clear about which direction he was taking things at each step of the way. The character development emerged through watching and listening, something that I'd been doing since my early birdsong-recording days. He'd invite us to pick someone to base our character on, then we'd begin to build the person through conversations and research. We needed to know the other person as well as we knew ourselves, who their family was, where they worked, their likes and dislikes. Towards the end of the process, before any performing in front of anyone – live audience or camera – he'd ask us to answer a list of questions that he had for each of us, and we'd answer them in character. It wasn't like a test or quiz that must be answered verbally or in writing; you answered them in your head and in that way you were truly getting inside the head of the person that you were creating. So Mike would say, 'Candice Marie, what's your favourite meal? What time do you go to bed on a regular basis? Who do you dislike? Do you dislike anyone? What's your favourite television programme?' It sounds random but it's the random things that make up the detail and we needed to have that detail in our heads. It's only possible to give truthful answers if you've developed the character so well that you know them inside out and outside in. Mike would then say, 'And now come out of character,' and we'd discuss the person from an objective point of view. He once described the method as, 'Discovering what the piece of work is through the process of making it.' I couldn't agree more. Steeping yourself in a deep psychological knowledge of a person enables you to play the part with a full understanding of what's under their skin. The swapping-clothes work that I'd done at East 15, although significant, was a lightweight precursor to being able to pretend to be other people and to cultivate a way of working that was to define the rest of my career.

Doing something for the first time can be quite scary and being the first person to do something for the first time doubly so. These two things collided for me when I was offered the role of Jackie in *Girl*, a TV play that was part of the BBC's *Second City Firsts*, which was produced by David Rose, who was such a trailblazer for TV drama at the time. *Second City Firsts* was a series of short one-off plays that offered the chance for new writers, including Willy Russell and Alan Bleasdale, to have their first television scripts produced (hence the *First* in the title) and produced by BBC Birmingham (hence the *Second City* in the title). It was such a brilliant series, not just because it showcased new writing but also because it offered great roles for young actors like me to get camera experience, as well as be seen in some substantial roles. The ensemble included Alun Armstrong, Julie Walters, Liz Smith, Michael Gambon, David Threlfall, Pete Postlethwaite and Bob Peck, and many of us were in more than one of the dramas over the series which lasted from 1973 until 1978. As well as Jackie in the aforementioned *Girl*, I played Helen, a young married woman who was having an affair with Vinny, an eighteen-year-old student who lived next door, played by David Warwick, in *Early to Bed* in 1975, the TV debut of my fellow Liverpudlian Alan Bleasdale. Like *Girl*, the play tackled a controversial topic that many regarded as taboo back then. I'm not sure that anyone realised how progressive the series was at the time.

Girl was written by James Robson, who had created a bold and boundary-breaking love story between two women. It wasn't a straightforward girl-meets-girl story by any means. My character Jackie is a young army recruit forced into leaving her job when it is discovered that she is both pregnant and in a sexual relationship with her superior officer, played by Myra Francis. There was a lot of action packed into the thirty-minute drama and at the time it was very controversial because it presented the first ever sexually driven kiss between two women on TV, as well as a post-coital bed scene that showed the women lying naked under the covers sharing a cigarette. Before transmission the controller of BBC2 had to come on air to give the audience fair warning of what was to come. I was offered the part by the director, Peter Gill, who had worked at the Royal Court, and when I read the script, it made me nervous, but I knew that it was something that I wanted to do. As usual there was very little budget, which meant very little rehearsal time; in the end that boiled down to four days rehearsing and working out all the shots, then on the fifth day we filmed it.

Myra and I didn't talk about the kiss as we were both anxious about it. Each day it would be a case of, *Oh my God, we've got to do this kiss, is it going to happen today?* I created such a fuss about it in my mind, much more so that when I'd had my naked reveal in *The Prime of Miss Jean Brodie*. This was different. It was being filmed, the audience would be much larger and I knew that it would be a talking point. Peter Gill, our director, was brilliant and didn't fan the flame of my apprehension; instead, when we got to that moment in rehearsal, he said, 'Okay, let's just do a quick kiss, just a quick one,' which we did, and then said, 'Carry on.' He didn't make a big thing of it and that made it so much easier. If he'd said, 'Alright, now we're going to spend some time on the kiss and you've both got to get it right,' we'd both have been in a state, purely because neither of us had kissed a girl before. We needn't have worried as all he said was,

'A quick kiss and then on with the dialogue.' Over the few days that we had left, both of us became more and more comfortable with it; the kiss became longer and longer, so there was no problem at all on filming day when we captured a moment of beauty and love.

My concern after that, as the broadcast date drew closer, was for people closer to home on Sherwyn Road. *Oh no, my poor mum. This will get the neighbours whispering!* And I imagined the over-the-fence gossip. *Did you see Marjorie's youngest was kissing a woman on television and is in bed with her too.* It was a big deal for me, and I was nervous about everyone's reactions. Once again, my mum and dad stood firm and supported me; even though it must have been a difficult watch for them both they were so understanding and complimentary. When the show was repeated my mum even watched it again and told me, 'Oh Alison, I'm so glad it was on again for a second time and I could be more relaxed. The first time I was so tense that I couldn't listen to a word anyone said so I'd no idea what was going on.' I loved her for that. *Girl* was a unique, breakthrough TV drama that didn't attach any stigma to the characters and the relationships between them. It was a carefully handled, innovative piece of storytelling and, as Peter said to us, *a love story.* I'm proud to have been part of the firstness of a drama that paved the way for many more progressive and liberal dramas on the small screen. It takes a leap of faith to do something for the first time and to allow your belief in the work to carry you forward.

The 1970s was a rich time for continuing TV shows, such as *Upstairs, Downstairs, The Two Ronnies, Are You Being Served?* and *The Goodies,* and this meant an opportunity for actors to earn a living that offered a bit more money than working in regional rep did. *Crown Court,* produced by Granada in Manchester, was one ITV's first continuing dramas. It ran from 1972 to 1984 and broadcast three afternoons a week, so there was a good amount of work available. Over the course of its twelve-year run it had an impressive roll-call of actors taking part including Tom Conti, Patricia Routledge, Ben Kingsley, Bernard Hill, Brian Cox, Juliet Stevenson, a young Mr Darcy (aka Colin Firth) and me.

To be honest with you, *Crown Court* was a bit of a trial for me and quite confusing. I'm sure that I couldn't have been the only actor to think so. The premise was an exciting one for the time: a real case, examined by a real jury, members of the public who were eligible for actual jury service, but with the barristers and those on trial being played by actors. That all sounds straightforward, doesn't it? However, for us actors, it wasn't, as although we were given the case information and a loose script, we weren't told whether we were innocent or guilty and this led to complications – at least it did for me. Not knowing the detail of whether I was innocent or guilty really bothered me. Surely to be able to do our roles justice (excuse the pun) we needed to know if we'd committed the crime or not? So, there I was standing trial for something that I didn't know if I'd done or not, being cross-examined by the prosecuting barrister and feeling so confused about which way to play it. A decision had to be made. To help things along, I decided that, given the evidence in the case notes and what the script was inviting me to say, I was most definitely guilty. *I've done this*, I thought *And now I must try and get myself out of this situation and be found not guilty. Isn't that what guilty people try to do?* So, I played it as best I could, trying to duck and dive around the questions and not incriminate myself as I was questioned under oath before the jury left us to deliberate things. These twelve good men and women returned a verdict of guilty so I thought that we'd all done rather well. In my mind the character was guilty, and the law had won out. However, my defending barrister was furious with me (remember, he wasn't a real barrister only a pretend one) and at the end of it all came up to me saying, 'What on earth were you doing? We should have won! If you'd have smiled a bit more then we would have!' And with that we began to walk out of the fictitious courtroom, but not before he said to the jury, who were still sitting there, 'Come on now, did you really think that she was guilty?' and they all nodded. He threw his hands in the air and stormed off. He was furious and his wig really was in a twist! It wasn't for dramatic effect either; he was truly cross that he'd lost and that he wouldn't be wearing the QC wig (as it was then) for the following case.

It was a tough gig as there was such a lot to learn, with hardly any rehearsal time and once again a budget too tight to allow time for second takes of any mistakes or fluffed lines. And anyway, the whole thing was set up to make the jury feel like it was real so as I was playing a supposedly real person in a courtroom situation, I couldn't really say, 'Oops, sorry, line please, I've forgotten what I'm meant to say!' So it was a relief to get back to London and rest for a bit afterwards. To ease the verdict I went out and treated myself to an expensive weekend bag with the money I'd earned. It was a knee-jerk reaction, as usually I had no money at all, but when you've no money and then a little bit extra comes in, you think, *Wouldn't it be nice to spend some of it on a treat or two?* The bag was an extravagant purchase for me, rather than just popping into Boots for a new lipstick because that felt like a treat when money was tight, and it cheered things up to be able to do that from time to time.

My time on *Girl* and *Early to Bed* had given me a taste of what good TV drama could be and so when I was offered a role in a new *Play for Today* drama I jumped at returning to the series for a bigger role than I'd had in *Hard Labour*. Like *Second City Firsts, Play for*

Today came out of the Pebble Mill Studios in Birmingham and was a mix of original television plays and adaptations of stage plays and novels. I don't think there's been a series like it since. It was an enhanced version of weekly rep but for TV and was far reaching and hard-hitting in term of the topics that it covered. Also like *Second City Firsts*, the ensemble of writers and actors was second to none, although that's not how we saw ourselves of course. Dennis Potter, Ian McEwan, Alan Plater, Andrew Davies, Trevor Griffiths and David Hare were just a few of the brilliant writers in the line-up. They attracted young up-and-coming directors such as Ken Loach, Roland Joffé, Lindsay Anderson and Stephen Frears. And these directors brought in actors including Anthony Hopkins, Donald Pleasence, Gemma Jones, Celia Johnson, Leonard Rossiter, John Gielgud, Janet Suzman, Joss Ackland, Liz Smith, James Bolam and Billy Connolly.

It was 1975 and *Through the Night*, written by Trevor Griffiths, was to be my first lead role in the *Play for Today* series, the others being *Nuts in May* and *Abigail's Party*. Of course, I hadn't a clue then about what an important impression the series would make on my career a few years later. 1975 was the year that saw Margaret Thatcher elected as the first woman leader of the Conservative Party, *Jaws* was the big-screen film and Queen had a number one with 'Bohemian Rhapsody'. The UK voted to continue membership of the European Community, and with the Sex Discrimination Act and Equal Pay Act both coming into force it appeared that society was making some sort of progress. If only we'd had a crystal ball to show us what was ahead of us!

Great writing is often a response to terrible situations and can yield both toughly expressed comedy and tender tragedy. Trevor wrote *Through the Night* to share his wife Jan's battle with breast cancer, and what she experienced during her treatment for it. Jan had kept a diary of her traumatic time in hospital that revealed the harrowing stay she'd endured, giving a unique insight into the NHS at the time, from a patient's point of view. It was a daring and touching chronicle of a terrible time but one that was so much more than a single woman's story. Jan's diary and Trevor's adaptation of it was the most powerful script of my career at that point and I was determined to do it justice. In the play, my character, Christine Potts, was shown becoming increasingly bewildered and frightened at the hands of various uncaring and dispassionate doctors who treat her as a number rather than a human being. It shows a hospital that is understaffed and overcrowded, *plus ça change*, where neither Christine nor her husband can get any information out of anybody. Taking her life into her own hands, Christine locks herself in a toilet cubicle and it's only when Dr Pearce, played by Jack Shepherd, does a set of Humphrey Bogart impressions that she comes out. 'Here's looking at you, kid.'

Michael Lindsay-Hogg had the challenge of directing the piece so that it captured the brutal realism of Christine's illness and of her operation, as well as the harsh hospital conditions. Everything about this piece was courageous. It was courageous for Jan to share her story and for her husband Trevor to adapt it for the screen. It was brave of *Play for Today* to commission it, and Michael followed suit with his filming decisions. As per usual there were budgetary constraints, and a location shoot wasn't an option. Michael's way around this was to film everyone on a video camera and from the character's viewpoint so that it brought the audience in closer to the action than the more static look that a four-camera set-up would have created. This was all very radical in 1975, and brilliant, as it exposed the drama in the way that it needed to be. I approached the character with the forensic detail that enabled me to feel comfortable in the role and found out as much as I could about the illness and its treatment. Breast cancer wasn't something that people felt they could talk freely about then, and a mastectomy was still largely a taboo subject. *Through the Night* treated both with care and respect. At any point when any of my shots required to show any nakedness the team always checked if I felt okay with it.

As bleak as the story was, we had some laughs too, mainly when we were trying to flatten my chest so that I looked like a person who had undergone a huge, body-transforming surgery. I wasn't amply endowed but without the flattening no one would have believed Christine had lost her breast. The make-up girls trussed up the area with cotton bandages as much as possible, so it felt like being mummified. But that wasn't quite sufficient, so during the post-operation bed scenes the two of them were hiding at the back of the bed, holding on and pulling each end of the bandage to keep me secure and flat. *Through the Night* was watched by over eleven million people and ignited an essential debate in the newspapers as well as on television about the need to take breast cancer seriously and to help women that were afflicted by it get the help that they needed as soon as possible.

Play for Today was both political and personal, and did what the arts do best: it shook things up. It pointed fingers at wrong-doing and ridiculousness, holding up a mirror to society so that we could see ourselves in our chaos and mess, as well as our glory. It's a tragedy that dozens of episodes were wiped during the BBC's massive archival clear-out so some important stories have been lost in time.

CHAPTER 16

Best of Times and Worst of Times

'Oh look, Keith, look at that bird. Isn't it lovely. I wonder what it is?' Roger Sloman and I are walking along a cliff path in Dorset plotting a scene as Candice Marie and Keith Pratt.

'Ah, yes, a lovely little bird. Do you want to get the bird book out, Candice Marie? We'll have a check what it is.'

It's an unseasonably hot day in early summer 1976 and we're on location developing, rehearsing and filming *Nuts in May*.

Everyone of a certain age still remembers that summer, don't they? If you say 1976 to anyone over fifty, the first thing that they'll say is, 'That was the year of the heat wave.' It was indeed, and between June and July the average daily temperature was 26.7°C while it peaked at 35.9°C. I can remember driving past Clissold Park in Stoke Newington when the grass was so dry that it was smouldering in the heat of the sun. The early part of that year was one of the happiest times in my career, as I had the opportunity to fully create and develop the character of Candice Marie, from *Wholesome Glory* at the Royal Court, for television.

Serendipity had played its hand again, as on so many occasions before, and being in the right place at the right time was how my next adventure with Candice Marie came about. Mike was working in the drama unit at BBC Birmingham, alongside David Rose, who had produced the two *Play for Today* episodes that I had been in, and they had bumped into each other. 'I'd like you to do a drama,' said David. He'd seen a few of the shorts that Mike had done and enjoyed them. 'I don't want it to be set in London or Birmingham or Manchester,' he continued. I'm sick of every television show being set in a city. I want it to be in the countryside and it might be nice if it was in Dorset.' David was from Swanage in Dorset, and he loved the county. 'Could you do something in Dorset, Mike?' And so, Mike got Roger and I together and posed the question, 'Do you think that Keith and Candice Marie would go camping in Dorset? You know, have a week's holiday or ten days there?' We didn't have to think very hard about our answer, as we knew the characters inside and out, and said, 'Yeah, definitely, they'd love that.' Mike went back to David and suggested *Nuts in May* to him, then he suggested it to the BBC, who said yes, and so it began.

'If they were going camping, what would Keith do?' Mike asked Roger. 'What would be his plan?' So, of course, Roger said, 'Well, he'd plan it all out, virtually hour by hour, so that he knew what they were going to be doing every minute of each day. There would be no perhaps or maybe to their itinerary. He would know exactly where they were going.' And that's what happened. Roger got a book and, as Keith, he created the whole schedule; where they were going, when they'd leave, how long they'd stay there, where they'd visit, what day they'd go to Corfe Castle. Keith's plan included what they ate for breakfast at 9.00 a.m. and when they'd leave for a walk, what they'd have for supper, 'Are we having raw mushrooms as a treat, Keith?' and when they'd go to bed. 'Say goodnight to Prudence, Keith.' It was incredibly detailed, and Roger worked so hard on it – as Keith would have done. Meanwhile Candice Marie was always painting, writing poetry and making up songs, some of which ended up on camera but not all, as there was limited time and budget, many of which I can still remember:

> Black smoke, crisp bags,
> Detergent in the river
> Cigarette smoke it makes me choke
> Litter makes me shiver.

We were in Dorset for eight weeks improvising and building these two characters having a holiday. The sun was shining, and I just loved being in my natural element. Everything that ended up on screen we had done for real and it was such a luxury to have so long to immerse ourselves in character. Candice Marie's childlike wonder could be a bit of a pain, but she had good intentions and was a dedicated eco-warrior. We wore our own clothes from start to finish but after it had been aired on TV one of the reviews criticised the jumper that Candice Marie was wearing, saying that it was 'high fashion', when in fact I'd bought it in a charity shop and had had it for years before wearing it as Candice Marie. It really annoyed me as we were so dedicated to being authentic. It's the only film that I've done without a scrap of make-up on and, given my lifelong love of lipstick, this wasn't easy. I won't even put the rubbish out without a touch of lippy! I can remember at one rehearsal I tried to sneak on a tiny lick of mascara and kept my eyes down so that it wouldn't be noticed but, alas, eagle-eyed Mike, who notices everything, said, 'What have you got on your eyes?' I said, 'Oh just a little—' and before I could finish the sentence he said, 'Get it off, get it off, she doesn't wear mascara.' He was right. It was important to ensure that all the choices that we made were in keeping with the character's truth, and mascara wearing most definitely wasn't very Candice Marie.

Even though we were on location for eight weeks the actual filming was completed over just eighteen days and so it was essential to know the detail of our characters. Mike would say, 'Okay, what happened on this trip, how did she feel?' Both Roger and I would have to be able to answer question after question. It was very precise: there would be things that we'd keep and develop for filming and things that were left behind. If Mike was rehearsing with some of the others, he'd ask Roger and me to do exactly as was written down in Keith's book, which usually meant going on a walk and doing some sightseeing. Our cliff-path walk was totally in character from start to finish.

When Roger as Keith said, 'get the bird book out, Candice Marie,' I, as Candice Marie, obediently went round to get it out of his rucksack, and on seeing that it wasn't on his back said, 'You haven't got your rucksack on, Keith.'

That wasn't something that Keith could fathom, and he replied, 'Don't be silly, Candice Marie, get the bird book out and we'll have a check what bird it is.'

I wasn't sure if it was Roger or Keith that didn't believe me, so assertively came back with, 'No, Keith, you really haven't got a rucksack on,' and I patted his back. We both began to laugh so much that we had to give into it and come out of character as we sat down at the side of the path and let it all out.

We must have been laughing for at least ten minutes at the silliness of it all when suddenly Roger jumped up and went, 'Right, come along, Candice Marie, let's continue our walk.' And so I got up and began walking again. Both of us went straight back into character. We didn't need to, there was no one around to make us, but we just did. It was only by keeping in role that we could discover what might lie ahead for Keith and Candice Marie.

The coastal path that was taking us to Lulworth Cove was quite a walk and even at twenty-nine I was exhausted by the end of it. The final stages involved climbing up a very steep path and I got panicky, as in me, Alison, got panicky – I'm not great with heights. I'm not sure when or why that began. I can remember being on holiday in North Wales and walking across the Menai Bridge when my mum said, 'Oh no, I can't do that, I can't walk across that,' and thinking, *Why not? What's there to be afraid of?* Perhaps it's something that I picked up from her over the years?

It's got worse and worse. Once, many years after *Nuts in May*, I was going to a show in the West End and my ticket was for the upper circle where the seating is very steeply stacked – I got myself into a real state. It was terrifying trying to shuffle along to the safety of my seat and once I got there the nerves just became worse so I couldn't look at the stage. Luckily, I had a scarf with me that I wound around my head, then left a tiny peephole so that I could look at the stage without fearing that I'd topple over onto it. The scarf made me feel more secure for some reason. So, if you were sitting next to a woman who wound her scarf around her head during a show many years ago, that was me, and I'm sorry if I disturbed you. It's a real fear and I could never do a show that required me to be hoisted into the air – they'd have to get a stunt double. Just thinking about being on a tightrope makes me jittery.

The Lulworth Cove coastal path was bad enough and Candice Marie's 'Keith, I'm really scared. I think I might fall' wasn't acting.

Roger, knowing that this was real, decided that as I'd kept in character that he would too, and from the top of the hill calmly said, 'No, no, no, Candice Marie. Don't be silly, you're perfectly alright.

Just go another two steps. You can take my hand, there we are.' I took his stretched-out hand. 'Now you've got my hand and you're quite safe. Come on. Up we go.'

I was really frightened and felt like stopping but Candice Marie said, 'Thank you, Keith. Thank you.'

And Roger as Keith said, 'Come along, let's carry on our walk.'

It wasn't until quite recently that I managed to control my foreboding of being close to the edge. I'd been made an ambassador for the London Wildlife Trust and in the same year was invited to present a three-part series called *Little British Islands with Alison Steadman*. It wasn't a job that I could say no to, as it promised the opportunity of getting up close and personal with my favourite creatures in their natural habitat, which for sea birds is a cliff face. I should have read the small print! At one point I was standing in the wind on top of a cliff and feeling incredibly wary as the drop, which was a few feet away from me, looked high enough to sky dive from and that's not a life experience that's on my bucket list.

The Scottish island expert who was with us was very soothing and patient and said, 'If you just take one step forward, Alison, no more than that, you'll be quite safe and you'll get the best view ever. Don't worry, I'm here.'

So, with some deep breaths, I moved along, then said, 'Okay I'm here too,' as I joined him nearer the edge.

'Right, now, Alison, look at the angle of my feet and do the same with yours. His feet were angled away from the drop and were apart rather than together. Never stand with your feet together as you'll get blown over, and always angle yourself away from danger.' Wise words for life, not just for standing on the edge of a cliff,

TOP: Joking around in my first West End show.

ABOVE: No laughing matter. Tony Sher's Tartuffe pulling at Elmire's heart strings.

RIGHT: Mrs Marlow about to meet her tragic end in *The Singing Detective*.

TOP: Me and my girl. With Jane Horrocks in *Life Is Sweet*.

MIDDLE LEFT: Brazening it out as Mari Hoff in *The Rise and Fall of Little Voice*.

MIDDLE RIGHT: My name in lights. Always a pinch-me moment.

RIGHT: On the other side of journalism as Jackie Johns.

ABOVE: Wedding day at the Bennets'. One down, four to go!

LEFT: Lucy Robinson, Anna Chancellor and me heading to the Net Ball.

BELOW: Oh, Mr Wickham! If you must!

TOP LEFT: Home is where the heart is. Back at 22 Sherwyn Road with Mum.

TOP CENTRE: A cherished moment on Mum's eightieth birthday.

TOP RIGHT: Twenty years later, at Sylvia's.

MIDDLE LEFT AND RIGHT: Let the transformation begin.

ABOVE: About to head into my favourite place: a theatre.

RIGHT: Look out for Alison and Michael!

TOP: As proud as punch to have met the Queen at last!

ABOVE: From *Fat Friends* to firm friends with Ruth Jones, James Corden and the rest of the cast.

RIGHT: One of the best times of my life, shooting *The Worst Week of My Life*.

TOP LEFT: *Enjoy*-ing myself in the 2009 revival of Alan Bennett's play.

TOP RIGHT: *Entertaining Mr Sloane* with Neil Stuke. Such a tough role but so rewarding.

ABOVE: Consciously trying not to laugh in *Blithe Spirit* with Hermione Norris.

RIGHT: Facing a career turning point in *Here* at the Rose Theatre, Kingston.

TOP: Mick and Pam taking a moment after doing some sliding to the left and sliding to the right.

ABOVE: The National Television Awards making Christmas special for *Gavin and Stacey*.

TOP: *23 Walks*: Preparing to sing in Spanish and hoping to not make a mistake!

ABOVE: Take Two. And the Jessop family are off again.

RIGHT: *Here We Go* birdwatching. Not another parakeet!

and an unexpected endorsement of my own step-by-step approach to life.

There are so many favourite moments from our time in Dorset. One of them is when Keith and Candice Marie arrived at Corfe Castle and Candice Marie immediately leapt into her fantasy world. 'Oh can you imagine, Keith, all the ladies in their frocks drinking wine out of goblets and eating fruit from the tables.' She'd travelled back in time in her imagination and was there amongst it while Keith, who wasn't listening to her and was keen to keep to his schedule and get it ticked off in his book, just said, 'So that's the B451, come on, Candice Marie.' Everything that we did was improvised first and then, if Mike felt that it worked, it was set in and prepped for filming. Working like this offers a great deal of creative freedom as well as allowing for the unexpected to happen, which can often, and when you least expect it, present comedy magic. This happened on our eventual arrival at Lulworth Cove. Roger, as Keith, decided to walk down from the top of the cliff into the cove and I, as Candice Marie, decided to stay at the top of the cliff and look down. Keith got down to the bottom and began to pick up bits of rock, rambling on about the marvels of prehistoric Britain for about five minutes to Candice Marie who was peering over the edge and looking down at him. It was like he was delivering a TED Talk on the Jurassic Coast. The only problem was that I couldn't hear a word Roger was saying, so my only option, as Candice Marie, was to keep saying, 'I can't hear you, Keith. I can't hear you.' Watching Roger be so earnest and committed to what Keith was saying was priceless.

We'd done such thorough work on both roles that we felt comfortable to keep within them to explore their reactions to fresh situations and people. Mike would introduce new characters to the environment and gently guide the action forward, so we had to react according. Ray, played by Anthony O'Donnell, was our first real encounter with anyone else. He'd pitched his tent close to Keith and Candice Marie's and, unbeknownst to me, Roger decided Keith would get it into his head that Candice Marie fancied Ray, which she didn't of course. This opposition created a hilarious dynamic between the three characters with each of them playing out their own truth. Candice Marie had some stones, so thinking that it might be good to break the ice with her fellow camper, wandered down to Ray's tiny tent, sat down beside him and said, 'Look at these lovely pebbles I found, Ray.' Tony, as Ray, joined in, albeit a bit bemused by it all. Meanwhile, Keith was furious as this wasn't in his book, and he didn't know how to respond. One of my favourite expressions from Keith was when he was chatting to Ray, trying to find out a bit more about him, and asks him if he eats meat. When Ray said that he did Keith replied, 'You do what you have to, Ray, but we don't because we're vegetarian.'

Not knowing exactly what someone might say or do was always exciting, so when Finger and Honky, played by Stephen Bill and Sheila Kelly, pitched up at the campsite the tension was ramped up even more. Roger and I didn't know anything about these characters, so we were finding out just as Keith and Candice Marie would have been. Their loud arrival into the field, bouncing over the uneven ground on their motorbike, was genius. They bumped down the stony slope and eventually fell off the bike but were okay, then Finger, in a broad Brummie accent, got out a football and said to Honky, who was all togged up in thigh-high white leather boots, 'On yer head, Honk.' It was hilarious – Roger and I would have laughed, but we couldn't show that, as Keith and Candice Marie were lost for words.

Being in the Dorset countryside and making up stories was heaven to me. I felt that my whole self was present and, even though I was in character, that there was nothing to hide. It was glorious and I delighted in it all. There was, however, an occasion that arose that wasn't quite so appealing. One day we were filming on a farm and I was just pottering about waiting for my call so I wandered into the farm shop, where, to my delight, there were lots of chickens running around outside pecking at the grass. I'd always wanted to keep chickens and was thrilled to see them looking so free and happy. Their eggs were being sold in the shop and everything appeared so perfectly idyllic. *It doesn't get better than this* is what I thought, as life and art blended so seamlessly for me. A few minutes later, as I continued my wander, I hit the ground with a figurative bump. There was a huge wooden shed with its door slightly ajar so I peeped in. To my horror there were hundreds of chickens in wire cages and when they saw me, they began to make this unforgettable screeching noise. Their poor necks were raw from having to reach through the cage wire to get to their food and most of their feathers were missing. It was horrific. They had no room to move and were crammed into tight rows so all they could do was feed. Suddenly the lady from the farm shop came stomping in, as my presence in the shed had set off an alarm and, thinking that I could have been a fox, she had rushed over. When she saw me, she spoke quite firmly and said, 'What are you doing in here?'

Still in a bit of shock I apologised, 'I'm so sorry, I didn't mean to I saw the door and ... Why have the chicken no feathers?'

Her answer appalled me. 'They're old and ready to be sent off for boilers.' The cruelty of what I saw that day has stayed with me and I vowed that from then on that I'd only buy free-range eggs, which at that time were only available in the health-food shops and not in supermarkets. The chickens that had been happily pecking the grass outside the farm shop had been placed there for cosmetic purposes, while round the corner was a torture chamber. Candice Marie was extremely upset, and so was I!

Nuts in May felt very complete, from the way we worked, to how it was directed and filmed, to how it ended up on screen. When my mum watched it, she called me, as she always did after watching me on TV, and said, 'You know that bit at the end? That was you as a child.' There's a beautiful moment towards the end of the film when the wind is gently blowing through the guitar strings and making a sound. Candice Marie begins to dance and says, 'When I was at school, Keith, the teachers put some music on, and we used to dance around with our silk scarves like this.' For anyone else watching, this may also have stirred their own memories of music and movement classes, and for my mum it was very particular and special. She continued, 'You were just like that as a child. I can remember giving you a silk scarf to take to school to use to dance to classical music with.' It was a wonderful reminder of the layers of history and story that are within us all, and the brilliance and power that improvisation offers to unearth them all.

Some jobs are harder to come down from or say goodbye to, and this was most definitely one of them. I found it very hard to return to our flat on a busy road near Euston Station. There was nothing wrong with the flat, but the air felt claggy and thick, and I can remember seeing our window ledge and being shocked by the amount of black soot and grit that was layered on it. We'd all shared eight intense, fun and creative weeks that felt like an oasis of special time, so coming back to reality was tough.

I want to get away she said

I want to get away

I'll take you on a trip he said

We'll have a holiday

We'll be in Mother Nature

And laugh and sing and play

I want to get away she said

I want to get away.

If I could do all of that again I would. It's not my job to give an analytical perspective of the film, that's for others to do, but I will say that, a bit like *Girl* and *Through the Night*, *Nuts in May* tackled some hot (excuse the 1976 pun) topics of the time and touched on issues that were to become increasingly important to us all. Keith and Candice Marie discovered that the grass isn't always greener. When Candice Marie expressed her concern about ghosts from the past coming back and being shocked by the coastline's abundance of litter, Keith's response, 'They'd find it difficult to comprehend all the changes that have taken place in the world,' was an eerie prediction of the future.

It was the best of times and difficult to let go of, so being able to gather everyone together again in 2021 for a special screening at the BFI, with a Q&A afterwards, was fantastic. Much to everyone's amazement, I brought along the scarf that I'd danced with all those years earlier, but refrained from doing any movement and music as Candice Marie may have done. I'm often astounded when people recall *Nuts in May* as it sometimes can feel dwarfed, though not by me, by *Abigail's Party*, which came immediately after it, but it is still remembered and very fondly. A few years ago, I was in the food hall of a store when a teenage girl and her nine-year-old brother stopped in front of me. The girl took a breath in and said, 'I'm sorry to bother you, but my brother is a huge fan and he wanted to say hello.'

Given their ages, I assumed that they knew me from *Gavin and Stacey*, so I said, 'Oh, that's great, do you like *Gavin and Stacey*?' He looked a bit blank, he obviously hadn't a clue what I was talking about. 'Oh no,' said his sister, 'it's *Nuts in May* that he loves.' It made my day. I think that any film that you've done that can be watched and loved by a nine-year-old decades after it first appeared must be extraordinary – not just because it's of its time, but because it's for all time.

Sometimes I wonder if the happiness that I experienced during the early summer of 1976 contributed to the worry and sadness that I felt during the autumn months. It's a question that doesn't need an answer, but I do wonder why I wasn't able to harness the joy that creating *Nuts in May* had fostered in me and carry it, and a renewed confidence, forward into my work at Nottingham Playhouse.

'Alison, are you okay?' I was in the world of my own head again. *I'm just not getting this, I'm not getting this* kept tormenting my mind, and I'd stopped mid-scene and broken down in tears in front of the entire cast. The whole room must have been thinking, *Why on earth is she crying?* It was our first run-through in the rehearsal room of *Othello* at Nottingham Playhouse and my first time back on stage after the success of *Nuts in May*. 'Let's take a five-minute break, shall we?' said Richard Eyre who was directing us. He was being so kind and patient with me, as he was with everyone. I headed outside for some fresh air and gave myself a talking to. *Come on, pull yourself together, you can do this. Don't muck it up. Desdemona is a great role for you.* The stage manager called us all back into the room when the five minutes were up and we began the scene again. I steeled myself and got through it. Little by little my confidence began to come back but that other voice in my head was still there, and I wanted to say, *I'm sorry, I can't do this. I'm rubbish. Can you please find someone else to take over?* It was agony; a very sharp feeling of fear, unlike any other that I'd experienced in rehearsal or on stage before, pierced me. It wasn't nerves. It was a much more visceral feeling, and I knew that I needed to shake it off somehow if I was to get through the run of the show.

I had been looking forward to returning to the stage especially as I would be sharing digs with Rachel again. We both had roles in *Othello* and Tom Stoppard's *Travesties* at the Playhouse that season. We took a couple of rooms in a large house near to the theatre, and we had our own bathroom, which was a relief after the Mr and Mrs Two Hoots experience. Apart from the fact that the damn toilet didn't flush properly. This was far from ideal as you can imagine. Not being able to empty a full toilet bowl is like a tormenting nightmare that comes back to haunt you so we would give the toilet a good old pumping each time. One evening we got back and there was a note from the landlady: 'Dear Alison and Rachel, please can you refrain from pumping the toilet.' That left us quite flushed!

Othello is a tough play and back in 1976 there was, quite rightly, a growing sensitivity about a white man playing the title role. Daniel Massey was possibly one of the last white men to play the part. Looking back I wonder if he felt uncomfortable about it as he wasn't the easiest of people in rehearsal or on stage, which didn't help the attack of deep-seated fear that had gripped me. After my shakiness in the rehearsal room, I managed to steady myself and the show got up and running successfully within the season's repertoire. I had also taken a TV job in Birmingham that I could do when *Othello* or

Travesties wasn't on, What I hadn't factored in was just how tired working in Birmingham during the day and being on stage at night would be. One evening I signed in at the stage door thinking, *How the hell am I going to get through the show tonight?*

Desdemona is determined, brave, resolute, faithful, honourable and confident. She doesn't have narcolepsy! The play began, I battled through it and the end was, quite literally, in sight as we headed into the moment when Othello strangles Desdemona and smothers her with a pillow. Neither of which were very pleasant for me, and sometimes Daniel's actions felt a little too real to be safe. On one occasion he had misplaced his hands; rather than placing them on top of mine to look as though he was grabbing my throat, he actually grabbed my throat then swung me up and round, and onto the bed. Shock took a hold for a few moments and I'd no idea where I was. Let's put it down to a fit of enthusiasm or a little bit of method acting but it put me on my guard. Anyway, the great thing about the death section was that I was thrown onto this enormous bed before uttering my final lines. Knowing that I could lie there for a bit before dying had kept me going. So, Daniel pushed me onto the bed and I lay there on my back with my eyes closed ... and fell asleep. I went out like a light. The problem was that I still had some final breathless lines to utter. Bridget Turner, who was playing Desdemona's maid Emilia, gave me a very long pause as she waited for the line from me that prompted hers. Hearing nothing but silence she reversed the order and ran on stage shouting, 'Hark that was my lady's voice,' as if I'd said it. I woke up with a jolt and uttered, in completely the wrong place, 'Oh, falsely, falsely murdered.'

It may have been the first time that I'd fallen asleep on stage, but it wasn't the last. Much later in my career, my character had to snuggle into a plump, soft pillow and the next thing I knew was when I woke up in complete darkness and it was the interval. I ran into the wings apologising, 'I fell asleep, it won't happen again!' And I'm glad to report that it didn't.

CHAPTER 17

Aahhhh, Love to Love you, Baby

'Alison, Alison, come here, quick, quick, look out the window,' said Mum every so often, and each time I'd dash to the window and see this woman, who wasn't like any of the other women on our street, getting out of her car. She had dyed red hair and fancy clothes and shoes, and didn't look as if she'd ever spent any time cooking and cleaning and looking after children. 'She's having an affair,' Mum would say knowingly. I was working at the probation office and marriage counselling service, so I knew what having an affair meant. 'Are you serious?' I retorted. It seemed so out of character for Mum to say something like this. However, it turned out that my mum knew quite a bit about this woman. 'I am telling you she is. It's on the quiet but she is having an affair, and with a doctor!' The woman was staying at her sister's house, which was down the road a bit and on the opposite side to ours, and so our front room, the one that we only used for special occasions, was an ideal bird hide of sorts to check the comings and goings of this mysterious redhead. Cars were few and far between on Sherwyn Road and so the sound of an engine pulling up in the wee small hours would always cause a bit of curtain twitching, 'See, see, I told you. Who gets home this late? Something is going on. I knew it.' The woman intrigued me, she seemed so out of place in her surroundings, and dressed and moved as if she was destined for better things. I only ever viewed her from afar, but she made an impression upon me and I must have popped her into the back pocket of my memory to reappear eleven years later in the rehearsal room of a new play that we were developing.

I'd just returned home to London after the season at Nottingham, when Mike asked me if I'd like to be in a new play at the Hampstead Theatre. At that stage we'd no idea what it was going to be about or the characters that would be in it, but I had no hesitation as this would be a return to working in the way that suited me best and I was excited to get going on this next adventure. My fellow explorers on our yet-to-be-titled piece were Tim Stern, Janine Duvitski, John Salthouse and Thelma Whitely – and off we went on our map-less journey. Mike outlined the kind of world that he wanted us all to create and the types of people that we might discover within in it. Then he asked us all to go away and think about individuals that we may know or had met, no matter how briefly, and pick half a dozen of them to bring back to the table.

This is where all that watching and listening from my childhood became so useful. As children we are so much more naturally alert to our surroundings, and see and hear in a highly tuned way. It's a natural survival instinct, but as we grow up and become distracted we can often lose sight of the detail in front of us. All these years on I'm still preoccupied with watching and listening, I know that it's part of my job, but I also think that it's part of who I am. Whenever I'm talking to students, I will always say that the best training is free as it costs nothing to watch and listen. I love looking at people and thinking, *Why is she wearing that dress and those shoes, and who is that with her, what's their relationship?* Nothing is ever boring when you allow yourself to be constantly aware and observant. Taking the time to tune into how someone speaks, *Why do they sound like that? Where is that accent from,* offers up so many other questions. If I'm on the tube, I might see someone's outfit that piques my interest so I'll note it down on my phone as I want to remember and try to understand why someone is wearing what they've got on. All the research that I need to create a character is usually just a stone's throw away; it's on the bus, walking down the street, at a party or sometimes even closer to home.

Mike constantly encouraged us to excavate the detail. When we all went back to the table and described our chosen cast of characters, he would listen and say, 'No, forget that, keep that, forget that.' Finally, having heard from us all, he'd say, 'Let's base it on that person.' One of the people that I brought to the table for this untitled piece combined the mysterious redhead from Sherwyn Road with a blend of some of the women who I'd seen around Loughton in Essex, when I was at East 15. In the late 1960s, even though there was a huge decline in industry, unemployment was rife and the pound had fallen, there didn't seem to be any poverty of aspiration in Essex at all. The girl in my year who had given me the advice about buying a smaller bra also told me stories about some of the women who lived in the area, and what they did to try and hook a man. On Saturday nights they would decide on a pub, then stand outside in the car park and look around. If there were a few expensive-looking cars there they'd go inside, swing their hips and hope for a catch, but if the car park only sported a Ford Escort or a Vauxhall Viva, they'd move onto the next place. It gave me a fantastic insight into a very particular survival mindset and a form of ruthless ambition that wasn't familiar to me at all, although I'm sure it wasn't only happening in Essex. I added all of this into our rehearsal mix and began to develop the character on my own.

Each morning, getting dressed, I made a very deliberate choice of clothes for the day, avoiding any of my usual rehearsal garb, and my make-up routine became a little more extravagant than a dollop of Nivea and some lippy. Mike noticed this and in rehearsals asked, 'What kind of job does this woman do?' and I found myself saying, 'She wants to be a make-up designer, work on the make-up counter of a posh shop like Selfridges and be the one in charge.' So, Mike suggested that I go down to Selfridges and spend some time there. I got lucky, as on the day that I went into the shop there was a lady giving a product demonstration in the make-up department. A group of women had gathered around her. She had a tiny little microphone that she held just below her lips and spoke into it as if she was going to kiss it. Once enough people had gathered, she purred, 'Now then, I need someone to come and sit in this chair and I'll do your make-up. Anyone going to volunteer?' There was an awkward silence – isn't there always whenever that question is asked – and the make-up lady began to scan our faces. 'How about you? Wouldn't you like to have a little treat today?' She'd picked out a woman who was standing on the edge of the group in her wet mac – she'd probably only come in to get out of the rain – and said, 'Yes, you, the very pretty lady with no make-up on standing at the back there. Would you like to come forward?' The woman in the mac had been put on the spot and was clearly too embarrassed to say anything but, 'Oh, okay then,' and moved forward to the high stool that was indicated for her. I watched the other woman. Her seduction technique was just brilliant. 'Okay,' she began, 'so now we're going to put on this eyeshadow, it's a beautiful colour, beautiful colour. This eyeshadow is very popular in Paris this week and whatever is popular in Paris is going to be popular here in London the following week. So, I'm telling you, ladies, this is what you want to be wearing.

Okay?' And she carried on applying this and that to her damp volunteer. She kept speaking into the little mic as if she were sharing a top secret with us. I absorbed her manner and brought it into the rehearsal room. Slowly, slowly, the character of Beverly began to emerge. The moment when Beverly says to Ange, 'Can you take a little bit of criticism? When you look in the mirror say, "I've got very beautiful lips," and then take your lipstick and put it on. You'll notice the difference.' All that section was inspired by observing the silky-voiced woman in the make-up department at Selfridges.

So much of the way that East 15 had trained us was so useful, and being able to move my way into a neutral walk that I could then apply another physicality to was invaluable during the process of developing what became *Abigail's Party*. In my head, as well as wanting to be a make-up designer and work in a posh shop, Beverly also wanted to be a model. She believed she was good enough to be one, so my question was, *How does Beverly walk if she thinks she could be a model?* I imagined that she imagined she was on the catwalk and on show all the time, and that every little gesture was done to demonstrate her style and high self-regard, so I began to experiment with this.

It all came together when we found her dress. Once again, our budget was very small and so all the clothes that we wore were bought off the rack. The costume designer and I went shopping in C&A Modes.

'How do you like this?' A bright orange dress was being held in front of me.

'That's brilliant. She'd love that. I'll try it on.'

I put it on and came out of the changing room. 'This is the one,' I said.

'Hang on a minute, we've only looked at one dress, let's carry on looking,' said the costume designer.

'We don't have to. This is the one, I'm telling you.'

And we bought it there and then.

When I had the orange dress on, my shoulders would rise a bit and I'd sashay around with my hips and top half swaying. Beverly was emerging. The dress really had its moment when Beverly opened the door to Ange who looks at her and says, 'Oh sorry, were we meant to wear long?' I just love that line, it's such a mixture of total innocence and confidence, and Janine delivered it with perfect pitch.

Like on our work on *Nuts in May*, there came a point in rehearsal when the characters that had emerged were ready to be woven into a narrative structure. It was at this point that Mike put Laurence, the character that Tim Stern had been developing, and Beverly together in the house as a married couple. For me this is when this approach gets interesting, the moment when you must navigate forward with another person to discover the lay of the land, and from then on Tim and I would improvise together to begin to develop their relationship. We'd each created our own back story and now we needed to shape a shared one. There were so many questions that needed answering. Where had they met? Why did she marry him? What did she hope for? Poor Laurence. He'd overplayed his initial seduction and Beverly had been lured in because he had a bob or two and was going to get a house. Her desire for the best, and having the most that she could get, put Laurence under huge pressure and it was soon clear to us both that he would never be enough for her. This dynamic tension allowed us to push into funny and dark corners with each of the characters. Even though they'd only recently married, she was bored stiff with him and was already on the prowl again. If someone came in that could offer her more then she'd dump Laurence immediately, swapping the Fiesta for a Ferrari in an instant. John Salthouse's Tony, an ex-footballer with much more swagger than Laurence, was an easy target for her and allowed Beverly to appear like the hostess with the mostess, while being ruthless and manipulative at the same time. She's sounding awful, isn't she? In many ways she is a monster, but she's also a person who is struggling and insecure – and her mask betrays her very revealingly towards the end of the play. The truth of a person will out.

We all wear masks in life, but as a performer it's sometimes mask upon mask, and when this is the case it can make it difficult to get to the truth of the character. However, I could see, hear and feel Beverly, with and without her mask, and this allowed me to build her into a character that was both strong and identifiable. Once the show had opened at Hampstead Theatre, people, mainly men, would come up to me in the bar afterwards and say, 'Oh God, I know that woman,' or, 'I've been followed by that woman,' and I often wondered what woman they saw. It's strange how safe we can feel laughing at someone else, whilst saying to ourselves, *Thank goodness I'm not like that.* But there's an argument to say that the reason we laugh is because we make a more personal connection, and perhaps, we've all got a bit of Beverly in us.

The show, which opened in April 1977, had an incredibly powerful impact on the audience and almost right from the start it was sold out, with people queueing around the block for return tickets. Due to popular demand, we did a second run a few months later by which time I was in the very early stages of my first pregnancy. Who would have thought that when we went dress shopping we'd find not only the perfect dress for Beverly but also that the dress, which had a voluminous drop of material from the bust line, would be ideal to cover my tiny bump. It was such a strange sensation to play Beverly for the second time knowing that my much-wanted baby was growing inside of me, and especially since the character was childless and this was one of the things that we'd explored during rehearsal. I was thrilled to be pregnant and loved dancing to Donna Summer and Demis Roussos knowing that I was expecting and only very few people knew. One evening I was standing between the tall sideboard, which held the record player and the drinks cabinet, and the back of the couch when I felt a new sensation in my tummy. I had to stop myself from declaring 'Oh, my baby has just kicked for the first time!' to the audience. It was a very firm kick that announced that my little one was on stage with me, and I nearly forgot my next line as a result.

The second run created another moment of serendipity for us all. The first run having proved so popular meant people were talking about it, resulting in lots of industry folk coming along to see what all the fuss was about. In the audience one evening was Margaret Matheson, a producer from BBC Scotland, who after the show said, 'This has got to be recorded.' She went back to the BBC and discovered there was a gap in the schedule. She was so determined – it was her faith and energy that helped to bring *Abigail's Party* to the screen and to a much wider audience.

By this time, eight years into my career, I was beginning to bank some good experience of acting for camera, but this was the first time that I'd taken a fully created character from the stage and translated it for the screen. It was different with Candice Marie as she became much more formed during the time on location in Dorset, and then we filmed her, but Beverly was already sculpted and so the challenge was a different one. Once again, the pressure was on, as there was very little time or money. But perhaps having less gave us more, as it forced us all to be positive, to find creative solutions and work collaboratively to the end. No one asked me to change the character that I'd developed – apart from getting used to the cuts and four cameras we were doing the same play.

It was a relentless shoot and Harriet Reynolds, who'd been thrown in at the deep end taking over the role of Sue, came in one day and said, 'Last night I said to my mum that I was tired and all she said to me was, "Well, if you're tired imagine how Alison must feel as she's pregnant as well!"' It was tiring but we were young and could cope with it. There was much more pressure on Mike, who had to make the cuts, change some of the music due to rights issues, work out the shots and ensure that what was captured on screen represented the stage play that had been such a hit at Hampstead Theatre.

Despite such a tight shoot schedule there was always a fixed start and finish time. It didn't matter what was going on, them was the rules and our latest finish time was 10.00 p.m. regardless of whether we were finished or not. All the props were then carefully locked away in wire cages so that they were safe but also easily accessible. This included the bottle of Beaujolais that Sue brought along, much to Beverley's approval, as her contribution to the evening, 'Beaujolais, how fantastic, I'll just pop it in the fridge.' However, towards the end of a day, when it came to filming that moment, the Beaujolais was nowhere to be seen. Someone had nicked it! It really made me cross, so I stood in the middle of the studio and said loudly, 'Whoever nicked that wine, you do know that you've really messed us up.' There was no choice but to run over and thankfully the crew all agreed to carry on, even though there would be no extra pay. I've been on other jobs when you're in the middle of things, then people just down tools, call it a day and walk off, as back in the day keeping tightly to union rules was important. On the last day it was the same, as there was still a way to go at 10.00 p.m. Everyone continued through until midnight, which was hugely appreciated by us all.

At the end of the shoot, the lead cameraman came over to me, held out his hand and said, 'It's been an absolute honour and pleasure to film this,' which I've never forgotten. Likewise, it had been an absolute honour and pleasure to work with all the team that we had on the production.

We had another bit of good fortune. On the evening of Tuesday 1 November 1977, when the show was broadcast on BBC, something went wrong with ITV (remember there were only three channels), so everyone said, 'What's on? Let's watch this thing called *Abigail's Party*. It sounds fun!' The audience figures were massive, and Beverly was rapidly catapulted into the imagination of the nation. One of the most touching responses to it came from Miss Brown, my headmistress from Childwell Valley High School, who had been so supportive to me during my awkward chat with the careers adviser. She wrote me a note saying that she had watched it especially and was so proud that I had followed my heart. That meant the world to me.

I felt like everything was falling into place and developing, including the tiny life growing inside of me. By the time that we'd finished filming I was four or five months' pregnant, and I half expected my baby to pop out singing, 'ahhhh, love to love you, baby,' or say in parrot-fashion, 'Ange? Gin and tonic? Ice? Lemon? Tone? Light ale?' Thankfully he didn't, but life did change from that moment onwards.

CHAPTER 18

Juggling

Toby, my first son, was born in the spring of 1978 and although he didn't come out singing any Tom Jones songs, he did arrive within the flurry of excitement, professional plaudits and acknowledgement that began after the November broadcast of *Abigail's Party* the previous year

The reaction to the stage play had been incredible – it had been the hottest ticket in town – but the response to the filmed version wasn't like anything any of us could have expected. Beverly became an obsession for people, and public property. Suddenly I went from being a jobbing actress to one who was recognised on the street and in demand, just as I was about to have a baby. Timing! In fact, it was perfect as it turned out.

The lot of anyone in the entertainment industry is to go where the work leads you, and this is as true for directors as it was for actors. So, it was unfortunate, but not a surprise, that I was on my own when the first signs that I might be in labour appeared. Mike was filming about a two-hour car journey away so he had arranged a number for me to ring as soon as I felt the baby was on its way. I was home alone, and like most first-time mums had no real idea of what 'the baby's on the way' meant. My pains had started in the late afternoon, so I made the call, not knowing what would happen next or when the baby would arrive. The message was relayed to Mike who jumped into a car. The initial contractions began slowly and didn't get any worse, but it was scary when my waters broke, a definite sign that things were progressing, so I called the person that I always did when comfort was needed, my mum.

'Mum, the labour has started. I think the baby is on the way.'

'Alright, you're going to be alright. Is Mike on his way? Don't worry. You'll be fine. You can do this. Just go and make yourself a cup of tea. It'll all be okay.'

It was great to have her voice on the end of the phone talking me into calmness. And it was all okay. Mike got back in time, we got to the hospital safely, and Toby arrived the following afternoon at around lunchtime.

Like most new mums, a waterfall of love flowed through me, and I was in heaven. The reaction to *Abigail's Party* had been like being whisked up into a whirlwind, but now I was going to anchor myself at home with my baby and enjoy watching this little soul growing each day. I hadn't realised just how much I would enjoy having a baby. In my heart I didn't want to go back to work and leave Toby, but sitting right beside that feeling was my love of acting and not ever wanting to give it up. In the end I took a whole year off. It was the best decision ever and I adored every second of it.

I was wrenched away by the opportunity to make my first appearance in a West End theatre, in Alan Ayckbourn's play *Joking Apart*. It felt like a physical tearing away from my baby bliss, unlike anything that I'd experienced before. Each morning, having got Toby up and ready for the young, local girl who was looking after him, I'd sit in the car just outside our house and cry so hard that I couldn't begin to drive for a least fifteen minutes. The thought of leaving him with someone I didn't know well who might not know his habits was excruciating – even though I knew Toby really liked her and would greet her with a hug, all I could do was worry.

Before the show opened in the West End it did a two-week tour of regional theatres to test the comedy out on audiences. I couldn't get home so each night spiralled into incessant catastrophising, dreaming that Toby had got hold of a bleach bottle and drunk from it. *Are the cupboards being shut properly? Does she know that the bleach needs to be put right to the back of the cupboard under the sink?* I drove myself mad with questions and I'm sure that I drove everyone at home mad as well as I bombarded them with phone calls. He was okay of course, and once we returned home and the show went into the West End, I chastised myself for not taking the opportunity to catch up on my sleep when I'd been away. The timetable was relentless, an eight-show week that included two matinees. When the show closed after four months, I have to say that I was relieved, which is a very unnatural thing for an actor to express, and utterly delighted to be back home again with my boy. Soon the memories of worry and drop-dead fatigue that come with a new baby began to fade away, so you can imagine what happened next!

When Toby was two and a half, I became pregnant again. I was excited to be able to share the news with my parents as being a mum of two was something that I'd longed for and now, all being well, was going to happen. But the phone call didn't go as I'd expected. Putting down the receiver, I replayed the conversation that had just taken place with my dad as it had seemed so out of character for him. *Why had he been so upset when I told him?* He had only ever been supportive of all my choices. His reaction to the news was concern, and I needed to think why. It wasn't that he didn't want me to have another baby – I was certain that he did. No, once again, and totally in character for him, his response was because he was so emotionally invested in me achieving my dreams. I think it was also about him. After a lifetime of work at the large electronics company Plessy, he had only been able to return to his true passions of music and art when he'd retired. He wasn't an unhappy man by any means, and never complained about his lot, but deep inside himself he must have known he had far more potential. And perhaps in those few minutes when I was excitedly telling him my news, his own mind flashed over a series of images that were linked to the day-to-day reality of his own mother, his grandmothers and my mum too, for whom keeping a home and raising a family was work in itself. Dad had good reason to be a bit anxious and when he said, 'A lot of actresses give up acting when they have a baby and a family as it's too hard,' he made me think about it a bit more seriously. It was true. A huge number of actresses did give up performing to have a family and never did return, which was heartbreaking for them. Many others chose not to have any children at all, which to me was equally heartbreaking. Surely it was possible for me to have both. It had never crossed my mind that it might not be.

Leo was born in the summer of 1981. It was very clear that if I wanted the best of both worlds then I'd have to reduce my juggling and invite someone else to come to help to keep the balls in the air. And thus we began our interaction with au pairs. Getting the right au pair is what I imagine using a dating app is like! We had to let quite a few go but we also got lucky. As the boys grew older I asked my agent to say that I didn't want to take anything on that clashed with the school holidays. It didn't always work out, so I made a colourful calendar that would clearly show the boys when their holidays were, and when I would be home. Occasionally I'd take them with me when I was filming away, but this wasn't often, and over time we all settled into a routine that balanced work and home life. Even though it never became easier to say goodbye it was all that the boys knew, and they also knew that I'd always come home.

I'm not sure if Toby and Leo were very much bothered by the fact that I was an actor or their dad was a director, but I do remember clearly the very first time that Toby came to see me in a play as it was the day after an incident that I prefer to forget.

The role of Elmire in an RSC production of Molière's *Tartuffe* at the Pit Theatre in the newly constructed Barbican Centre was one of my first forays back into live theatre since becoming a mum of two. It was exhilarating to be on stage again, albeit an exhausting juggle what with the early morning wake-ups and the late return home, but I felt like I was in my prime and invincible. I had two amazing roles to play – one off stage and the other on.

On the day Mike brought Toby to the matinee, I was in the dressing room stepping through the process of discarding my day, my concerns, aspects of me, and beginning to harness my character and enter her world. I love taking my time to get ready, doing my make-up, getting my hair done, and then quite literally stepping into someone else's shoes and clothes. I always adorn the walls and mirrors of my dressing-room with good-luck cards and on the countertop is always a framed photograph of my mum as a young woman, which travels with me everywhere. My dressing room becomes home, for a while. I picked up a previously ignored pile of envelopes without any concern. It's wonderful getting notes from people who've been in the audience saying that they'd seen the show and loved it. Among them was an off-white envelope without a stamp that made me curious. *Who could it be from? I hope I haven't missed out on seeing a friend after the show.* Closer inspection, however, made me think otherwise as the neat copperplate handwriting had the tone of one of the stricter teachers at my secondary school. 'Dear Alison Steadman,' it began. I could almost hear the writer clearing his throat before going on to say, 'You seemed to find the show very funny last night.' Then on a weary out breath, 'I however did not!' Followed with the indignant flourish, 'and I paid £28 for my ticket!' My whole body deflated like a burst balloon as my thoughts flipped back reluctantly to the previous evening's show when I had got a fit of the giggles. It was like a series of burps that kept being torpedoed from the depths of my tummy that didn't stop but just got worse and worse and worse; even though I managed to quash the snorting, my shoulders took on a life of their own. The heat of it had drenched me in sweat and although everyone could see me in the intimate surroundings of the Pit, I convinced myself that no one had noticed and flounced off stage promising myself that it would never, ever happen again. Ever.

Why does this feeling of having the freedom to laugh when I shouldn't rise in me? I blame my lovely English teacher Miss Davies! During one lesson a girl called Pamela had had a fit of the giggles – it wasn't me for once – and just couldn't stop. We were all expecting Miss Davies to shout at her and tell her to be quiet. She didn't though. She walked over to laughing Pamela and said, 'What's so funny? What's making you laugh? Come on share it with us so we can all have a giggle.' We all began to laugh, the whole class and Miss Davies too, then she said, 'Alright, girls. that's enough. You okay now, Pamela? Let's carry on.' And we did. That was the sort of woman that she was. She gave us permission to laugh when we weren't meant to, and I suppose that must have remained within me in some way or other.

I looked down at the stern, disapproving words of the letter and promised myself that I'd get through the show without bursting into a bubble of giggles again. It was especially important with Toby in the audience. He was only five years old and him coming along to see me in a show for the first time felt like an important moment for us all. I made it through, and during the curtain call Toby stood on his seat and cheered, 'Hooray, hooray!' It was wonderful to have him share in the occasion with us as he did.

My dad needn't have worried about me giving up the thing that I loved doing and was earning a living by, as he'd quietly taught me the value of being resilient, taking it step by step and doing what needs to be done to keep all the balls in the air.

CHAPTER 19

Read All About It

'Alison Steadman upset by Mary Whitehouse!' blazoned the headline that was attached to a three-page article in one of the daily newspapers late in 1986, after the airing of Dennis Potter's *The Singing Detective*. I'm not sure how the journalist managed to create the story at all, since our encounter as I'd walked into a theatre to see the opening night of a show had been very brief indeed. 'Alison, Alison,' I heard my name being called and innocently turned my head. 'Alison, I suspect you were really upset about Mary Whitehouse and her reaction to your sex scene in *The Singing Detective*, weren't you?' There was a split second of processing what he'd said before saying, 'Well of course I was,' and then I walked on. How daft was that! Also, how clever he was to quite literally put words into my mouth and tell me how I must have been feeling.

Mary Whitehouse, the conservative activist who campaigned against social liberalism, had kicked off a huge fuss about one of my scenes in *The Singing Detective* saying it 'made voyeurs of us all' and that 'we must ban this filth'. She went berserk and, as we had anticipated, so did all the papers. There had been nothing quite as explicit broadcast on the BBC before and the controller, Michael Grade, had viewed it very carefully before allowing it to be transmitted. It didn't matter to Mary Whitehouse that the scene in question was an integral part of the story and that we had filmed it all very carefully. All she could see was that a young boy was watching on as his mother and a man were having sex in the woods and she, Mary Whitehouse, was outraged!

The night that the scene was due to be aired, I went out to get a Sunday paper from my local shop and splashed across the headlines was 'BBC braces itself for biggest sex shock ever'. After it aired I had the press calling me around the clock, and when I wouldn't speak to them, they managed to get hold of my parents' phone number and began to harass them. How shameful to cause such worry and upset to two elderly people who had only ever lived quietly and privately. My spilt-second hesitation before replying to the journalist with the few words that gave him his scoop came after all the fuss about the show had died down and so, thinking that I was safe, I'd begun to go out and about again. It just goes to show how careful you must be and how easily baited people are. It certainly taught me a lesson. I should have totally ignored him and kept walking. Hindsight is a great teacher! It's morally corrupt to use simple, honest statements from people and then enlarge them into some other truth. It's fake news that does a great deal of harm and in some instances can put people in danger too. Why anyone would want to participate in activity like this is beyond me.

Dennis Potter was a genius and his writing was unlike anything that I'd read before. We all knew that we were in the middle of a ground-breaking television drama and that the ensemble was dream fantasy casting made real. What a line-up it was: Michael Gambon, Janet Suzman, Joanne Whalley, Patrick Malahide, Jim Carter, Imelda Staunton and a young David Thewlis, amongst many other wonderful actors. It felt an honour to be in it. The script was so, so good and for once we had proper rehearsal time built into the filming schedule. It was a case of two weeks of rehearsal, two weeks filming, two weeks off, and then repeat. That's not something that would ever happen nowadays when everything is bang, bang, bang. It was a luxury to have the time to settle into our creative choices and to be on top of things before facing the cameras.

The part of Mrs Marlow in *The Singing Detective* immediately spoke to me. She arrived on my lap when I was just the right age. Forty back then was a dangerous milestone for an actress, as not many women were offered decent parts after hitting the big four-O and many left the profession. Thank goodness there's no restriction placed against maturity now and that great parts for women in their sixties and seventies these days are on the up, or I'd have been out of the game years ago. Age aside though, it was brilliant to have the opportunity to get stuck into a role that allowed me to challenge myself as a performer and to be seen taking on yet another type of woman. After *Abigail's Party*, all that people had wanted me to do was a version of Beverly with knobs on and I was constantly being offered parts that were a pale imitation of her. This wasn't what I wanted to do, so the opportunity to play Mrs Marlow was a refreshing challenge. In writing her, Dennis Potter had brilliantly captured the essence of a woman who was discovering that the earlier choices that she'd made in her life no longer suited who she was now. Mrs Marlow is married with an eleven-year-old son, trapped by the conventions of the 1940s. She's an extremely sad and vulnerable human being who is caught between doing what's right for her son and doing what's right for her. It was so accurately written. As in life, she makes a series of decisions without playing out what the consequences of her actions might be. Mrs Marlow feels trapped in her marriage and is yearning for more when she is reeled in to what she thinks is a love affair with another man. She's looking for passion, she's looking for love that is meaningful. She's not a woman that is looking for sex in the woods. The much-talked-about scene in the woods is a pivotal moment for Mrs Marlow as she goes from feeling special and sexy to feeling stupid and used as the realisation dawns that her lover, Ray, has taken many other women to the exact same spot in the woods before. It's devastatingly raw, beautiful and exposing all at the same time. It's a grotesque scene that was filmed with tenderness and care, and despite Mary Whitehouse's protestations there was very little showing of flesh, and none of the choices that we made were gratuitous. The camera choice when Ray, played by Patrick Malahide, pins her down for the second time was to close into Mrs Marlow's face; even though there are no words, the emotion was in the silence and it was all written in her expressions. It was a complex and challenging scene, and to hit the right notes I needed to be able to stand back from it as well as be in it. I was also able to draw from my own memory bank of darker experiences. My overriding recollection though is of getting twigs stuck in my knickers and of it being very prickly to lie there for the time it took to get the take that the director, Jon Amiel, wanted.

It's sad that Dennis Potter was taken from us too soon, as his writing was bold, courageous and dangerous. Cutting between fantasy and reality, past and present made for compelling viewing as well as an exciting acting experience. In one of the dream sequences Philip Marlow, played by the irrepressible and much missed Michael Gambon, imagines that his mother, played by yours truly, is a tragic film star whom he shoots by mistake. It was a complicated sequence: Michael and I were in position lying on the floor waiting for the shot to be set up, which was was taking some time. I was doing my best to keep focus and not laugh, which was easier said than done, given that Michael was so mischievous and known to be expert at making others laugh when they shouldn't.

Suddenly I heard a muffled voice saying, 'Oh God, oh God, oh, oh, ouch.'

'What's the matter, Michael? Are you okay? What's the matter?'

Michael pointed to his pocket that had the prop gun in it. *Are you just pleased to see me?* It's one of the oldest jokes in the book and I fell for it. Through my chuckling I pleaded to Michael, 'Will you stop it now, please stop.'

Then I heard Jon Amiel saying, 'Alison, can you concentrate please and stop laughing'

I was whispering, 'Michael, can you stop it. Just stop it.'

Then Michael in a less muffled voice said, 'It's not my fault, it's just this thing in my pocket.'

He was absolutely brilliant and wonderful to work with, even though he was so naughty and got me into trouble for laughing, again.

Playing Mrs Marlow was a return to my love of working with great writers, those who execute their craft so sublimely that very little acting is required – it's all in the clarity and detail of the text. Dennis Potter's gift to me was the economy of the phrases he gave to Mrs Marlow. After the episode in the woods and the realisation that she's been a fool and that her life is in a mess, she knows that there is no choice but to move on. The scene on the train as she leaves, which is a cutback to Philip Marlow's childhood, is a brilliant example of Dennis's less-is-more writing. The train pulls out of the station and Mrs Marlow and the young Philip are sitting opposite each other in a carriage, both in a daze. Mrs Marlow turns from looking out of the window to looking at her son, who begins to itch his arm. 'What are you doing?' she says, but she may as well have been asking herself the same question. When she turns away again and looks out of the window as the countryside speeds past her it's as if her memories are doing the same. No need for any more words. For me, the absolute genius of this scene was the arrival of some soldiers who join them in the carriage. It's a tight squeeze, and the physical presence of the men makes her feel uncomfortable. The proximity of these men being close to his mum also agitates her son and he flips back to what he witnessed in the woods. How brilliant to have the two of them share the same memory without the need to speak about it. Both characters are trying to contain themselves in the silence of the strained atmosphere and then, without any indication, the soldiers begin to sing. I knew that they were going to sing, but not what they would be singing, and when they began 'Paper Doll' by the Mills Brothers I dissolved and had to look out the window as the tears streamed down my face. The train is moving on and so is Mrs Marlow. The song had been a complete surprise to me, and so it brought all the emotion to the surface. Being on a real steam train just added to the drama of it all as they sang, 'I'll tell you, boys, it's tough to be alone.' I can still see David Thewlis sitting opposite me singing. That was the shot. So much said in so few words. Just perfect. That was what the press should have been writing about!

The journalist outside the theatre wasn't my first run-in with the press though. In 1975, I was cast in a new TV series for ITV called *The Wackers*. The show centred around the Clarkson family, who were divided by religion and football – and, given that it was located in Liverpool, there was a plentiful dose of Scouse banter and humour. I played the daughter, Bernadette, and before the show aired there was a great deal of interest in it on the back of the success of *The Liver Birds* and the fact that Ken Jones, who'd been in *Porridge* as well as *The Liver Birds*, was one of the leads. It's a given to expect to have to do a certain amount of press and PR around the launch of any new piece of theatre or TV, so when I was invited to do a press shoot to generate excitement in the lead-up, I duly agreed. It was only when I was asked if I would bring along a bikini that I began to think twice about it! A bikini? The show was set in Dingle, an inner-city area of Liverpool and not the Costa del Merseyside! I didn't pack any swimwear. When I arrived at the venue and was ushered into the room allocated for the shoot, my worst fears were confirmed. The space was full of multicoloured balloons and looked like a ballpark for some sort of grown-up entertainment that I didn't want to play. Before I could turn my back and walk away, an overly smiley photographer emerged from the latex jungle and cheekily said, 'Alison Steadman, bursting into the 1970s!' I didn't smile back and when he said, 'Did you bring your bikini?' it became apparent what they wanted me to do and equally clear to me that I wouldn't be doing it, as I would never get involved in any sort of gratuitous interplay of this kind for love or money.

It's always fascinating to walk in other people's shoes and many years later, in 1990, when I was asked by the TV director Les Blair to be involved in *News Hounds*, his Screen One film for the BBC, I jumped at the chance. It was about a group of journalists who worked on a tabloid newspaper and was developed through improvisation, which, of course, I loved. My character, Jackie Johns, was a celebrity interviewer, a bit like Nina Myskow was at the time. Even though I'd had a lot of experience of being interviewed, I needed to know what it was like being the one pressing the record button. I began, as always, by doing my research and arranged time at newspaper offices and chatted to journalists. I think that it may have spooked a few of them as it was quite widely known that I often based my characters on people that I'd met, so they were all very kind and accommodating to me, but perhaps not quite themselves! My own experience of reporters came in handy too, so I was able to turn the irritation that they induced into how Jackie behaved, to replicate the way news hounds, who are after a story, chat to you. It's horrible and very clever, as they start off very friendly and don't ask any intrusive questions, then once they think that they've got your confidence, they begin to push and then push a little more firmly to poke around. Before you know it, something is revealed that shouldn't have been. I established for myself that Jackie chain-smoked and finished people's sentences by putting words into their mouths. It was the era of big hair, shoulder pads and frosted lipstick, and so I had a ball with working out her style. Once I had a handle on her, I did some in-role interviews with real people.

During the actual show I interviewed Edwina Currie, the former Under-Secretary of State for Health, appearing as herself, and I asked her not just about losing her job over the salmonella-in-eggs contro-versy but also about who she fancied in the House of Commons. In the edit they made a brilliant cut at that point so that the question was left dangling in the air to continue the intrigue for the audience. It was a bizarre occasion as Edwina didn't seem to quite get that it was Jackie Johns, not Alison Steadman, who was interviewing her. *News Hounds* was fun and even though I was playing a role it did confirm what I already thought about the unsavoury nature of some more manipulative journalistic tactics.

I'm of an age now that journalists aren't interested in my private life anymore and that suits me down to the ground. They're not going to see me wobbling in a pair of stilettos on the red carpet anytime soon, and even if they were interested, I'd give them short shrift. Perhaps I'm being a bit too harsh, I have to say that, generally, my experience of late has been okay. But it's in a journalist's nature to be on the hunt so they can go back to their editor and say, 'Look what I've got.' They're more interested in the bad story, the salacious story, the is-he-having-an-affair story than anything else, and it does take a while to get used to this and to learn to be careful.

Much worse are the scammers that make up stories about other people and try to sell them to the tabloids. It is shark-infested water and sadly I was once bitten quite badly. A few years ago, I was out having a pizza with my partner, Michael, and the four-year-old son of a friend of mine. It was all fine until the guy who was serving us did a bit of a double-take of me. *Oh she's off the telly.* The next thing, I noticed him deep in conversation with the young woman at reception. It seemed a bit odd, but I decided to ignore it. Five minutes later, the girl brought over the glass of wine that we'd ordered. We were quite happily chatting away and eating our pizza as she put the glass down and moved to stand directly behind Michael. She then placed her hands on his shoulders and began to move them down onto his chest and then further down onto his thighs, right in front of me and this four-year-old boy. I was so shocked but, not wanting to cause more of a scene, very quietly said, 'Excuse me! What do you think you're doing?'

She stood up straight again and said, 'Oh sorry,' and walked off.

It didn't feel right, so I went to the manager and had a word with him. 'Your waitress has just come over and rubbed her hands all over my partner. This is a family restaurant, it's Sunday afternoon, it's not some strip club on a Friday night in Soho. What does she think she's doing?' The manager just shrugged his shoulders.

I was enraged so, as we were leaving, I said to the girl, again very discreetly, 'Your behaviour is unacceptable and you should not do that to customers.'

She replied, 'Oh sorry, I know. I'd feel the same way if someone did that to my husband.'

I was stunned at the turnabout, and so said again, 'You do not behave like that in a restaurant with customers,' and walked out thinking that was that.

It wasn't.

At 11.30 that evening, there was a knock at the front door. I'd had a bath and was watching some television in my nightie and dressing gown, so, no way José, was I going to answer it. Michael went to the door and there was a guy standing there.

'Hello, can I speak to Alison Steadman?' He didn't seem to entertain the fact that it was nearly midnight.

'Why, what do you want?'

'Well, I believe that she had a row in a restaurant today and that something happened that really upset her.'

Of course that set alarm bells off so Michael said, 'Can you go away please,' and then shut the front door.

Oh my God. They're looking for money, the two in the restaurant, and they think that the papers are going to pay them for a story.

The door went again, so I said to Michael, 'Just say that we'll call the police if he doesn't go away.'

Michael opened the door and said, 'You're intruding on our privacy, and we'll call the police if you don't go away,' before shutting the door.

I ran to the closed door and peeked through the keyhole only to see this guy, obviously thinking, *Shit, shit, I've come all this way. What a waste of time.* Then he turned and walked off. It would be comical if it wasn't so pathetic and upsetting. If we had opened the door again and I had made the most casual of remarks it would have been blown up and inflated beyond recognition.

It's a depressing situation that this is the sort of story that is being hunted down. There is always something far more important to talk about than what did or didn't happen in a pizza restaurant! Read All About It: Alison Steadman upset by doorstepping tabloid journalist! Well, who wouldn't be?

I wonder which programmes Mary Whitehouse would take to task these days. Can you imagine? And would the implementation of trigger warnings satisfy her desire to clean up TV? I doubt it. I wonder if she ever contemplated her complicity with the press and how, in some instances, her unregulated and often misunderstood comments about programmes that were not to her taste caused innocent bystanders like my parents a great deal of distress as they were caught up in the wake of her watchdog crusade. The more I think about her comments about *The Singing Detective* and how ill-informed she was about how we shot the scene, the more I actually concur with the journalist that caught me on the hop just when I thought it was safe. Alison Steadman was indeed upset by Mary Whitehouse and her thoughtless caustic comments, which she knew that the news hounds would grab at to pick up the chase, not stopping until they had gnawed into someone's life without a care for the aftermath.

CHAPTER 20

Character Building

'Alison?' It was 8.00 a.m. and I was in LA promoting our 1991 film *Life Is Sweet*. 'Alison, is this a good time to talk?' It was 4.00 p.m. in the UK and my agent was on the other end of the phone. 'I've an American agent who wants to see you and since you're in LA do you want me to arrange a meet-up?'

A few hours later I found myself sitting in the back of a posh car being driven through downtown LA to the agent's office. The car was comfortable, the sun was shining outside, the fronds of the palm trees that lined our route were swaying alluringly in the balmy wind and it was persuasively seductive for a hot minute, before I snapped myself out of the momentary lull in sanity. *What am I doing? Why am I going to this meeting? Why would I want to come and work in America?* It's not something that I had considered or that had ever appealed to me. It's just not me. I like playing British parts. I know that I know British women and how to play them authentically. I don't know the sensibility of American women and I'd not want to do anything that felt like a caricature. However, my agent had persuaded me to do the meeting on the back of the critical success of *Life Is Sweet*, in which I'd worked with Mike again, this time developing and playing my first leading role in a feature film. So I'm sitting on the soft leather back seat of the car and trying to be as open minded as possible without jumping to all the problems that might arise if a too-good-to-be-true offer came in. *What about the boys? They're happy at their school. Would it be reckless to bring them with me?* The car pulled up against the sidewalk (sidewalk!), the black-capped driver stepped out to open the door for me and I headed decisively into the reception area of the office where the meeting was scheduled. It felt immediately hilarious, as the carpet was so thick and spongy that the small heels that I had on were being sucked into it and it was a struggle to not fall over. The perma-tanned, healthy-looking receptionist took me through to the office, which felt more familiar. There were messy shelves of files and books, and boxes and boxes of tapes. *Oh dear, all those poor actors. No one is ever going to look at those tapes and they don't know it. Why is there such false promise from people?* There are so many gatekeepers and at that moment, staring at the mountain of celluloid hope, I felt so lucky that my career was beyond this now. There are hurdles that you will need to find a way to jump over, push through or knock down, but I do believe that talent will out, eventually. It's a series of stepping stones and if you step forward and find your balance and then step forward again, then you may well forge the career that you wish for. *Why on earth am I sitting here? I like my life and work in the UK.* The door opened and in came a guy in shorts and a crumpled T-shirt. I immediately felt overdressed. He sat back into his own chair – it was one of those that can tilt back and swivel at the same time – and said, 'Okay, okay,' sounding a bit like Jeff Garlin from *Curb Your Enthusiasm*. 'So I started to watch your film last night and sorry, but I fell asleep.' Any amount of enthusiasm that I may have had for the meeting evaporated completely. 'Not because I was bored,' he explained. 'I'd had a long day, and the kids were playing up. But I will watch it. I will watch it.' He then got up and opened an adjoining door saying, 'John, John, come in here, come in here.' John, also in shorts and a T-shirt, stepped into the room. 'Come over here, John. I want you to meet Alison Steadman. This is the British actress, Alison Steadman. Say hello.'

So this guy, who was very clearly feeling awkward went, 'Hi.'

And it then went from bad to worse. 'Have you seen any of Alison's stuff?' What a cheeky thing for him to ask when he hadn't even bothered to watch *Life Is Sweet*.

'No, no I haven't.'

'Oh, she's great, she's great, you gotta watch her stuff. Okay, thank you, John.'

John and I smiled at each other in a way that suggested that we could read the speech bubbles above our respective heads: mine, *What on earth am I doing here?!* John's, *What on earth is she doing here?!* It didn't fill me with glee.

'Okay, Alison, so here's the plan.' *Have I missed something?* The meeting was going terribly, and I just wanted to make a speedy exit. 'I want you to come back for three weeks, maybe a month. I'm gonna get you interviews here, there and all over the city – all over, all over. That's how we'll start off. Okay?'

He got up. It was time to go, and I walked out onto the spongy carpet and made my escape. There was no way that I'd be coming back. *Wow, I've dodged a bullet there. There's no way that I'm going to be pushed around by that guy.* I didn't want to entertain the thought of conquering Hollywood for a moment longer. On the car ride back, I remembered an actress friend of mine who'd been persuaded to relocate to LA on the promise of great things happening for her. When she returned to the UK for a visit she didn't look like the same person. They'd told her that she needed to lose weight, which she didn't, and she'd practically starved herself. She looked awful. If she'd stayed in the UK, she'd have got far more work. *No*, I thought. *That didn't feel right.* Once again my instinct kicked in and guided me. *I want to work in Britain and be close to my family. I've got the boys and I'm staying put but I do know what I need to do when I get back – change my agent.* It was time to move on.

Mike and I had travelled to the US to promote the release of *Life Is Sweet* buoyed by the critical acclaim that the film had received in the UK. Our first pit stop had been New York, where a private screening at a cinema club in Manhattan had been scheduled. It sounded so good on paper, but the reality wasn't quite what we expected. We should have known from the abundance of expensive handbags and pearls that these ladies who lunched had very different appetites from ours. It was the blue-rinse brigade. We introduced the film and then, just before it finished, we crept into the back of the cinema ready for the Q&A. We were sitting there quietly, when a woman in front of us said to her neighbour, as loud as you like, 'Can you understand what they're saying? I can't!' And then someone else piped up and shouted across to her, 'I don't know what they're saying either.' There was an initial burst of hushed whispering that then became out-and-out normal chatter and it was very obvious that they hadn't been enjoying it. I wanted to creep out and not come back, but that wasn't an option. These well-heeled Housewives of NYC felt under no obligation to be polite about things.

The Q&A began with, 'I thought it was going to be a sweet film about teaching little ones to dance and it began okay but suddenly it changed, and it wasn't like that at all.' Well, you can imagine how uncomfortable we began to feel sitting up on the stage as she went on and on. There wasn't one word of compliment, which was a first.

The film had been reviewed very favourably in the UK, and there had always been stimulating and rewarding conversations with audiences at the screenings we'd attended. The floodgates had opened and she barked out, 'Mike Leigh, why did you take this poor, vulnerable sick girl and put her in a film that made her reveal her problems? This was a child that needed care and love, not putting in a film for the world to see.' Well, by that time, I'd had enough. Mike had been doing his best to answer the questions, but I just lost it and cut in, 'Can I just stop you for a moment?' The woman looked at me and it was clear that I wasn't going to take much more from her. 'Jane Horrocks is not a sick, vulnerable girl. She is an actress who is healthy and absolutely one hundred per cent mentally fine. She's playing a part. She's a character. There is nothing wrong with her at all.' Things wound up swiftly after that. Honestly. It was absolute nonsense.

When I told Jane she laughed and said, 'What? You have to be kidding me. You mean she thought that I was actually unwell?'

'Yes. That's how good you are. She wanted to believe that you were really ill.'

We were all proud of *Life Is Sweet*. Once again, Mike had assembled a group of actors – Jim Broadbent, Timothy Spall, Jane Horrocks, Claire Skinner, David Thewlis and Stephen Rea – who, when I think about it now, were possibly the only combination of actors who could hit the notes that the developing story required. It's such a poignant piece with so much discovery for each character. 1990 was a very political time when the UK was going through a period of social and cultural change so there is turbulence within the piece, but there's also a great deal of hope and positivity. There's a great deal of love within it and Wendy, my character, is one of the nicest and warmest women that I've ever played. This was refreshing as most of the others had been quite monstrous in their own way. It was lovely to make this family together. This isn't to say that she was bland or *nice* and that there weren't conflicts between the characters. It had to feel like a real family and that was what we tried to achieve. Wendy was complex, masking concern and disappointment, and trying to work out what to do for the best for her girls, especially troubled Nicola, the character that Jane Horrocks played. Like all my work with Mike, I didn't know what the piece would be or who would emerge from me when we began the process. It very quickly became about family, relationships and healing. Jim Broadbent, who played my husband, Andy, and I became very close and the connection between us felt very real. Even though years have since passed, we still slip back into the dynamic that was between our characters whenever we meet.

My boys were nine and twelve in 1990 and came on set during filming. It wasn't as exciting as it might sound as there is always a lot of waiting around but the make-up team were brilliant and to amuse them gave them fake scars. It was good to have them there and interesting for me to play a mum, having now been one for quite some time and, as such, living with the ongoing umbilical connection to my children, and the unparalleled joy and worry that this brings. That's the truly satisfying thing about acting, the more you know about life and the more you've experienced, the better prepared you are to mine the depths of another person and make connections with your own psyche that may be helpful. Wendy was the glue of the family, a brilliant mum to her girls and, a bit like my own mum, Marjorie, she put everyone else before herself. It was heartbreaking putting myself into her shoes and feeling the terror and sadness of trying to understand her daughter's view on the world. The Wendy who emerged through the collaborative work with the others is utterly wonderful as, unlike Candice Marie or Beverly or Pamela Shipman or Mrs Bennet, she isn't at all bothered about doing the done thing. Wendy is only concerned about doing the right thing by her family; there was a transparency to her that brought out both her humour and her vulnerability. I felt this very keenly in one of the final scenes, when, at her wits' end, she shouted at Nicola, 'We don't hate you, we love you, you stupid girl!' It was emotional and character building, a phrase that is bandied about without much thought at all. Creating character through a process of improvisation and research is truly character building, and our shared time on *Life Is Sweet* was just that. The six months that we spent on creating the film was an opportunity to deepen empathy and strengthen all those unseen muscles of compassion, listening and understanding, all of which are vital for creating an authentic character. It was a privilege to have the time to keep practising until it felt right.

Creating Wendy had taught me a great deal about myself. After the meeting with the agent in LA and encountering the well-heeled ladies of NYC at the screening, I was surer than ever of where I wanted to be and how I wanted to put all my accumulated experience to good use in the work that I did.

Almost immediately after *Life Is Sweet*, Jim Broadbent and I were cast together in *Gone to the Dogs*, which was broadcast on ITV in 1992, and the follow-up *Gone to Seed* immediately after. Both were written by Tony Grounds, who was unlike any of the writers that I'd previously worked with. Rather than standing aside once his script had been handed over to the director and actors, Tony would join us on set, which was always useful and also fun.

Coupling actors who have recently appeared in something successful together is quite common as it builds audiences as well as affording the next project a small guarantee of commercial good fortune. From my point of view though it can bring comfort and ease to the job when I have already established a rapport and know how to work to get the best results. So it was a joy to be working with Jim again in my next two television jobs.

The cast of *Gone to Seed* also included Peter Cook in his last professional appearance. Peter was a natural clown, off and on camera. At the end of the shoot the production company hosted a party with karaoke. Peter was adamant that he wasn't going to attend and there was no sight nor sound of him until at midnight a tall, skinny figure stormed the stage, took the microphone and gave his own rendition of the Elvis Presley song 'Heartbreak Hotel', complete with gyrating hips and lip curl. Then Peter jumped off the stage, ran out of the room as quickly as he'd run in, and we didn't see him again. It felt just like a scene that Tony would write, and at first I wondered if he had. He hadn't. There are just some people, places and things that write themselves, as my next adventure, back in theatre, was to show me.

CHAPTER 21

Rewarding

'I want Wendy back! I want Wendy back!' comes the plaintive chanting through the darkness. Jane Horrocks and I are standing in the wings of the Cottesloe (now the Dorfman) which is the National Theatre's smallest and most intimate performance space, and we're about to go on. It's 1992, a couple of years after *Life Is Sweet,* and my first time on stage in quite some time. It's opening night and the air is full of nervous energy that needs to be released. We're all feeling it and gathering our focus as we wait for the cue to go on stage. I'm happy to be back doing live theatre again and even though there is a familiar rising anxiety within me, it's also thrilling to know that we're about to share this new play with an audience for the first time. *What will they think of it? Will there be a chemistry between us all?* I've left the comfort of my dressing room and the touchstones that help me to remain grounded, such as cards, family photos and a coin – don't ask me why – that I keep for good luck. Those few minutes in the dark of the wings are both intensely private and personal, as well as practical. It's an in-between moment, when the wig, make-up and costume teams are doing their final checks and props are being picked up from their allotted place on the props table. Precision is essential and everyone is on high alert and ready to go.

'I want Wendy back! I want Wendy back! She's a great mum!' comes the wistful cry in the dark and it makes me smile. Jane and I have been reunited as mother and daughter in Jim's Cartwright's new play, *The Rise and Fall of Little Voice*, which has been directed for the National by a new young talent that everyone is talking about, Sam Mendes.

Mari Hoff, the mum that I played, was another woman whose voice on the page I could hear immediately. I knew that Jim Cartwright's text would be fabulous to interpret and that I could bring this character to life. Being the first performer to tackle a role is exciting, as even though the dialogue is there in black and white and the writer knows who the character is and their purpose in the piece, it's not quite locked in, so there is a moment when it's possible to add to the development of the role. I was the first actress to step into Mari Hoff's shoes, literally and figuratively. *This is a person who has hardly any money*, I thought. *And when she does have it, she doesn't spend it on expensive shoes, even though she wants to look nice.* I'd had a chat with the wardrobe team and asked if they could get me a very cheap version of a stylish stiletto. What a mistake that was! My feet were protesting in agony as it was so uncomfortable to wobble around in the twig-thin heels, so after a few weeks we ditched the fashion option for something a bit more workable. Mari Hoff was a tough nut to crack and a million miles away from any mum that I knew personally. She's not interested in her daughter or bringing her up; she regards her as an inconvenience that must be put up with as she pursues sex and alcohol, and finding ways of turning a trick. She's a strong, rough character who takes no prisoners and it was rewarding to play her, even though I didn't particularly like her. That's an exciting challenge. *I don't like this person, but I need to find a way of understanding her.* I needed to see life from her point of view and work out why she was the way she was. *Why does Mari Hoff mouth off all the time? Why does she continually get herself into complex situations?* You must keep digging and digging until you find what you need and a path to follow. Having the writer in the rehearsal room is brilliant for this, and Jim was so helpful when I was unsure of the reasons behind some of Mari's actions.

I love and hate rehearsal rooms. I love them because this is where the work is made, it's where collaboration and creativity come into their own and where we can also all have a laugh together without the worry of an audience looking on. I hate it too, as it's a place where at so many times over my career I've felt stuck, doubted myself and walked into a head space that was torturous and unhelpful. This happened on *The Rise and Fall of Little Voice* at the end of the first run-through. Sam had been lovely and continuously reassuring as all of Mari's lines were jumping around in my head. But still I remember sitting there, flushed with stress and tiredness, and so unsure whether anything I was doing was worthwhile or not. I was in too much of a state to drive home, so I walked down onto the Southbank, sat on a bench by the river and breathed my way into calm. It was something that I ended up doing most days, as Mari Hoff was one of the heftiest stage roles that I'd ever played, and I needed to find some peace of mind.

It was important to get into my body, be less in my head and to be as fit as I needed to be. So I went swimming each morning in the weeks leading up to the beginning of rehearsals. I'd drop my sons off at school, be in the pool by 8.00 a.m. and then swim for an hour each day. It was necessary and worth it, as the role is full-on right from the moment that the lights go up and there's not a moment to sit back and take it easy. I had loads of dialogue and Mari's constantly in and out of conflicting moods as she is drunk a great deal of the time. Acting drunk is very physically draining because to make it seem realistic you need more control of your body than if you weren't inebriated. Mari is the sort of drunk that falls over and so my legs were sore and bruised all the time. My mum would look at the clock at the time I was due on each night and say to herself, 'Oh, poor Alison has to do that part again,' because it was such a strenuous and exhausting role.

She was a gem of a character to play though and I relished it. Jim's text was so sharp and funny, and Mari had some great lines. 'What's up with you lot? Never had a shag in a Chevy?' She was fun to play. There is a great moment towards the end of the play when Mari hugs a friend who has been through all these traumas with her and she says, 'Come 'ere, love, come 'ere.' She goes into the hug and pulling her friend close says, 'Yer all lard and love, ain't yer. All lard and love,' swiftly followed by, 'Oh, put some deodorant on will yer,' as she gets a whiff of her poor friend's armpits. It's such clever and funny writing that I knew there was a risk that I might find it funny on stage when I shouldn't, so I needed to ensure that I didn't tip into laughter land. The role was very special to me, and it was wonderful to be at the National and performing with Jane again, so I didn't want to mess it up.

Once the show was up and running, we were all a bit more relaxed about things, So much so that one night when Mari had to open the on-set fridge in amongst the expected fridge items was a statue. The lovely stage-management team had put it on the shelf as a lark. My task was to move it and put it somewhere else where another person would be surprised by it. I left it where it was and during the interval said to the stage manager, who was a decent chap, 'Look, I appreciate everything that you all do, and I know that the show is going well, but please can you not do anything like that again.' It was one of those, it's-not-you-it's-me chats. 'If I start laughing, I just won't stop. It's like a disease with me, it spreads like wildfire, and I don't want to ruin the show.' He was so understanding. The statue was never seen again, and I managed to hold it together for the entire run.

It was wonderful playing at the National, being surrounded by theatre history and the traditions of the building. The dressing rooms there wrap around an internal courtyard, and they all have windows that face each other. The tradition on the opening night is to slap your hands on your window to drum up good luck for the show. Judi Dench was working in the building at the same time as us on the day that she learnt that she'd been made a dame and everyone leant out of their window and sang, 'There ain't nothing like a dame, nothing in this world.' It was so enriching to be a part of all of that.

The show transferred from the Cottesloe to the Aldwych Theatre in the West End. Frequently we'd be surprised by special guests who would come along to see it and then join us in our dressing rooms for drinks afterwards. I would always have a bottle of fizz in the small fridge in my room just in case. I had a dresser who once said to me, as she was taking off my wig and costume, 'I've never known anyone open a bottle of wine as quick as you do when you come off stage.' I just love having friends pop round if they've seen the show so I always make sure that there are enough glasses to go round.

The Rise and Fall of Little Voice is a mother-and-daughter story in which the drama and humour is driven by the fact that you couldn't get two people who are as far apart as Mari and her daughter. It's a fairy tale of sorts with both people dreaming, one about what could have been and the other about what could be. It's about managing expectations, and it shines a light on hardship, growing up and finding your voice. Jane was astonishing in it. I can remember being shocked when we were both nominated for an Olivier Award for Best Actress after the show had transferred to the Aldwych. We laughed about it a great deal and as the ceremony got closer and closer, we'd joke about what we'd do if the other person won. I'd say, 'If you get it, I'm going to be sitting at the end of the row and when you walk past me, I'm going to put my foot out and trip you up.' Jane would say, 'If you get it, I'm going to run to the back of the theatre and slam the doors really hard as I flounce out.' We'd laugh a lot but the reality of both being nominated for the same show in the same category was awful and we used to think that it would have been wonderful if we could have shared the award instead.

Nothing prepares you for the moment that your name is called out. It's as if the body and mind numb themselves; you're both there, sitting in the theatre, and not there at all. Jane and I had given a supportive look to each other as the nominations were read out, then I stared straight ahead. It was a surreal few seconds, and my mind went into freefall.

It had been one of the most difficult and unimaginably sad years of my life as my beloved dad, George, who had struggled more and more with emphysema, had died. The childhood illness, and subsequent operation that had robbed him of being able to join the RAF, had taken its toll, so we were so very lucky to have had him for a long as we did. We were all in a state of shock, trying to find our way forward without his guiding influence and constant kindness. Dad championed me so much. It was devastating to have got to this moment in my career, to be nominated for an Olivier for a role that I was immensely proud of, and not be able to share it with him. Mum had braved coming to London on her own to see the show and support me, as both she and Dad had done all of my life. It must have been so tough for her to be sitting there watching a show that I was in, without him next to her and without being able to lean over to say, 'What has she got on?' or, 'She's doing so well, Dad.'

I felt Mike nudge my side, and I tuned myself back in to hear, 'And this year's award for Best Actress goes to,' – there was the customary beat of silence to ramp up the tension – 'Alison Steadman.' Oh. My. Goodness. I stood up and moved along the row. Jane didn't trip me up or run out of the theatre, slamming the doors on her way – she hugged me. I made my way to the stage. My knees were shaking as I looked out into the sea of faces and tried to remember who to thank. What I do remember saying was, 'I hope to be acting for many years to come and doing many more plays, but I doubt that there will be many as good as this one or roles as wonderful as Mari Hoff. Thank you to everyone.' And in my heart, I thanked George Percival Steadman, whose faith and belief in his youngest daughter were now being rewarded with the West End's equivalent of an Oscar. My dad's love of opera soared above the rock 'n' roll tunes of my growing-up years. His favourite was Giuseppe Verdi's *La Traviata*. One of its most famous arias, 'Sempre Libera', translates as 'always free'.

> Free and aimless I frolic,
> From joy to joy
> Flowing along the surface of life's path as I please.
> As the day is born,
> Or as the day dies,
> Happily, I turn to new delights,
> That make my spirit soar.

This is how my dad parented me, always looking to the future and encouraging me to be free. This was his greatest and most rewarding role. I clutched the award, looked upwards and said to myself, *This is for you, Dad.*

CHAPTER 22

Causing a Scene

There was a perfunctory knock on the front door of 22 Sherwyn Road but before I could get to it, it was pushed open and I was pushed to the side as my Aunt Mary strode past me saying in her distinctive voice, 'Where's Marjorie? Where's Marjorie?' Her arrival was always unexpected. Aunt Mary, my mum's younger sister, always made her presence felt, she was always getting into a strop about something or other and would fall out with my mum over the most ridiculous and trivial of things. 'Oh, Mary's at it again,' Mum would say, and we all knew what this meant. She had three sons, my cousins Maurice, Steven and Colin. Maurice, who was named after my grandpa, was eight years older than me. When he was born, Mum had leant down to take a look at him in his cot and said, 'Oh, he looks like he's a little toon,' and from that day on he was known as Toony, which he loved. Once he was waiting for a bus with Aunt Mary and she shouted out, 'Toony! Toony! The bus is coming!' She then overheard a couple of chaps say, 'Listen to that. His name is Tony but she's trying to say it posh.' We laughed for years about that. But Toon stuck.

Mum loved words and language and would constantly either make up words, like toon, or mispronounce them for her own enjoyment. Lasagne was 'lasarney', muesli, 'muselay' no matter how many times I corrected her. One evening, when I was a teenager, I came downstairs all dressed up and she said, 'Oh look at this one. Better with a stick of rhubarb!' What she meant we'll never know, but it made us all laugh.

Steven and Colin were younger and even when they were grown-up, Aunt Mary would never call for them in a normal voice. It was as if the two names had blended into one and she trumpeted them out like a morning bugle call that was loud enough to awaken the troops. 'Col-in Stev-en!' It never changed and neither did she.

Aunt Mary was a larger-than-life, one-of-a-kind character who only ever did things her way. As I was looking through the role that I'd been offered in a new period drama by Andrew Davies, it was Aunt Mary's voice that I could hear. I knew the role could be brought to life drawing upon her as my inspiration.

'Oh hello, you're playing Mrs Bennet, is that right?' It was a sunny afternoon in early June, and I was sitting, minding my own business, in a pub in the town of Malmesbury in Wiltshire. I had noticed a group of elderly women – well they were older than I was at the time – chatting away like clucking hens.

'Yes, yes, I am.' I didn't really want to get into a chat and so had kept my response short, but to no avail.

'Remember, the eyes of the world will be upon you.' It was like she was the soothsayer from *Julius Caesar* saying, 'Beware the ides of March.'

I nodded politely and forced my face into a strained smile. *The eyes of the world will be upon me!* What a thing to say. This was the last thing that I needed to hear two weeks before we began filming *Pride and Prejudice*, and as we were about to have our first read-through.

'Thank you for that. I will,' I said hoping that my assurance would shut her up.

'I'm just saying,' she went on, 'that the eyes of the world will be upon you.'

Again? Honestly? She was obviously an enormous fan of *Pride and Prejudice* and her passion had spilled over into ownership. In scholarly terms it's called a novel of manners and I needed to keep my own in check, but what I really wanted to do was to throw the book at her. Like other much-loved novels, everyone has their own idea of what key characters might look and sound like. That's the magic of literature. It transports us to places and times that we can only imagine and introduces us to people that we may never meet or would like to meet. As a reader we cast the scene as we see it in our mind's eye and colour in the detail with our imagination. This lady had clearly got a very different actress in mind for Mrs Bennet and her tone suggested that she didn't approve of me at all.

She began to try to engage me once again and I'm sorry to say that my reply was curt. 'Can you please stop saying that. You've said it three times now.' What was I supposed to say? 'Oh thank you very much for telling me that the eyes of the world will be upon me. That's very helpful indeed.'

Why do some people feel that they can invade a stranger's personal space and assert their unsolicited and unwanted opinions? I'm always going to be at odds with that, even though I do understand that being in the public eye comes with a requirement to stop, chat and exchange pleasantries. I'm always more than happy to do this, and so delighted when the work that I've done has resonated with people and grateful for their kind words. However, this lady's intention wasn't to be kind, and I needed to leave the premises before I said something that I might regret or that could be misconstrued.

Mrs Bennet had been offered to me several months earlier and it was another of those immediate 'yes please' jobs. The creative team of screenplay writer Andrew Davies, director Simon Langton, producer Sue Birtwistle, composer Carl Davis, designer Dinah Collin and choreographer Jane Gibson, was par excellence, while the cast and production team that had gathered around their expertise were equally exciting and impressive. It was just what I needed to try and take my mind off the news that I'd had in between being offered and accepting the role, and the beginning of production a few months later in June of 1994.

My mum, our wise old owl, had been diagnosed with pancreatic cancer, which had floored us all. She'd been lost after Dad had died two years earlier and, even though she put on a brave face as ever, she was utterly heartbroken. I found it unimaginable to lose someone that you loved so completely and lived with so well since you were nineteen years old. My parents' was a union of sixty years and the loss of the young man that she had knitted a blue scarf for, the man who had shielded her family from the ferocity of the bombings of the Second World War, the father of her three daughters and her constant companion was too much for Mum to bear.

Since then she hadn't been as well as she usually was and so she'd had a few tests. It soon became clear that the situation was serious. Sylvia, Pam and I made the trip to Liverpool to accompany her for further tests. I'll never forget the day when the consultant told her that the cancer was terminal. He told her that there was nothing to be done and then just walked out! There was no such thing as a kind bedside manner with that doctor. Mum said, 'It's like he'd got a hold of me and thrown me against that plate-glass window.' It was unbelievably careless, so when he called me and my sisters back in and said, 'I have to tell you that your mother's got between two and six months to live,' I told him in no uncertain terms that he wasn't to tell Mum that as it would finish her. Whether it's a real thing or not, I totally believe that our spirit needs to have hope to hold on to.

When we got home to Sherwyn Road, Pam said, 'You're the actress, you'll need to take care of it.' It was one of the most challenging performances of my life, but we needed to look after our mum and be strong for her as she had always been for us. I dashed upstairs to the toilet to compose myself and become ready for the questions that we all knew were coming. 'Any hope?' Mum asked me as we were all having a cup of tea. It was the saddest question that she'd ever asked me and the most difficult to answer. My instinct kicked in and I said, 'What a prat the doctor is. He may be a brilliant surgeon but he's not God. How does he know how long you've got to live? What you've got to do is just take care of yourself and enjoy your life.' Afterwards, Pam hugged me and said, 'You deserve an Oscar for that.' It's complicated, isn't it? When someone that we love dies, we face our own previously ignored mortality and perhaps this is the time when we need to get things in order and share our wishes with our nearest and dearest. But after Dad died, Mum didn't really talk about her own death, and we took her lead of always being positive, as we were so keen to keep her alive.

The sun was shining and embarking on this next adventure was just the tonic that I needed to help me through the complexities of my own real-life dramas. The read-through of Andrew Davies's script was one of the most enjoyable of my career and it was obvious that everyone was totally up for being immersed in Austen's world and having a great deal of fun along the way. Before we began filming, I took a trip to Jane Austen's house with a friend who was also in the cast. We idled the day away looking around the house and soaking up the period. It was fascinating to learn that the household was all-female and Jane, her two sisters and mother all lived there comfortably together. The house in Hampshire was where she wrote and revised her six novels; being there and imagining that helped me to develop a sense of the way of life that Mrs Bennet and her daughters may have had, and how they occupied and entertained themselves.

It is a truth universally acknowledged that there's nothing as beautiful as a honey-coloured Regency manor house and we picked the lucky long straw that located the Bennet family's Longbourn estate in the glorious architecture and grounds of the Grade II-listed Luckington Court just outside Chippenham in Wiltshire. The lady who owned Luckington Court was in her eighties and had been living there for decades. She was always welcoming and friendly whenever I bumped into her. One morning, I was in my costume ahead of time and sitting waiting for my call in the comfort of the space that had been designated as our green room, when she popped her head into the room and cheerily said, 'Good morning, Alison, how are you?'

I turned and said, 'Good morning. I'm fine thanks. Feeling a bit tired but I'm fine.'

She stepped into the room a bit further enquiring in a concerned voice, 'Are you staying at the hotel in Malmesbury?' The hotel was only four miles away from where we were filming.

'Yes,' I nodded.

'And have you travelled all the way from Malmesbury this morning?'

'Yes.' This almost felt like a trick question, and I hoped that my answer would help to solve the mystery and reveal more.

'Well,' she exclaimed, 'it's no wonder you're exhausted.' And off she went.

I've laughed so much about that ever since. She was such a lovely woman. I liked her even more when she told me that she wouldn't allow foxhunting on the large estate and that the hunt had to go round the outside. *Good for you.*

Lots of people have asked me if I read *Pride and Prejudice* in preparation for taking on Mrs Bennet. I didn't. This was a very deliberate choice on my part. Andrew knew the book inside and out and had lived with it in his creative imagination for years before he handed over his finished screenplay to all of us. It was important to me to trust and respect his knowledge as a man of language, so I chose to stick to what he had written as it was his interpretation of Mrs Bennet that I would be playing. I was also worried that if I began to read the book the two would blend into one and I'd become more and more muddled, rather than more and more detailed, with the character. I was forty-eight, my brain was still sharp and there was no worry about not being off book when I needed to be, so I could enjoy the period of rehearsal that we were given and look forward to filming. That's not to say that there weren't challenges – there were, but I felt able to face them head-on and without too much concern as by that time I was much more at ease being surrounded by cameras at all angles and on-set conditions.

It's not too much of an exaggeration to say that Mrs Bennet is extremely gabby. Think of the most talkative, neurotic, hypochondriac person that you know, then imagine them with far too much caffeine in their system and you'll have a sense of the volt of energy that courses through Mrs B. Performing at such a high octane level can't just be achieved with the flick of a switch and it was when the schedule for my first day of filming arrived – the shoot was a scene when she comes out of the church on full throttle – that I knew that I would have to muster myself and fuse her fully charged highly strung nerves with my own first-day ones. It proved to be a creatively successful combination.

Mrs Bennet is a nightmare in lots of ways, but you can't blame her for it. She has five daughters that she needs to marry off to secure their future and now that they are all of marriageable age, or nearly, she is panic stricken and almost always in a state of frenzy. 'Oh, Mr Bennet' is her default phrase – she probably says it in her sleep – but thank goodness for him though. Our Mr Bennet was beautifully played by Benjamin Whitrow, who was as calm and grounded as his character, and the Bennets were such a wonderful double act to be a part of. Mrs Bennet would buzz around and jab and poke and try to get him to rise to her, but Mr Bennet would sit back, not react, request to be left alone for a moment and not join in with her hysteria. It was much like how my family dealt with Aunt Mary. It was wonderful to be a mother to five daughters, albeit fictional ones, and we all became so close over the filming period. In the photograph of us standing waving off Elizabeth and Mr Darcy, played by Jennifer Ehle and Colin Firth respectively, the happiness on all our faces is real – there was no acting required at all.

The attention to detail on the production was magnificent and every department was working at one hundred per cent. It helped that we were filming a six-episode series, which allowed for wonderful detail across all aspects. Diana, our designer, even created a completely new parquet floor, which was stunning, There was nothing off the peg in any shape or form, and I was particularly struck by the fact that our dresses were created from scratch using fabrics that were dyed to the required colour with special pigments and then hand embroidered and embossed. Each dress was created first from a light toile fabric to ensure that the cut and fit were absolutely perfect, then, once the prototype was signed off, the actual dress would be made. Everything was tailor-made in the true sense of the word.

We were all involved in the creation of a very different world so to transport our audience, as well as ourselves, back in time, the research and application that we were immersed in was imperative. There was such care given to every aspect of our preparation including lessons in the etiquette of the period as well as dance and movement classes. Even though Mrs Bennet didn't dance I was allowed to join in, and it was so invigorating. All the food that we ate at the Bennet family mealtimes, or when taking tea in the parlour, was entirely of the time and if mutton stew was on the menu, then that's what was on our plates, to ensure that we created a believable world. We'd rehearse with our corsets on to allow us to feel the constriction and how this affected our posture and movement. In between all this there were costume and wig fittings. Even though I had plenty of hair to style it was more effective to give me a wig, and so, sadly, those pin curls are not my own.

For once, the budget was generous, and we were able to rehearse and film from June to November which meant that all the outdoor scenes could reflect the seasons. In many ways, I felt cocooned being on set as Mrs Bennet and filming over a time when in my own life there was a great deal of worry going on. This was almost as if I was living two lives at once and quite surreal. This is an actor's reality but I felt it very acutely during *Pride and Prejudice* and, on reflection I wonder if the total joy that I felt during filming was my mind and body numbing the pain of everything else to enable me to get through it all.

We had fun on and off set, and I launched myself into it with gusto. One evening we all went out to play skittles after work. It was great to let our hair down and step back into modern life for a while, as well as be out of wigs and corsets. The person who had organised the event planned the teams and I was in one with the young gentleman whose job it was to set all the real fires in the house and to keep them alive. The next day when I saw him on set, I said to him, 'That was good fun last night wasn't it?'

His reply took me aback, 'Yeah, well, it was except for this woman on our team. Every time I went up to bowl she was going, "Come on, come on you can do it!" She was determined to win and just kept going, "Come on, we can do this," and all that. She didn't stop.'

Turning away I quickly said, 'That must have been so annoying,' and ended the chat.

It was me. I was the annoying woman, but out of costume he hadn't recognised me, thankfully. It wasn't just Mrs Bennet and my Aunt Mary who were brilliant at creating a scene, I was obviously very capable of it too, and for that moment had taken the character home with me and into the skittles tournament.

Mum's diagnosis hit us hard and when I wasn't working my focus was on ensuring that she had company if we weren't able to be there, and that she could remain in the comfort of her home for as long as possible. One day we came back from a shopping trip in town, and she'd enjoyed herself but was exhausted.

'Do you think I'll still be here by Christmas?' she asked me.

'Of course you will. I've just bought you a new black skirt, a new jumper and a pair of slacks. Of course you'll be here.'

It was my way of helping her cope as well as avoiding facing the truth of our situation. Death is something that always happens to other people, until it happens to you, and no one can truly prepare you for it. We managed to keep Mum at home until it was clear that she needed some extra care from time to time and this is when we found a place for her at one of the Marie Curie centres in Liverpool.

Her indomitable spirit was still intact and she put her best dress on for her first day with them. As soon as we walked through the front door, we all felt a sense of relief and I was calm about leaving her with the doctor for a while. Afterwards the first thing that she said was, 'What a lovely doctor I met. Do you know what the first thing she said to me was? "I love that dress."' Straight away her spirits had been lifted, and she felt a bit sunnier about things. Mum's love of looking her best remained throughout, even though the illness was causing her great pain. One of my saddest memories, and also a wonderful insight into her tenacity, is of when she said to me, 'Oh, Alison, look at my nails. I need to do my nails.'

So, I said, 'Okay, Mum, that's a good idea,' and I went to get her nail polish.

I set it all up as she would usually do, putting down tissue and placing the small bottles of colour in front of her, then she just looked and looked at them, and said, 'I can't remember how to do it.' She was on extremely heavy painkillers that were affecting her mind.

'Okay, Mum, I can do it for you. Don't worry about it,' and I painted her nails for her.

We didn't know when the unimaginable was going to happen and so I continued in rehearsals for *When We Are Married*, a J. B. Priestley comedy that I was doing at the Chichester Festival Theatre, and tried to keep my head in the job. The dreaded call came, when I was told that they didn't think she had long, and I had to get back to Liverpool as soon as possible. It was such a relief to get home and be by her side as she became weaker and confused by the medication. One evening, I was heading to bed and on saying goodnight to her, she looked at me and said, 'I don't like you. I don't like you. Go away.'

My heart just broke. 'Mum, Mum, it's me. It's Alison. Please don't say that. It's me.'

She looked at me again and said, 'Oh no, I love you. I didn't mean that.' She put her arm out to me, as she had done so many times before, and said, 'I love you, I love you.' During the last week her mind travelled all over the place and I reached out to people that she was fond of to try and bring her back to us. I rang Mike, who was in London, and said, 'Mum's in a terrible way, she's so distressed. Will you speak to her?' And he said, 'Of course.' I don't know what he said to her as I couldn't hear but she was nodding and smiling on the phone. It was so nice to see, and for that minute or so, her light shone again and I felt grateful to him for giving her that momentary respite.

The thing about life and death is that they co-exist. Death happens, and life goes on. That is the tough bit. We are required to continue living when all we want to do is have time to stop and grieve. When I returned to rehearsals there was only one person in the cast who acknowledged my loss and everyone else acted as though nothing had happened. Where does that embarrassment come from? Why aren't we afforded the displays of deep emotion in our real lives that we see on stage and screen? We're so very stiff-upper-lipped and it's such a contradiction. This wasn't an easy time for me as life and art were at odds in many ways and a great deal was in flux. But the show must go on, as they say, and that's what I did to see me over the troubled waters and the deep grief that I felt after my mum's death. Over the years I've played so many different sorts of mums but none quite like Marjorie – although at that point I didn't know who was coming round the corner. Mum, unlike my Aunt Mary and Mrs Bennet, never caused a scene, she only ever created good ones.

CHAPTER 23

Between the Lines

I like to call myself an actress. I'm a woman who acts and so that's how I'll always describe myself. It's important to me. I'm not an actor, I am an actress. Even though it's what I've been doing for a very long time now I still have a fascination with other actresses and how they do what they do. I can remember when I'd just started drama school seeing Ingrid Bergman playing Natalia Petrovna in *A Month in the Country* at the Cambridge Theatre in the West End, and the whole theatre gasped when she made her entrance. It was a magical moment. This is what I adore about theatre, the alchemy of it all, so even when television and film became a larger part of my repertoire it was important to me to keep doing live stage roles too – for as long as they were being offered to me, and if I was able to.

I'm aware that I've been open about certain moments of anxiety, self-doubt and worry in relation to some of the theatre work that I've had over the years. Once I'd trained myself how to stop the words jumping around on the page in the first read-through, I was always fine in rehearsal, but the dark cloud cover of worry would usually begin as we headed towards the first run-through and then took the play onto the stage. However, I'm equally aware of the joy and thrill that it brings so there must be something in me that thrives under the pressure that being in a live performance stimulates. It's like being on a tightrope and holding your balance as you move from one end of the high wire to the next. The feeling on entering an unknown place as the lights go down and a group of strangers share a darkened room, a feeling that anything can happen, is gripping.

A really good example of loving and loathing a role was my time as Kath in Joe Orton's *Entertaining Mr Sloane*, which opened at the Arts Theatre just off Leicester Square in 2001, with Neil Stuke, Bryan Pringle and Clive Francis. Doing the show at the Arts had the added pressure that this was the theatre where the play had first been presented during the 1960s, and here we all were reviving it in amongst all the ghosts from that production. Despite it being a small theatre, and by that time I'd played in many much larger ones, my experience of bringing Kath to life was one of the most terrifying of my career. It's a complicated role, as Kath begins the play as a quiet rejected person who is still living with the guilt and trauma of bringing up a child out of wedlock, which in the 1960s still had huge stigma attached to it, and then she transforms into a dominatrix landlady. That's quite a journey! It was important to me that the audience believed that Kath was the same person at each stage of the way. The line learning held some challenges for me and seemed harder than usual, and Act 3, which was like a jigsaw puzzle with mismatching pieces, was almost impossible to get into my head. I entered a tunnel of worry and self-doubt. At the curtain call each evening, surges of emotion would well up and down in me, and I'd say to myself, *Why did I decide that acting was a good way to earn a living? Why am I putting myself through this agony and scrutiny? Why have I made this choice?* But it was a wonderful play and once I got the hang of it, it felt like flying.

The possibility of things going wrong and unexpected interruptions has always added frisson to live theatre. You rehearse and rehearse, and then go out on stage with absolutely no control of what the audience might do. It's a wonderful mad adventure and you've no idea if you're going to end up loving it or loathing it or both!

In 2009 I was invited to be in Alan Bennett's *Enjoy* at the Gielgud Theatre. It was a revival of a play that had originally opened in 1980. Alan wanted to give it another go and I'd been invited by the director, Christopher Luscombe, to play Connie. While we were in rehearsals for *Enjoy* for some reason or other my shoulders were very painful, and I'd been sent to see an osteopath in Primrose Hill. Alan lived nearby, and I was thrilled to bump into him and share a chat over cake and coffee as he is as brilliant in person as he is on the page.

There was one performance early in the run that I'll never forget. At the end of the play my character had a soliloquy and one evening, as I was standing on stage giving my all, I suddenly heard, 'Taxi!' being shouted loudly to the right of me. *Gosh, that's really penetrating the building, it must be coming from outside on Rupert Street*, was what I thought, whilst trying to stay on track with the speech. I kept on going. 'Taxi! Taxi! Taxi!' kept being shouted. *Who the hell wants a taxi so badly that they just can't stand and wait for one to come along, we're in the West End for goodness' sake!* I said to myself, trying not to show any irritation. Then there was a kerfuffle, at the side of the stalls, as this man got up and slid his way to the end of the row and other people got up so that he could move past them. Meanwhile he was rummaging in his pockets and hauling his coat on while I was trying to get to the end of my speech. By now I'd realised that it was the ringtone from the guy's phone that was disturbing us all. After what felt like an age, he managed to head up the aisle with 'Taxi!

Taxi!' blaring from his pocket. I hope he got one. Actually, no I don't!

Alan is as good at saying a throw-away line as he is at writing a one-liner, and each time he hits the mark perfectly. Once the show was up and running, he came along to watch a matinee performance. Afterwards somebody wanted to take a photograph of the assembled cast with Alan on stage. The stage-management team brought some chairs for us to sit on and as he was going to sit down next to me Alan said, 'I'm wearing a very posh coat.' There was so much meaning in that short phrase, it revealed a great deal about how he was feeling at that moment, as well as that he was a master of the spoken as well as written word.

Enjoy wasn't the first time that I'd worked with Alan. Our first encounter was much earlier in my career, in 1984, when I was cast as Mrs Allardyce in his film *A Private Function*. I've been lucky with the film and TV work that has come my way, even though sometimes a role can be cut short even before filming begins. This can be frustrating, but it's also par for the course, and when the script is by Alan Bennett, it's a joy and a thrill to be a part of it, no matter the cuts, as his writing is so good and so funny. On *A Private Function*, they were cutting like crazy and Mrs Allardyce turned out to be quite a small role in the end – remember, there are no small parts, etc. But, luckily for me, they'd left in a classic one-liner that was pure Alan Bennett genius. The piece is set in the late 1940s and everyone is sitting around a table having a meal. Dr Swaby, played by Denholm Elliott, is sitting at the other end of the table from Mrs Allardyce. Alan had written into the script that at one point during the meal, Dr Swaby farts, leaving an awkward silence, before Mrs Allardyce chimes in with what must rank high up as one of my favourite lines ever. So, imagine if you will, everyone is eating and it's all quite formal, then Denholm makes a farting noise – I'm not sure how he did it – then there's a beat before I come in with, 'More sprouts, Dr Swaby?' It was a priceless line and so Alan Bennett. For once, I managed to just about contain myself and deliver the line over several takes as the director needed, but the poor girl who was holding the boom mic had to stuff a hanky in her mouth each time and turn her head away as she held the equipment over the table. More sprouts, Dr Swaby?

Unscheduled and unexpected laughter is one of the most cathartic and life-enhancing feelings off stage, but, as I have found many times, on stage it's the stuff of nightmares. You never know it's going to happen and it's never intentional. At no time in my life have I ever been on stage and thought, *I know, why don't I make everyone else on stage laugh?* although I know people that do. That's not in me though. I've never done it because as I've already shown I'm such a terrible corpser and really have to get hold of myself to control it.

In 2011 I took it into my own hands to attempt to put an end to the bouts of irrepressible, not-in-the-script, laughter that I'd been prone to all my career. I'd been cast as the clairvoyant Madame Arcati in Noël Coward's *Blithe Spirit* with Hermione Norris, Ruthie Henshall and Robert Bathurst. Although I didn't feel that I was natural casting for the part, it felt like a challenge that I wanted to take on. I was excited to discover who this woman was and find her in a way that best opened the door to her character. On this occasion, it was from the outside in. I needed to find the right frock, the right stockings and shoes, and the right bag. Once all that was in place, I was able to feel her getting closer to me, or should that be me getting closer to her. However, it was when I put her hat on that I felt that it all came together and that I knew who she was. Madame Arcati had several large entrances to make, and one of them was after she was supposed to have cycled seven miles and then turned back, as she'd forgotten her bicycle pump, and do the seven miles again! It feels exhausting just thinking about it. It's a lot of cycling and we worked out that on a good day that was about fifteen minutes of effort in total. I wanted the audience to believe that the cycling was real and so I would stand backstage, hike up my long skirt so that I didn't trip up, and spend fifteen minutes going up and down the steps. By the time it was my cue to go on stage I was properly exhausted, genuinely out of breath, and looked like a middle-aged woman who had exerted herself a bit – so not much acting was required at that point!

Blithe Spirit is described by Noël Coward as 'an improbable farce in three acts' but the truth is that as the run got going it felt like it was becoming farcical for the wrong reasons and all getting slightly out of our control. One day, before a matinee, Hermione and I were going over our lines and we began to spot double entendres all over the place. Once we had seen them, we couldn't unsee them and this was a problem as it ignited my uncontrollable laughter. I was dreading going on stage for the show, and, as I could have predicted, as soon as one of the double entendre lines came up, I began to feel that familiar surge of bubbles rushing through me and erupting as my shoulders shook and an unstoppable giggling took hold. It was contagious and Hermione caught the bug too. I don't know what the audience must have thought. I began to shout, 'No, no, no,' which wasn't in the script, and managed to plug the laughter and get to the end of the scene. It was like an exorcism and, as my character was a medium who made connections with the spirit world, my repeated 'no' possibly didn't look as out of place as it felt.

'Hermione, that was dangerous, we nearly lost the plot completely this afternoon – we've got to find a way to put an end to it.' I just couldn't allow the laughter to creep in, as it had so many times before, as it would ruin things and the rest of the run would be a disaster. This was serious for me. 'Right, I want us to meet on stage between the two shows and we'll sort it out once and for all.' We met as agreed and I stood on one side of the stage and Hermione stood on the other. 'Okay, repeat after me,' and I shouted across at her, 'I am not going to laugh. You are not going to laugh,' and she shouted back at me, 'I am not going to laugh. You are not going to laugh.' And then we both said, 'And that is agreed,' shook hands and left the stage trying not to laugh. Goodness knows what the ushers, who were in the auditorium preparing for the evening show, must have thought of us. It worked though. We managed to get through the scene without laughing that evening and for all the rest of the performances. A few years later I was working on a job and a friend of Hermione's was on the same project. It was the first day and the first thing that she said to me was, 'No, no, no!' Hermione had obviously told her about our disgraceful, pardon me, *my* disgraceful behaviour, and it had come back to haunt me. Given that Madame Arcati was a medium, that didn't surprise me one bit.

After that, it didn't happen on stage again. I wish that I could say the same about the rising feeling of fear that had cloaked me during *Othello*, *Entertaining Mr Sloane* and some other theatre roles. After *Blithe Spirit* that feeling gripped more tightly and really began to cripple me in a way that it never had before. It was 2012 and *Here*, a play by the magnificent writer Michael Frayn, was being revived at the Rose Theatre Kingston and he'd asked me to be in it. It's a lovely intimate theatre and I took the job for the same reason that I agree to all the work that I do, because I could hear the character's voice, the writing was strong, and I knew that I could play this woman. Mine wasn't a large role but it was a good one – I was playing another landlady!

The main action centres around a young couple, played by Zawe Ashton and Phil Beckett, who rent out the very cramped studio flat that my character, Pat, owns. Pat is a lonely and isolated older woman, and this is reflected in the text by there being very little interaction between her and the other characters. I'd come on and make a speech, say another couple of things and then go off again, then fifteen minutes later come back on and make another speech. I became very anxious about the onstage and then offstage nature of what I had to do. I found it unnerving, my confidence began to slide away, and this just got worse and worse. I began to doubt if I could carry on and really had to give myself a stern talking to reminding myself of all the reasons why I should.

This was both a surprise and a shock as being on stage felt like being at home to me, a safe place. Theatre acting was my favourite thing in the world and to contemplate stopping was like shutting off a vital organ. I shared my worry with one of my sons, who said, 'Look Mum, you love being on stage, you love entertaining people. Being in a show is when you're at your best.' He was right, it was my best place or at least it had been. The feeling of dread was a challenge to shake off this time though. Whenever I arrived at the theatre, I couldn't go in, so I used to walk along the River Thames and go over my speeches in my head. Over and over and over again. Then I'd dump my stuff in the dressing room and go over everything once more. It was torture, absolute agony. I was lost in this tunnel of loneliness, and I couldn't tell the director or the other actors as I didn't want to alarm them.

If it hadn't been for the lovely dresser that had been assigned to me, I'm not sure I would have managed to get through the run. She didn't come across as a typical theatre dresser, attired all in black, wearing trainers so that they can run up and down the stairs, and with no nonsense about them. She wasn't like this at all, with her short skirts, high heels and very bubbly character, and I wasn't sure if we'd get along together. I couldn't have been more wrong. There was something in her that got me and when I recognised this, I knew that she'd be there for me. There was no fuss, she wasn't at all over the top, but when she saw that I was struggling, and what I masked from the others all the time, she'd whisper, 'You can do it, it's okay.' That's all. She just knew. Often she'd stand backstage waiting for me to come off and when I did, I'd hear her voice in the dark whispering, 'You did it.' On the final night of the show, she left me a card, which I've kept as she was such a special support to me, and I'll never forget it.

Dearest Alison,

Well, here we are, last day and we made it all in one piece, believe it or not. I just wanted to say that it has been an absolute honour and a pleasure to work with you. To me, you are one of the very, very few highly talented and extremely professional artists I've ever met. From the bottom of my heart, I wish you all the best for all new things. May they all be beautiful. And please always remember that anxieties and difficult times do pass as much as they seem eternal when one is in them. Time always goes by in the same way. The tips of your toes are where they should be. And at the end of the night there is always a glass of wine waiting for you.

E. x

As my Grandma Steadman, would say, she was 'sent for a reason', and I truly believe that she was. The show ended and that was the last time that my dresser and I had any contact. I hope that she knows how important she was to me and how much she helped me.

The show might have been distressing to do but it was a special time because of her.

The whole experience was a marker in the sand for me, and I've only done one play on stage since, taking on the role in 2014 of Madame Raquin, the mother in *Thérèse Raquin*, who becomes wheelchair bound and can't speak, but is desperately trying to communicate her love and affection for her son, Camille. Taking on a character like this was a first and it was a humbling insight into the challenges that people can face when they are suddenly afflicted by the changes that a bleed to the brain can bring on.

Playing Madame Raquin meant that when, three years later, I was offered the role of Mary Taylor, a woman who suffers a devastating stroke, in the television drama *Care*, written by Jimmy McGovern and Gillian Juckes, I knew that this would be an important piece of storytelling to be involved with. My main ambition with all the women that I play is to be able to tell their story accurately and for *Care* I needed to do a deep dig into a medical condition that I had no personal experience of to ensure that I honoured the writing and subject matter.

Mary is full of life, a mum, a granny; she's bright, independent and strong, but then in an instant the rug is pulled from under her. It could happen to any of us at any time and we have no control over it. It must be terrifying to go from being able to communicate to being locked in and stuck, and it was vital for me to understand the reality of this. I've never taken any aspect of my work lightly, and research, no matter if the role is scripted or created through improvisation, has always been my bedrock. It's what enables me to meet the character head-on and transmit who they are to an audience. The weeks before I began filming were spent with doctors and in hospitals so that I could fully comprehend what happens when there is such a seismic shift to a person's inner system and how this affects how they see the world and how the world sees them. With a role like Mary it wasn't good enough to just *act* it, but nor was it about method acting. My way inside the character was to grasp the physical changes – *How does she move? Eat? Communicate?* – and allow these outside factors to determine how Mary communicates.

It was a challenge and a privilege; my experience of playing the part has stayed with me. Roles like Mary make you value life as you know it and not waste a second of it. There's no sleeping on the job of living!

CHAPTER 24

Enough Love

'Get back from the road, Alison. Come on. Come and stand up here at the back with me,' and reluctantly I step back from my pole position and go and stand by my mum. I am five years old and watching the TT Races on the Isle of Man is one of the highlights of our family holiday there. The island is packed full of holidaymakers from Liverpool who've taken the short boat trip across the Irish Sea and, even though we are still within the UK, it feels foreign and exotic to me. 'Take my hand and stand on your tiptoes so you can get a better view,' says Mum. I've never seen anything like it before nor been in such huge crowds of people. The noise of cheering and roaring, the sound of the motorbikes whizzing by and revving up, the smell of the oil on the road all bombard my senses. It's thrilling. My dad has told me stories of accidents and injuries and lead riders, and now standing, looking down on the road, I am part of that drama. The rider we all give the biggest cheer for is Geoff Duke who zooms past us, top to toe in leather, looking like a motorbike-riding Zorro or the Lone Ranger. I cheer and wave and wonder if the Queen is in the crowd watching her husband race! The 'Iron Duke' – although always the Duke of Edinburgh to me – is a fearless rider and a true old-fashioned sporting superstar with many admirers, including me.

I loved our holidays on the Isle of Man and the trips on the old steam trains to take us out and about around the island. There are some places that we pass through in our lives, where we may spend time but are of no consequence to us, and there are other stopping places that make you feel that you've been there before or need to return to at some point. It can't be explained. The Isle of Man is that sort of place for me.

It's the same with people. Just think about how many people you encounter in a week, a month, a year. Over the years how many of those people stick only for a moment and how many people end up travelling through large parts of your life and make a significant impact on you? The latter is true of my first encounter with Ruth Jones and James Corden when our paths crossed on the Kay Mellor series *Fat Friends* in the early 2000s. Ruth and I had previously spent a couple of days working on a radio play together, but hadn't got to know each other. As for James, well, our first encounter set the tone for a relationship that has followed since.

'Can I help you with your bags?' The train had pulled into the station at Leeds, and I was struggling to get my luggage and myself off in one piece. *That's nice customer service*, I thought as I lifted my head to the person on the platform who had made the kind offer. Standing in front of me was a boyish-looking young man who was not a station attendant.

I laughed, as I recognised him immediately from the cast sheet for *Fat Friends* that I'd been sent a few weeks earlier. 'Yes, you can,' I replied feeling grateful for the offer, 'and don't ever stop asking people that.'

He smiled and said, 'I'm James Corden. I know who you are.'

This was our first encounter, and I didn't anticipate that what lay ahead would be any different to most of my other work in theatre and TV; that we'd be friends and colleagues for a fixed period and that would be that. Well, I got that wrong didn't I!

Kay Mellor's writing was full of energy, vitality and determination and she always knew the story that she wanted to tell. She was an actors' writer who consistently encouraged all members of the cast to discover the full truth of the characters that she'd created. Kay understood the human condition, the complex layers that are within us all. When the role of Betty Simpson came my way, I knew that it would be a rich experience, but I could never have predicted the considerable impact that it would make on my career further down the line nor how, in retrospect, my character's story was to be a fore-telling of a momentous revelation in my own real life one.

Betty Simpson is another of the great mums that I've played. She's loving and kind, and puts her husband Douglas, played by Barrie Rutter, and two daughters, played by Ruth Jones and Jessica Harris, first. That is, until she doesn't. Betty and Douglas work in the family fish and chip shop, Big and Battered, which isn't ideal for a person struggling with their weight. In the first episode, brilliantly titled 'Love Me Slender', we met Betty who, having lost five stone, was through to the regional finals of Super Slimmers and Kelly, Ruth's character, who was determined to lose weight so that she can fit into her wedding dress.

During the filming of *Fat Friends*, my Aunt Mary, the woman inside my Mrs Bennet, died. She was such a lovely woman, despite all her eccentricities, who, alongside her mother, my grandmother, had shared her love of birds with me. She particularly loved starlings and the last time I saw her, which was just after Christmas 1999, she was putting out turkey scraps in the garden so that the starlings could enjoy their own festive dinner. The birds swooped down, and she chirped, 'Col-in Stev-en, Alison! Look at them, look at them, they're really enjoying it!' It was compelling viewing to watch these tiny birds strip off all the bits of meat that you can't carve off, and there was nothing left by the time they had finished with it.

The following year our location for one of the scenes in *Fat Friends* was in a field. It was just after lunch, and I hadn't been able to finish mine so I'd wrapped it in a paper napkin and shoved it into my pocket to give to the starlings that I'd noticed were in the field. As I was walking back, I began to unwrap the meat. A man walking towards me in the opposite direction said, 'I hope you're not going to throw that meat into the bin.' It was such a random thing for a stranger to say to me.

'I'm not actually, I'm going to put it out for the starlings.'

'Ah good,' said the man and carried on walking as I began to shred the meat into tiny pieces and scatter it.

Coincidentally, later that day filming was delayed because a starling had flown inside Big and Battered and couldn't get out. This really worried me, and I couldn't settle until it was released safely.

After a long day of filming, I got back to my hotel and a message telling me that my bird-loving Aunt Mary had died that morning. It stopped me in my tracks. It was as if she had come to me that day, right from the man talking to me, to feeding the birds in the field, to the trapped starling. I took it as a sign of the enduring family bond that was between us and felt comforted by it.

There comes a point in many people's lives, men and women, but especially women, when they've given so much of themselves away that they don't know who they are anymore. It's often once any children have grown up, flown the nest and are now leading their own lives so there becomes a pressing need to reclaim their own. Betty reclaims hers by losing a colossal five stone, even though her husband doesn't see the need for it and isn't too happy that she has. Betty's weight feels like a burden that she needs to lose. The moments when the character looks in the mirror and hates what she sees are so powerfully touching and real. How many times do we all look in the mirror and wonder where the time has gone and where we have disappeared to? Kay understood this completely and reflected it so accurately. Her lines always had heft: 'Inside this comfortable woman is a wild woman who wants her hair and nails doing and to be held in somebody's arms and told that she's beautiful.'

The brilliance of the series was that it set up the world and then established story lines that interweaved as the drama unfolded and the secrets and shame of key characters emerged. For Betty, losing weight is her way of turning back the clock. which set the action for the second series when Betty came face to face with her past when her childhood sweetheart, played by James Hazeldene, joins the slimming club and the dark secret that she's held onto for all her adult life begins to take hold. The wider context is, that much to her annoyance, Betty has been putting on weight, only to discover that she's pregnant. This unplanned, unexpected, late pregnancy completely derails her and once her little boy is born, she finds it difficult to love him but no one knows why. Why wouldn't this mother, with enough love inside her, not connect with her first-born son? Those of you who have watched the series will know the answer, and spoiler alert coming up for those that haven't. It's because the little boy isn't her first son, but her second, as she had her first decades earlier when she was a teenager. Betty has carried the shame that this secret makes her feel all of her adult life. In trying to get under her skin I had to put myself in her shoes and think about what it must have been like to find yourself pregnant, unmarried and under twenty during a time when such things were frowned upon and young girls were put under pressure to give their newborn babies away. Her only way of coping was to make herself believe she was doing the right thing, 'If I loved him, I'd let him be adopted. Have a proper life with a proper family.' Little did I know that I was circling a secret from my own family's past.

After the success of *Gavin and Stacey*, Larry Lamb and I were often asked to pair up for documentary series or reality shows, and in 2022 we took part in ITV's *DNA Journey*. The premise was that Larry and I would go on a road trip to find out about our family histories. We'd meet our own family members as well as new ones that we never knew existed, who had been found using a mix of DNA evidence and genealogy. I've always been intrigued by family history and about twelve years earlier the BBC's *Who Do You Think You Are?* team had approached me to test my interest in doing the show. I'd agreed, but the way it works is that nothing is set in stone until their team have done some poking around. I was on tenterhooks. *What would they discover? Were there some professional entertainers or artists in the family? Was I related to the Queen?* Sadly, it was a no-go as nothing of interest had been discovered. So, when I agreed to join Larry on *DNA Journey*, I was 99.9 per cent certain that it would be a straightforward revelation of my Welsh and Scottish heritage and that a few distant second cousins might pop up for a bit of surprise. Just before filming began, the producer asked if they could have a Zoom call with me to go through things. Nothing seemed untoward, so when on the call she said, 'We think that we've found out that your father was adopted,' I rebuffed with, 'No, absolutely not, that's not the case.'

She replied, 'Okay, we just wanted to run it past you and to say that we may bring it up in the programme.'

It was brought up in the programme and on film they had shown me the documentation that turned any sense of who I thought I was upside down. Unlike the previous search a great deal more could now be accessed, as more census information had been released, and this told the story of my family that no one apart from my paternal grandparents knew. The form had been filled out by Richard Steadman, my grandfather, and he had registered, his wife Agnes, his son Ron, his daughter Hilda and then 'George Percival Steadman, adopted'. Adopted, was written clearly. It wasn't an error. It was definite. We continued filming and all that was going through my mind was, *Who knew? This can't be true. My relatives aren't my relatives. All these people that I've felt connections with are not connected to me at all.* It was completely overwhelming, and I felt shattered and very lost. It took a while to settle in but as it did many things began to make sense, such as the fact that my dad looked nothing like anyone else in his family. Also there was suddenly clarity and meaning to, 'We were glad to have him,' which is what my 101-year-old Uncle Ron said to me when I asked him if he remembered his brother. It was a huge shock, but as more was revealed and I stood at my dad's birth mother's grave on the Isle of Man, what helped me to reconcile it all was that love was at the centre for everyone involved.

When I told my sisters they felt the same way, but Sylvia said, 'This is nobody's business but ours and it shouldn't be made public.' I understood her point of view and respected the fact that she is a very private person and said all of this to her, but I also stressed that the news was nothing to be ashamed of. Sylvia came from a school of thought that attached shame to illegitimacy and she didn't want to be associated with this. 'What matters,' I said, 'is that he had a loving family, was happy and cared for, and well brought up. I couldn't care if his birth parents were married or not and it must have been so traumatic for his mum to give him away.' I took comfort from the fact that he'd had a lovely childhood and was adored by all his family. Agnes, my Grandma Steadman, had said I was 'sent for a reason', and it was clear that her youngest son was too.

As devastating as it was at the time to uncover all of this, I take comfort from the fact that my dad was adopted by the kindest and most loving people that anyone could hope to have as a family. The sadness comes when I think about the young woman who had no choice but to give her baby, my dad, away. *DNA Journey* revealed that his birth mother was a girl called Brada 'May' Craine, and that she came from the Isle of Man, the location of so many of our happy family holidays where we'd enjoyed ourselves so much and always felt at home. May left the Isle of Man for Liverpool in 1911, entered service and at some point between 1911 and 1912 she became pregnant with my dad. My heart goes out to May: she'd arrived in Liverpool full of hopes that were dashed when she became pregnant out of wedlock. She had no choice but to give her precious boy to others. Dad was born in a home for unmarried mothers on Edge Lane in Liverpool. He and May were together for eight months until my grandparents took him into their care. We know that he was baptised when he was a month old and that May gave him his name, which feels so profound to me. The fact that my grandparents kept his name is such a wonderful act of respect. We also know that May remained in Liverpool for another eight years, and only lived three miles away from my dad's family, before returning to the Isle of Man, where she went on to to have a daughter, my dad's half-sister. It's odd to think that May and my dad could have walked past each other and might even have been reunited. Who knows? She was close to her boy though. Perhaps she did know where he was and perhaps she had looked on from afar. The fact of the matter is that we'll never know what happened after she gave him up for adoption or how she felt, and these secrets remained locked with her.

Betty Simpson, on the other hand, released hers, and sought to find the little boy that she'd given away at birth. In doing so she realised that she had enough love to share around, which was certainly also true of Richard and Agnes Steadman, who always displayed more than enough of it to us all.

Fat Friends ran for four series, but the years immediately before *Gavin and Stacey* weren't just about playing Betty and dishing up fish and chips, as towards the tail end of the period there was overlap with *The Worst Week of My Life*, a comedy series that aired between 2004 and 2006. It's a show that I'm extremely fond of and it was fun playing Angela, who prided herself on serving a haute cuisine menu at breakfast, lunch and dinner, hosting elegant gatherings whenever the occasion required her to and, first and foremost, ensuring that she kept up appearances as the Lady of the Manor. Like *Fat Friends*, the writing, by Mark Bussell and Justin Sbresni, was too good to resist, as was the ensemble of Ben Miller as Howard Steel, Sarah Alexander as Mel, Angela's daughter and Howard's fiancée, and Geoffrey Whitehead as the much-tested husband Dick. The show was a full-blown comedy of errors that saw Ben's character Howard lurch from disaster to disaster as he found himself totally unintentionally in a series of unfortunate situations that were always made worse as he attempted to make things better. Mark and Justin also directed each series, and this was as sharp as their writing, which made it such a fulfilling job because every aspect of it slotted into place perfectly. It was fast paced, and a great deal of the comedy was physical. Ben was wonderful as the hapless Howard – or as Angela pronounced it, 'Howrd', which sounded more like 'Hard' than

Howard – clowning about and wreaking havoc. I trusted Mark and Justin completely and was happy to jump into anything that they required Angela to do. On one occasion, this was, quite literally, into the deep end of the indoor swimming pool that was part of the house.

In the scene Howard loses Angela's blind sister, Yvonne, while taking her to the lavatory. She takes a wrong turn and plunges into the pool, so Geoffrey and Angela jump in to rescue her. Yvonne was played by Anna Massey, the sister of Daniel Massey who had been Othello to my Desdemona. I knew from the get-go, when Anna asked me in a conspiratorial fashion, 'Do you ever eat meat when you're out of your home? I don't,' that we were in for an interesting adventure. So, full transparency now, Anna didn't plunge into the pool. She refused to and so a body double was brought in to make a splash. The body double, Geoffrey and I got wet through and shivery cold jumping into the pool multiple times to get the required action shot. Once that was in the can, the next scene was at the poolside attending to the unfortunate Yvonne. Anna had also been adamant that for this scene she wouldn't wear a wet costume or wig and no water must touch her. Honestly! Filming always takes the time that it takes, and we were all in position: Anna on the floor (bone dry) with Geoffrey and me standing beside her as we waited for the cameras to be lined up. I looked a fright, as you would do if you'd spent a good amount of time in a pool with your clothes and make-up on. Mascara was running down my face, my clothes clung unflatteringly to my body and I was dripping from top to toe, which was all fine with me, as it was what was required to make the scene believable. Suddenly, as if awakened from the dead, there came an irate screech from the floor. 'I said in no uncertain terms that there was not to be any water on me and there is!' I looked down to see

Anna staring angrily up at me, and at the same time noticed the offending drop of water on her cheekbone that had dripped from me onto her face. I couldn't believe what I was hearing and very unlike me, or very like me when I feel that something or someone is totally out of order, I gave as good as I got and told her off. Before she had any chance to reply, the director of photography shouted, 'And action.'

Angela's circumstances were totally unlike Betty's in *Fat Friends* but a gentle scratch upon the surface revealed that they have a good amount in common. Both are women of a certain age who are waking up to the need and feeling of wanting more from their lives and from those around them. *Worst Week* was full of brilliant slapstick comedy but it was also full of pathos and tenderness, and whilst Betty may have looked in the mirror and then raged with passion at her husband, Angela's outburst of frustration, disappointment and longing after doing the same was quieter but equally clear.

Betty and Angela were alive in me at the same time, and I've often thought that there is an evolutionary link between myself, my age and stage of life, and the order in which I've met and played the women that I have. Betty and Angela co-existed for a while and when I consider how their two might become one I begin to get an outline of the fantastic female that emerged next and the following chapter of my professional life.

CHAPTER 25

I Know What I Saw

Let me introduce Pamela Andrea Shipman née Gryglaszewska – 'To go from that to Shipman, you know, Ship-man, I felt quite flat the day after we got married!'

Pam, aka Pamalaar, was a gift of a part for me, which would never have come my way if James and Ruth hadn't met on *Fat Friends* and decided to try and write something together, and if I hadn't been in the show playing Ruth's character's mum, Betty Simpson. Serendipity strikes again. Ruth and James had mentioned that they were writing something and that there was a role that I might like, but beyond that I didn't know much until they sent me a script with a note saying that they were hoping to get this off the ground so would I have a look at it and consider the role of Pamela. As soon as I read her first scene, I knew it was the role for me. There was no hesitation at all. It was brilliant. How could I resist this? Pam is lying on her sofa with cucumbers on her eyes and her only son Gavin, played by Matthew Horne, comes in the front door.

'Hi, Gav.'

Not noticing her he says, 'Alright, Mum?' whilst he's fussing about in the kitchen.

'No, I'm not really, I'm absolutely shattered, I've been crying all afternoon,' she says sitting up.

'How come?'

'That *Pet Rescue*. There was this badger and all its litter died and you could actually see the mother badger crying.'

Gavin looks at Pam and says, 'I don't think badgers can cry, Mum.'

Then came the classic line that sold it to me: 'Nor did I, my little prince, but I know what I saw and it's knocked me for six. Still, life goes on.'

It just sprung off the page. How could I not want to play her? It just clicked. The series was commissioned straight away by the BBC, which was amazing. They knew how good it was too and set a tight delivery deadline for it, which meant that James and Ruth had to get their skates on to write it. James was in Alan Bennett's play *The History Boys* in New York at the time so that meant Ruth had to go over there so that they could spend the days writing, then he could go and do the show in the evening.

I knew that I was playing Pamela, but it wasn't until I did a chemistry test with Larry Lamb that I knew who'd be playing her husband, Mick. The scene that we had to do together is one of my favourites from the first episode, let's just call it the Three Steaks Pam scene. Again, another classic that reveals the personalities of each character so quickly and precisely. Pam has three steaks on her plate as she's on the Atkins Diet (other diets are available). She explains to the perplexed Mick and Gavin that one is the actual steak and the other two are substitutes for chips and peas, which to Pam is completely logical. Mick's having none of it, so much so that Pam pushes her plate away saying that if she eats it, she'll be known forever more as Three Steaks Pam. The irony is that people will often refer to her in this meaty way when they're talking to me about the character. Larry and I had such a laugh, we were easy company with each other and all of us knew that this was a relationship that would work on and off screen. We had worked together years before on the BBC comedy *The Missing Postman*, and had become friends. The producers sent Larry a script, as they had to me, and I can remember he called and asked me, 'What is this *Gavin and Stacey* thing then?' They were looking for a Mick and they couldn't have found a more perfect one.

Casting is key to the success of theatre, television and film, and the casting director on *Gavin and Stacey* brought together an ensemble of actors that were a perfect fit for the characters that I'd read on the page. I can remember thinking on our first day together, *This is the beginning of the best job ever.* When Joanna Page came up to me on that day and said in her lovely sing-song voice, 'Hiya, I'm Jo and I'm playing Stacey,' I thought, *Oh my God, you are perfect, you are the best casting ever.* And then my little prince came over and in his understated, gentle way went, 'Hi, I'm Matt,' and again I thought, *And you're perfect as Pam's son and a perfect match with Jo.* It continued like that as all the characters came into the room. There was magic in the air, and we all felt it.

When we began the first series, we didn't know how well we'd all get along, or not. Experience has taught me that finding moments to let your hair down together and have a laugh early on can make an invaluable contribution to any show. The first season of *Gavin and Stacey*, although a straight commission, almost felt like a pilot and the pressure was on as the budget at that stage was low. None of us had any expectations of being afforded any luxury treatment and it was a surprise for us all when we were booked into a rather plush hotel and not a Travelodge, although I've spent many a comfortable night in the latter. The hotel was one of those places that has warming fake fires in every nook and cranny to lull guests into a feeling of *at home cosiness*. I've always had a fondness for a glowing log, no matter if it's an imitation, and it was pleasing to find an inviting corner of the main bar that had enough space for us all to gather and relax. I found myself going into full event-organiser mode at the end of each day in an attempt to bring us all together and the bar very quickly was christened, Ali's Parlour, by the producer Lindsay Hughes. Very soon there was no need to herd the troops as people could be heard saying 'Ali's Parlour?' to each other, which became our recognised shorthand for an end-of-the-day drink and get-together.

It was such a happy cast. Through the brilliance of the writing everyone had their moment and we could believe in all the characters leading full lives. Being able to have such confidence in the writing is so liberating as it allows you to be playful with your part within the script, with no need for improvisation at all. On most TV comedy-drama series there are rewrites but on *Gavin and Stacey* over the three series and the Christmas special there wasn't a single one. There was a gap of ten years between the end of season 3 and the first much-hoped-for Christmas special, and I can remember feeling nervous about things again. It had been some time since I'd walked in Pamela's shoes and I began to question whether I could get the character in the same way as I had previously, Plus, I was older, my hair was shorter and I felt fatter. But I needn't have worried as the script reflected the passing of time and we'd all changed just a little, including Neil the Baby who was now ten or eleven years old but was still called Neil the Baby, which always made me laugh.

If laughter was like a virus, then on this show no matter how inoculated I was I had a tendency to succumb to it. This was by far the worst of any of the times I've had to stop myself corpsing. In fact, with my hand on my heart I don't think that I've ever dissolved quite as badly into a soggy mess of unscheduled and inappropriate laughter as I did on *Gavin and Stacey*.

Oh, my Christ!

It was dreadful and I hang my head in shame just thinking about it, although it's such a cherished memory too from my time filming the show. On the page, it all looked so innocent, unfunny even, but getting any of the words out became an increasing challenge for me. The moment in question was the night before Dawn and Pete Sutcliffe's wedding-vow renewal with everyone gathered in the Shipmans' kitchen in Billericay. Julia Davis and Adrian Scarborough, who played the in-and-out-of-love-struck couple, are comedy gold together. they're a magical combination, and although I adored being on set with them both, I also dreaded it. There were so many times over the series when I'd hope that the camera wouldn't turn on me, as I'd be standing there rocking and saying to myself, *Keep breathing, don't laugh, you must not laugh, don't laugh*, when all I wanted to do was howl with laughter. The offending sequence, or should that be the sequence that I offended in, was quite low key as sequences go. The Sutcliffes were round at the Shipmans' (even those names set me off) to chat through the stag and hen dos that were planned. Julia, Adrian and I are sitting around the table in the kitchen, I'm directly opposite Julia and Larry is standing just to the left of me. Dawn asks Pamela what she has planned and my bit was to tell her about some films that we were going to watch, including one called *Doubt*, which Dawn doesn't remember, and Pam says something like, 'You know the one. Meryl Street plays a nun and it's got that big strawberry-blond fella from *Patch Adams* in it.' Well, I just couldn't get the words out. It was impossible. And so, taking a deep breath in, I went again, 'Meryl Streep, plays a—' and then I was gone. Julia was holding a wine glass close to her lips, but I could see that the corners of her mouth were turned up and this set me off for the umpteenth time. She's one of those people who can keep a poker face, but their laughter is all in the twinkle of their eyes, and she had the worst twinkle in her eye at this point. I tried again, 'Meryl Streep—' Gone. By this time Adrian had caught the bug too. It's like a disease. Julia managed to keep it together, just about. She was laughing hysterically inside but kept her composure on the outside and every time I looked up, there it was, that twinkle, and I was a goner whenever we made eye contact – which we had to. The more together she was, the worse I became. It was torture. It was all so involuntary and there was no controlling it. There were tears, there was sweat, there was hooting, and no matter how much I attempted to deep breathe, and reprimand myself out of it, the waterfall of laughter just kept spilling over and over. It must have gone on for at least twenty minutes and, after trying my best to get over myself, the director Christine Gernon said, 'Okay, everyone, we're going to take a break now to give Alison the chance to sort this out.' She broke the whole set, which never usually happens. Larry, who is the epitome of patience, even ended up saying to me, 'For God's sake, Alison, just say the fucking line will you.' As we walked off set, I turned to Chris, full of apology, and said, 'I'm surprised that you haven't thrown a bucket of water over me.' Some fresh air and a cup of tea sorted me out and, somehow or other, I managed to get through it. When I watch the take of that scene now, it looks far more serious than it should, as we're all desperately trying to recover from what had just happened and not to laugh again. Which lasted for a hot minute of course. It was hard work not to laugh from start to finish and as we were all enjoying it so much there were many filming days when I wasn't sure if I'd get through them without dissolving into laughter.

The scene when Dawn came round saying that she's having no more to do with Pete because he's a drug addict was a tough one for me, especially when they begin to sing together after Pete persuaded her that he was innocent. I don't know how Adrian Scarborough managed to look Julia Davies in the eye. I was standing there thinking, *Just breathe, don't laugh, keep breathing* and, once again, all that I wanted to do was howl with laughter as Julia sang, 'If you fall, I will catch you, I will be waiting, time after time.' Pam and Mick were standing looking on as the song singing led into kissing, with both of them feeling like the oddballs at a party. Thank goodness the camera only came on to me and Larry once or twice because, by trying to keep straight faces, we both looked very strange indeed.

It was such a relief when I was allowed to laugh because the script required it. One of my favourite Mick and Pam scenes was when they were in bed together laughing. It was the only scene that we ever filmed twice, but not because we'd made any mistakes. They've fallen out so Pam isn't speaking to Mick. He says, 'Oh come on, Pammy,' in the way that only Larry can, but it's no good and she replies, 'No, Mick, no. You know I'm not speaking to you,' then he goes, 'Oh, Pammy, please,' but she still doesn't respond. So he does the thing that works every time for him when she's in a strop and reaches over to put on these enormous pink ears then says, 'Oh come on, Camilla,' and she (and I) begin to laugh. We did the scene once with lot and lots of laughter, then we did it again as we weren't sure if it was a bit OTT and we wanted to get it right without it being offensive. That's the only time in the entire run that we gave ourselves two takes (not three steaks) and I was happy to be Two Takes Pam. It was always efficient. The script was handed over to us, we read it, we acted it and they filmed it. It's wonderful when it happens like this though it's rare that it does.

If my laughter was hard to contain, tears were equally hard too. It hadn't taken any of us very long to form close bonds with each other and towards the end of the first series, when Gavin and Stacey get married, just before they all set off there is a scene between Pamela and her little prince when she comes into the bedroom to see how he's doing. They just look at each other and she fixes his tie. A bit like when laughter surges up in me, I could feel the emotion rise and my eyes welled with tears. Matt was the same. In that moment he was my son, and this was his wedding day. Another moment of teariness was much later in the series at another wedding day. It is Nessa and Dave Coaches' big day and everyone is there. Ruth and Steffan Rhodri, who played Dave, are having a tender moment as they are about to do their vows. The emotion in the church is palpable, and then in walks Smithy carrying Neil the Baby. It could have been so gushing and sentimental, a sort of *An Officer and a Gentleman* moment, but it wasn't. When James as Smithy said, 'And we've got him,' and the baby, without direction, looked at James, I became a soppy mess. It was gold.

Most of my filming sequences took place in Pam and Mick's home and so it was always exciting to head off further afield when we had to do a shoot in another location or, even better, outdoors. Going down to Barry's Island – no one will ever convince me to call it anything else – was always a hoot, whether it was for a family Christmas, hosted by Gwen, played by Melanie Walters, with Uncle Bryn, the inimitable Rob Brydon, cooking up a feast as well as reaching boiling point under the stress of it all, or for weddings and christenings. Being with the extended family, as it were, was always such a treat and it also gave us time with Margaret John, who played the minxy Doris, Gwen's wild-living elderly neighbour. Doris knew how to live and so did Maggie, so it was wonderful to get to know her better when we were scheduled for three days of filming on the beach. It might not have been such fun if the sun hadn't shone down on us, but it did. Maggie and I, who were sat beside each other on deckchairs and didn't have many lines, were able to spend the time nattering away together and discover a bit more about each other. Maggie was an impressive eighty-one years old when we began filming; she was such a bundle of energy and always had a story to tell. She'd had a long and successful career on stage and screen before becoming much more widely known due to the success of *Gavin and Stacey*. She'd married at bit later in life at forty-eight and her musician husband, Bill, was the love of her life. She was clearly incredibly proud of him. He'd played the viola with the London Symphony Orchestra and had performed with Frank Sinatra. Theirs was a love story, and it was so sad to hear her talk of his untimely death just three years after they were married. Even though she was just in her early fifties at the time, she never remarried. Bill was very much still in her heart and this was palpable during our filming of the bank holiday barbeque hosted by Uncle Bryn. Doris picks up a guitar saying, 'Here's one you'll know,' and just before she began to sing, Maggie quietly uttered to herself, 'Come on, Bill, be with me,' which I noticed, and suddenly the song, a rendition of the Smiths' 'There Is a Light that Never Goes Out', took on a deeper meaning as she sang that to die by your side would be such a heavenly way to die.

Maggie passed away in 2011 but she is forever a part of the *Gavin and Stacey* family; for me, the song will always belong to her and Bill. In the 2019 Christmas special we all raised a glass to her, and the incomparable Doris. She is a light that never goes out.

Ever since Beverly appeared on the screen, I'm often asked, 'Where does the character come from?' When it comes to Pamela, Pamalaar, Pammy or Pam, I have to say that it came from Ruth and James and their writing. My job was to lift it off the page and add colour to their black and white. They gave Pam some cracking one-liners which always came out when you least expected them to, such as, 'What you said then was really boring, I switched off after banana,' to Stacey. And, 'You're a leek-munching sheep shagger,' to poor Gwen. I especially love, 'My little prince, you're the victim of a victimisation.' Then there's the phrases that are in her DNA such as 'Oh my Christ!' and 'You and me are going to fall out today, Mick, Michael.' One of the wonderful things about Pamela is the conviction with which she says everything. Her many malapropisms feel completely correct and not to be doubted – ours is not to question while!

There are many magic moments but one of my favourites is when she's just come back from the shops and is jamming ham into her mouth before anyone comes home as she needs to keep up the pretence of being vegetarian. Stacey comes in just as Pam has thrown her head back and is shoving it in and says, 'You're eating ham, Pam.' It's so simple and so funny. But what really cracks me up in the scene is Pam's response when she goes into ye olde English and says, 'Do you think ill of me, my child?' and, 'Promise me that thou shalt speak of this to no one, swear it, forsake me not.' Honestly, writing like that is such a delight for an actor like me to play; perhaps Ruth and James knew this and wrote to my strengths.

I've been in the business a long time and have had to say goodbye many times as jobs come to an end, and we all move on to other things. It's never easy, very rarely a relief, but it's something that's part and parcel of the job that you become accustomed to. Saying goodbye to everyone on this job was entirely different though and the only time in my career when I've dissolved into tears at the end of my final scene on hearing, 'That's a wrap for Alison Steadman.' Everyone involved had become like a family and our investment in each other was more than just doing a job. This continued through to the very last day of filming, and it was so tough to pack Pamela away for good along with the relationships that had been forged. It didn't feel like it was over, however, and there was still one gargantuan question that all of us, and all of you, needed answering – *Will you marry me, Smithy?*

POSTSCRIPT

A few weeks after I wrote this I got the news that we all had been expecting: everything had come together, and I could finally share the fact that the *Gavin and Stacey* family would be reuniting for a final time. I'd be returning to Billericay and no doubt to the infamous Barry's Island. It was a huge relief as rumours had been circulating for weeks and it had been hard to keep a poker face whenever anyone asked me about it, which they frequently did. Ruth and James had approached us all to see if we'd be up for it again and my heart had soared. I had just signed the contract for a third series of *Here We Go*, so I had also had to try and quash the mild concern about the fact that the filming was slated to take place at exactly the same time. *Oh, my Christ!* I'd referred to it as Gilbert and Sullivan but you'd not need to be a Bletchley Park codebreaker to guess what we were talking about. The prospect of stepping back into Pam's life is an exciting one. I've missed her. However, it'll be weeks and weeks before we get to see any scripts. I wonder how life has treated her and how's she's feeling about being eligible for a bus pass – I wonder if she's even picked hers up! What will it be like going from Sue Jessop to Pamela Shipman? And what about all the lines?! It's not a bad problem to have. I can hear Martin Duncan, the then stage manager at Lincoln Theatre Royal, saying, 'Well, I aren't grumblin'!'

CHAPTER 26

Dance Me to the End of Love

H it the right note. Hit the right note. Not too low. Not too high. Remember to take the coat off. God. It's bloody freezing. Do I have to take the coat off? You have to take the coat off. Just keep your eyes on Dave. My mind raced with multiple thoughts as I tried to tune myself into what I was doing before a voice from the side said, 'And action.' I looked at Dave, opened my coat, dropped it to the floor and began to sing.

Bésame
Bésame mucho
Como si fuera esta noche la última vez
Bésame,
Bésame mucho,
Que tengo miedo a pererte, perderte despues.

I don't know any Spanish and I'd driven Michael mad as I had been singing it night and day to get it into my head. The song, although it wasn't familiar to me, is a famous Mexican love song by Consuelo Velázquez. Apparently Paul McCartney sang it during early Beatles sessions in the Cavern Club, which must have been just before my

289

illicit lunchtime visits there. Even though it was in Spanish and hard to learn I felt more comfortable singing the original lyrics than I would have if they had been translated and I'd been asking Dave to 'kiss me a lot'.

Dave Johns and I were standing opposite each other in character as Dave and Fern on an outdoor shoot for the film *23 Walks*. It was freezing, we were in a public space with people jogging, dog walking and doing what people do in parks, and I had to drop my coat and sing. I could feel that others had stopped to listen, as well as Dave, but I kept my attention on him. The filming was taking place when the production team knew that the park would be quiet, but with just enough people who might be inclined to slow down a bit and linger a little when they see a woman in her seventies drop her coat and begin to sing huskily to the man standing opposite her. It all went perfectly. When the singing stopped and Fern had to say 'Oh God,' as she realised that it had been more than an audience of one listening, her feelings of relief and embarrassment certainly rang true!

It was the tail end of 2019 and it had been a busy and productive year proving the truth in the saying, you can wait half an hour for a bus and then half a dozen come along at once. The year had been like that for me, as the roles that I'd been offered had all appealed, so I'd said yes to them all. Thank goodness for that, as 2020 was going to be very different indeed! It was thrilling to still be working, given that there is never any certainty of that in my business, and to be getting under the skin of women of my own age, whose lives had been rich and full, was particularly rewarding. Age is a great leveller; when a person arrives at seventy it feels like a significant milestone, and you can be certain any character will have had to face some extraordinary things even within the context of a seemingly ordinary life. It's the same for everyone. We are born, we know we will die at some point, but we don't know when or how or what will have happened in between. We hope for a good life, a safe and happy one, one that includes relationships and responsibilities that we might desire. However, it's not mapped out for any of us; not even looking at which side of the road the puddles are on can help here. Life has a tendency of throwing several curveballs at us over the course of a lifetime and we learn to travel forward by navigating the highs and lows. By the time we reach our seventies, most of us know a thing to two about what we will and won't accept from ourselves and others.

All of this can offer meaningful storytelling for writers who choose to ignore age-related restrictions and instead focus on the human being that is behind the grey hair, the untoned body, the creased and saggy skin, and look to the lives that they have led, the choices that they've made and the emotions that may have been stored. Life doesn't stop until it stops, and everyone carries the essence of who they are with them right to the end. I can remember being fascinated about how it might feel to be old and would ask my grandma, 'How do you feel now that you're sixty, seventy, etc. ...' And her reply was always the same, 'I feel the same as I did when I was thirty,' which I never understood then, but do now.

Fern's 'Bésame Mucho' moment is a courageous one. It's when she says yes instead of her usual no and it's huge for her. This is a woman who's now alone, her children are gone, she's retired, worrying about money and is trying to cope. She's been fooled by a man and can't afford to be fooled again, so she is wary about talking about her stress or sharing it. She knows herself well enough to know that she can't jump into another relationship as she couldn't handle things if it failed. It's a common story, not just for women, that reveals our frailty as well as our faith and need for connection. Paul Morrison, who wrote and directed *23 Walks*, is a very gentle person and this is reflected on the page as well as the screen. He wanted to offer the audience a sense of how time passing can alter a person's perspective.

We filmed it over ten months and waited for the seasons to change so that we could film the mood changes and circumstantial shifts within the script. It may have been low budget, but it was never rushed and in filming it as we did, I could feel the character beginning to unfurl and place trust in herself until she takes a leap of faith. I love to dance, more than I love to sing, and the dance scene, when Fern first allows herself to be held, is so delicate and sensual – hopefully – that it leaves the audience wondering if she'll take the next step, so to speak. She's full of fear and that's something that I can connect with. It's a strange one because on the one hand there is an inner confidence that comes from experience and on the other there's a looming sense of what's next. The notion of time running out is a very powerful one for any drama to convey – it's one that can propel a character into taking action and doing things they might not have usually, or may have always wanted to do, just in case time does run out. Fern is a romantic at heart; it's unnatural for her to be alone, so she takes the plunge and agrees to spend the night with Dave and share a bed. It's quite a scene. I can remember going on *Woman's Hour* on BBC Radio 4 where they never stopped talking about the sex scene, which made me realise that, even though it wasn't rampant, it did take risks. Who would have thought that old people having sex would create such a stir! It wasn't as if they'd ripped each other's clothes off and were hanging off the end of the bed. What we ended up with was the result of both Dave and I saying, 'Shall we try this, what do you think, is that okay with you?' I knew that I wouldn't appear naked, those days have long gone, and that it wouldn't be something that Fern would do either. She'd be self-conscious and pull the covers up over her. It was important for us to remember that this was their first time together after a fair amount of pain in both of their lives. There is a great deal of unspoken apprehension; the fact that she cries at the end of their intimacy is because it's such an enormous release for her. There's such truth in the script. I loved the moment just beforehand, when she puts the toilet seat down and sits there in a lovely negligée that she's bought especially, facing the fact of what's about to happen. I wasn't being me and this wasn't my story, but I could understand her, and Paul gave the character some lines that resonated, as I'm sure they did with other woman of my age, including when Fern says, 'We've both lived a lot of life and we have a chance of something.'

Having a chance of something but not taking it isn't in my DNA. Sometimes we have to be brave, don't we, and push ourselves a bit further than we think we can go. Afterwards, we look back and think, *I've done it. That was good.* That was my 2019. I was lucky to have had the offers that had been made to me and didn't want to turn any of them down, even though I knew that the schedule might be gruelling. *Gloomsbury*, the wonderful radio series by Sue Limb, was recording. I was booked to do the long-awaited *Gavin and Stacey* Christmas special, there was *23 Walks* and then *Life* came in. They were all back-to-back and my initial reaction was, *No I can't do it, I can't do it*, before I switched to, *I've got to do it, I've got to do it*.

I have always felt a sense of freedom throughout my life, which I value and never take for granted. So many women of my mum's generation and beyond didn't have the opportunity to be themselves and achieve what they wanted to, as I have been lucky enough to do. My parents were a happy couple, but I do know that my mum found life frustrating sometimes because she'd never had a profession. She was living during a time and in a place, when most women were at home bringing up their kids and they were expected to be happy doing that. Mum was happy, but later in her life she would say to me, 'Oh, Alison, I wish I'd had a better education. I wish I could have done something more.' Her sacrifices enabled me to have choices and I was determined not to squander them, so taking on a bit too much in 2019 didn't feel like anything that I should complain about.

Every job that year had its challenges, but playing Gail Reynolds in Mike Bartlett's *Life* posed the greatest. Here is a woman on the cusp of her seventieth birthday who is experiencing a dawning realisation that time has passed her by and that she's become like a piece of comfortable furniture to her husband and family. So many women wrote to me after the series had aired to say that this was exactly how they felt, or had felt, before they had decided to take action. Mike wrote some gritty and painful material for all of the characters, and I needed to be on top of my lines so that I could serve Gail well and get my teeth into playing her. The whole script was like a tightly woven tapestry and even though my main connection was with Peter Davison, who played my husband, as the story unfolded there was an entwining between all the people living in the four flats in which the show was based. All the characters were trapped in stories that they had concocted for themselves, so that their lives seemed bearable.

Gail only begins to truly question her reality after her husband reveals details of an affair that he'd had years earlier with a colleague, which leaves her reeling. There was proper camera time given to close-up shots so that the interior of how Gail was feeling could be captured; it was like being put under the microscope or looked at through a set of binoculars. It was an exciting challenge to try and reveal Gail's confusion as well as her epiphany. Henry, her husband, had become lazy in his communication with her, cruel even. I thought back to my mum and dad and their truly supportive relationship; also the times that Mum would talk about the husbands of some of her friends who constantly put their wives down when she'd say, 'How dare he speak to her like that.' Ben Gosling Fuller and Kate Hewitt, who directed the series, made some bold choices that only enhanced the drama. When they asked me during the party scene, after the affair revelation, just to dance and dance and keep on dancing, as if Gail was trying to dance back to a former version of herself, it was so liberating. There was no rehearsal, they just put the music on and said, 'Just go,' then let the music play on and on. To be given this trust and be able to do what I felt was right was empowering; for the character it was a pivotal moment, and she left the scene changed.

Life, as in real life, does change and shape us. Gail is pushed to the point of no return. She looks at her situation and thinks, *No, this isn't enough, this isn't good enough*, then walks away from a marriage that, on the surface and to their friends and family, has always seemed happy. She becomes braver, able to confront and reveal the truth. If *Life* made some women of a certain age take a look at themselves and their situations, then good. If it made their partners take a harder look, then even better. It was a stand-out job in a busy year that helped me to evaluate my own life; to coin one of Gail's phrases in response to living how she chooses to, 'I've just got started.' This is how I feel about keeping on working and pushing myself to dance right up to the edge of time. There's no reason not to.

CHAPTER 27

Dear Woman in the Mirror

'And that's a wrap.'

My shoulders drop slightly as they settle back into their at-ease position and we all begin to stand down from our day on the set of *Here We Go*. We put our inner gear sticks into reverse as we begin the process of ending the working day and heading home again to our respective lives. It's not late, but it's been a full-on day for everyone and there's still the journey home to come which takes about one and a half hours in the rush-hour traffic. I dawdle back to my winnebago and wrestle with the notion of not getting out of Sue Jessop's costume but instead getting straight into the car and zooming off home a little earlier. It's the same each day. It's always exciting getting into costume and heading to make-up, then lighting up as Granny Sue, but it's tiring the other way round and sometimes the clothes feel like they are carrying the weight of the hours that have passed since getting up at 4.30 a.m. I never succumb though. It's important to me to get out of character, and no matter how tired I am or how eager to get into the waiting car, I always take off my clothes and take care to hang them up properly.

There I am. I catch a passing glance of myself in the mirror as I hook the clothes hanger on the rail before returning to sit down at the dressing table and stare straight in front of me. *There she is.* The woman that's reflected back at me is still Sue. I reach over and pull out a couple of cleansing wipes to begin the process of altering the image. Taking off her make-up is like peeling off a carefully crafted mask and the ritual of sweeping the wipes across my eyes, to remove the vibrant eyeshadow, and then over my face, loosening and soaking up the foundation that's now fairly set into my skin, is like gently taking a canvas back to its neutral base colour. It's an important part of my routine that enables the separation between me and her. After a few minutes of deliberate coaxing I begin to appear again and the face that I face each day and recognise stares back at me and there's a momentary reflection on the day.

Dear Woman in the Mirror

It's been another good one. No complaints. It's brilliant to have the chance to get to know Sue a bit more this season and it looks like there will be a third one too to keep me on my toes. Who would have thought, eh? Yeah, I'm playing the granny but so what, I am one now, to my own gorgeous grandson Freddy, with another one on the way, and I love it. Granny Sue is making her mark on the family, and I hope that I'm doing that for the show too, as working on it has become such an unexpected and happy experience during this chapter of my life. I'm learning a new way of working with the camera and I'm surrounded by a company of people that I'm now so very fond of. I feel seen and heard, and not put out to pasture or left to exist in the margins of my career. It's a rich and full life, and I'm immensely lucky. No. I've no complaints. I don't feel stuck in any way at all, and I feel sure that I've yet to drive through some more wonderful moments. I really like Sue Jessop; she's not got an ounce of malice in her and does her utmost to move with care and kindness.

Even though she can be quite a handful at times, she tries her best to make the world lighter. Yes. I like being Sue Jessop, but now it's time to be me for about nine hours or so before returning to set again tomorrow.

I reach down into my bag and rummage around for my own lippy to add a bit of brightness and familiarity as I return to me. I stand up, pick up my script for the following day, drop it carefully into my bag, then check that I've got my phone as I haven't had time to finish today's Wordle and might try to on the journey back. Wrapping my coat over my shoulders, I switch the lights off and head out to the car. My carriage, not a golden one, awaits and the six-seater people carrier pulls up outside the caravan to save me a walk. There's a chill wind in the air so I appreciate the gesture, although I'm less happy about the family-sized wagon that will only have me as its sole passenger. The early part of the journey is through a residential area and there's an obstacle course of speed bumps for us to bounce over – I dread to think what it's doing to the rear undercarriage as I can feel my own being challenged! The last vestiges of light are disappearing as my one-person carrier accelerates up to a speedy 40 mph as we exit the controlled traffic area, and the homeward journey begins to feel a bit smoother. The roads are far busier at this time of day than they were on the journey in. The lights of the oncoming traffic glisten then flash past; sometimes there's a bright glare and then a dip to darkness as a passing driver realises that they've got their full beam on. I cross my fingers and hope that there will be no hold-ups to delay us, as the time to decompress at home for a while is short enough as it is.

I sit back and look forward to the G&T that I'll make myself so I can add a tiny drop more gin, and the indispensable accompanying bowl of olives that my boys always tease me about. They send me up something rotten about the olives and always say that I can't have a drink without a bowl beside me! I'm comfortable in my consistency though and it's this simple indulgence that can make getting up at 4.30 a.m. each morning a little easier to keep going with. Home has always been my safe haven, first 22 Sherwyn Road in Liverpool and now the home that I share in London with Michael. I always look forward to hearing him put his key in the door, as he does mine, and then settling down for a catch-up on our respective days. We all have our ways. If it's a Monday evening, then Michael and I get into competition mode with a TV quiz show. These simple pleasures are invaluable to me. I daren't close my eyes on the journey as I'd drop off into a deep sleep and there's still things to be done when I get home in order to prepare for tomorrow – I also want to have a quick go over of my lines before aiming to be in bed by 9.00 p.m.! There's very little time to switch off on a job like this. It's like being a light that may have been switched off at the neck but remains plugged in and is still switched on at the socket so that there is still a low electrical current being emitted. Doing any job, especially one with a demanding schedule like *Here We Go*, requires me to be hardwired for the duration and any unplugging will only truly happen once the filming has ended.

The car begins to slow down again as we head into central London. Sometimes we take a route through the West End, which I adore as it brings back so many happy memories of my years on stage. Charing Cross Road, the Garrick Theatre, then a turn down Shaftsbury Avenue passing the Gielgud and the Lyric before heading into the neon brightness of Piccadilly and up along Regent Street and onwards to my side of the city. Seeing the names of friends and former colleagues up in lights never fails to make be proud and excited to be part of a band of troupers, who try to live a life while providing for themselves and their families through storytelling. It's what we all do, though, regardless of how we earn our living. We present ourselves to the world and to each other, and hope to find our way through the traffic with the stories we tell of ourselves.

We've stopped at a red light, and I think back to today's filming. It was a huge scene, Robin and Cherry's wedding, and there was lots going on for everyone, including Granny Sue having to sing an impromptu song to replace the music for the first dance. I like singing but I wouldn't describe myself as a singer; whenever it's required, I'm aware of needing to sing while still being convincing as the character, as well as not making a fool of myself. It's a fine balance. Tom, our writer, who also plays Robin, had given me a 1940s song that had been made popular by Dean Martin, 'You're Nobody till Somebody Loves You'. My initial choice had been to sing it as if there was a big band playing behind me and go all Las Vegas and clicky fingers on it. But that felt all wrong as I thought that's not the true Sue, that's not the Sue who would step into save the day out of love for her family. So I decided to sing it without fuss, no finger-clicking or jazz hands, just a woman and the words.

Red turns to amber then turns to green and we cross over the traffic lights then turn right into the street where I live. I look out the window as we head on slowly. It's pitch black, apart from glints of artificial light seeping out through the shutters and curtains of the homes that line the street, as I contemplate how much we shut ourselves away and hide from each other. Acting is brilliant at making you face yourself and come out into the open. There are no other cars on the road as we pull up outside the house that I left nearly fifteen hours earlier. The driver, sensing how tired I am, gets out and comes round to open the passenger door for me, holding it open until I get out. The latch on the gate squeaks as I lift it, then the only sound is of my footsteps crunching on the gravel path that leads to our door. The birds are sleeping, safely nestled in the hedgerow and I'm sure that Mr Fox is close by just waiting for the coast to be clear before he begins his nighttime foraging. I hope that I see him again in the morning. I know that Michael will have heard the car pull up, the lifting of the latch and then my footsteps eagerly taking me to the front steps. Before I can get my key in the door Michael opens it. I'm home.

EPILOGUE

The Unsinkable Molly

*O*h, *my Christ! Oh, my goodness! My phone's on. My phone's on. What am I going to do? If it rings, it'll ruin the play. If I switch it off it'll make that silly noise. I'll ruin everything. Oh God! Why did I bring it with me? What am I going to do? I know. I'll sit on it. Oh why didn't I wear trousers. I knew I should have worn trousers. What if it makes that vibrating noise that just gets louder and louder the longer you leave it? Everyone will know that it's coming from me. I know, I'll take the batteries out.*

This is what was going on in my head when Michael and I were attending the 2003 press night of *Pretending to Be Me*, Tom Courtney's one-man show about Philip Larkin, and realised that I'd forgotten to switch off my first ever mobile phone. On reflection it makes me wonder if the skin between me and Pamela Shipman is a touch more gossamer thin than I've previously thought.

Writing this book has invited me to question my own character in the same way that I've interrogated the characters of some of the 'other women' that I have shared my life with. Even though I hang up their clothes at the end of a run or shoot, parts of them must be left in me, as there are parts of me in them. It's a weirdly evolved DNA of sorts that endorses just how porous we all are and it's clear

303

that what makes me who I am is the blend of people, environment and circumstance that I have been nourished by and exposed to, and this in turn is what enables me to pretend to be other people. But the loaded question is, *Who am I?* What, reading between the lines of this story, would I do if I ever had to *pretend to be me*? What questions would I be asking? What would I discover? The cover is not the book, as they say. Remembering my yesterdays hasn't felt like treading upon foreign ground or like reading a fiction about someone else, and although it's out of character for me to share as I have, giving my mind a good old shake-up has enabled me to bring so much back into technicolour. My past remains a *home* of sorts and acts as a foundation stone for my future. Who I was, who I am and who I will be are intrinsically linked so I would like to think that these recollections are also a forward projection of what's to come, as I keep on keeping on, forging forward and holding dear all that I love.

'The Unsinkable Molly is at it again' was the regular refrain from my classmates at secondary school whenever I'd shower them with an abundance of positivity and encouragement saying, 'Come on, everyone, we can do this.' This term of endearment was originally given to Margaret Brown, one of the few survivors of the *Titanic* disaster, and as time passed it became more widely used as a nickname for people who weren't pulled down by life. It's interesting to reflect on this and think about the energy and positive outlook that I must have shown to my friends. I'm not so sure if I could muster the troops in the same way now. Do I still possess that Unsinkable Molly in me? I find myself needing to check back in with that younger version of myself more and more, especially when any sense of reluctance stirs.

From an early age I've only had positivity ingrained into me, both at home and elsewhere. Our school motto was 'Think on These Things', and Miss Brown, our headmistress, would always encourage us to look to the good things in life and not the bad, in the same way that my mum was always drilling in 'Always say you can, and you will,' and both heartening beliefs have stayed with me.

> Whatsoever things are true,
> Whatsoever things are honest,
> Whatsoever things are just
> Whatsoever things are pure
> Whatsoever things are lovely,
> Whatsoever things are of good report;
>   if there be any virtue,
> And if there be any praise,
> Think on these things

So why, as I've become older, do I seem to be grieving more than ever before? Is it for times gone by and people and parts that I'll never encounter again? My tendency is to shake off this feeling rather than allowing myself to become swallowed up in it. My life has been a full one, for which I'm grateful. That's not to say that there haven't been blips, there have, but I've pulled through them and I am happy. I love working, but equally I adore coming home to what I know and where I feel most comfortable. Being able to watch my boys grow up and now have families of their own has brought an inordinate amount of happiness. Even though the juggling was tough at times, I swell with pride knowing that being a mum and being an actress weren't mutually exclusive.

I'm immeasurably proud of the nearly six decades of tenacity that has led to non-stop work, of having remained true to my roots and to still be standing with my feet (in flats) firmly on the ground. At the end of the day, though, it doesn't really matter who you are or what's been achieved, what matters is how you've chosen to behave. I'm not perfect by any means but I've always tried my best and have regarded everything that's come my way as an addition to the story that began with my parents. I miss each of them every day but even though I'm not religious, I do have faith that they are still a guiding influence upon me.

When Mum died, my sisters and I chose the intermezzo from the opera *Cavalleria Rusticana* as the funeral music, as it was one of the records that our dad, George, played to her when they were courting. I thought that I'd splinter into a thousand pieces listening to it, but in fact I felt proud and immensely strong that we were able to bring them both together to say our farewells. Several years later, after Mum had passed away, Pam, Sylvia and I were sitting in a restaurant in the Lake District and were just about to head back to our hotel when a new track came onto the sound system. 'Listen,' I said as the strains of the intermezzo floated towards us, 'it's Mum, she's come to us.' We stood still and remembered one of the final things that she'd said to the three of us: 'When I'm gone, make sure that you always stay close and that you don't drift apart.' It felt like a convergence that was meant to be, and in the unravelling of certain parts of my life, in telling this tale, I realise that so much of it has been moving towards the same point and has come together at the right time.

Once work had become more established, my mum would express how proud she and my dad were of me for taking a road that was different to what had been expected and she'd say, 'Oh, Alison, I was only thinking the other day that you've climbed to the top of the tree. You really have. You've climbed to the top of the tree.' That's a mother's loving pride talking, and it's not how I see myself at all. There are much taller trees that have been climbed. I'm not a big

Hollywood star, that's not the route that I chose to explore, but within my own world, I've done okay and I'm happy with that. 'Never say you can't. Always say you can and you will' is inscribed on my heart and I hope that my mum knows that I proved to myself that *I could* and that *I did*.

The Unsinkable Molly of my youth is still afloat and who knows where the compass will point next, but whatever the direction, I'm ready to step forward and, if doubt creeps in, I'll remember the wonderfully reassuring phrase that my dresser wrote to me: 'Time always goes by in the same way. The tips of your toes are where they should be. And at the end of the night there is always a glass of wine waiting for you!'

Let's think on these things, and thank you for travelling over these pages with me.

The Other Women

In the idle moments of train or car journeys or when I'm home alone and talking to myself, I've often wondered what it might be like if some of the women that I've inhabited were to find themselves all together. I'd love that, I think that you might too, but would they? Over to you, ladies:

Mrs Bennet: Nobody can tell what I suffer but it is always so.

Pam: You are the victim of a victimisation, Mrs Bennet.

Beverly: Can you take a little bit of criticism?

Pam: You and I are going to fall out, Beverly.

Mrs Bennet: You delight in vexing me. You have no compassion for my poor nerves.

Beverly: Sometimes a little row can add sparkle to a relationship, Mrs Bennet.

Fern: Ladies, we've all lived a lot of life.

Sue: I haven't scampered since the late nineties, Fern.

Gail: I used to do things.

Pam: What you said just now was really boring, Gail.

Mrs Bennet: Those who never complain are never pitied, Pamela.

Pam: I'm not being funny but you wanna get a life, Mrs B.

Gail: *Who am I? Who was I?*

Fern: *Oh, I don't like mysteries, Gail.*

Pam: *Let's do some shots, ladies.*

Sue: *My bladder is very suggestible, Pam. I can barely do three minutes on a toilet.*

Candice Marie: *Are we having raw mushrooms as a treat, Pam?*

Pam: *No way, José.*

Beverly: *A little bit of ice and lemon?*

Candice Marie: *Would you like to hear my poem?*

Pam: *Oh my Christ!*

Candice Marie: *A gentle flower that grows in spring,*
That feels the sun upon its face,
It's free to smile and laugh and grin,
It knows no guilt or hate or sin,
It has no battles it must win,
Oh, how I love and envy him.

Pam: *What you see is what you get, everyone.*

Candice Marie: *Say goodnight to Prudence.*

Pam: *Give it a rest, you.*

Acknowledgements

Mike Leigh for opening up the door to improvisation for me, and allowing me to be creative and find my feet in this world.

Margaret Matheson for coming to see *Abigail's Party* at Hampstead Theatre and insisting it should be filmed for television.

David Rose for producing *Nuts in May* and insisting it should be filmed in Dorset.

Rachel Davies for her friendship and her relentless kindness and patience over the years running my lines.

Philip Hedley for giving me my first job and believing in me.

Margaret (Maggie) Bury for seeing something in me and giving me my first chance at East 15 Acting School.

Jim Wiggins from my Friday night youth theatre, who said I had to go into acting. He said he wouldn't want to meet me in twenty years' time stirring a pot of stew and saying, 'If only I'd become an actress.'

Michael Elwyn for his love and for being my rock over the last thirty years.

Fiona Lindsay and Luigi Bonomi for planting the seed for this memoir, and being so supportive and kind throughout. My editor, Emma Tait, for her attention to detail, and Sarah Emsley and the team at HarperCollins for all their support and faith in my story.

'Do not stain today's blue sky with tomorrow's clouds.'
Edna Spears

Picture Credits

While every effort has been made to trace the owners of copyright material reproduced herein and secure permissions, the publishers would like to apologise for any omissions and will be pleased to incorporate missing acknowledgements in any future edition of this book.

Section 1

Page 2 (middle) © Gordells Art Photographers – Page 3 (middle right) Edwin Sampson/ANL/Shutterstock; (bottom) © Hartley and Laurence – Page 4 (top left) © Hartley and Laurence; (top right) © Colin Osman; (middle) Bill Sharples; (bottom left) © Len Davis – Page 5 © Rachel Davies – Page 6 (top left) Steve Wood/Daily Express/mirrorpix; (top right) BBC Photo Archive; (left) Dave Pickthorn/BBC Photo Archive; (bottom) ITV/Shutterstock – Page 7 (top) BBC Photo Archive; (bottom left) Kobal/Shutterstock – Page 8 (top) Donald Cooper/Alamy Stock Photo; (bottom) Moviestore/Shutterstock

Section 2

Page 1 (top and middle) Donald Cooper/Alamy Stock Photo – Page 2 (top) Thin Man/Film 4 Int/British Screen/Kobal/Shutterstock; (middle left) Alastair Muir/Shutterstock – Page 3 (top) PA Images/Alamy Stock Photo – Page 5 (top) John Stillwell/PA Images/Alamy Stock Photo; (middle) ITV/Shutterstock – Page 6 (top left) Tony Larkin/Shutterstock; (top right) Alastair Muir/Shutterstock; (bottom left and right) Donald Cooper/Shutterstock – Page 7 (top) © BBC/Courtesy Everett Collection/Alamy Stock Photo; bottom Anthony Harvey/Shutterstock – Page 8 (top) © Parkland Entertainment/Courtesy Everett Collection/Shutterstock; (middle) BBC Studios; (bottom) Jonathan Browning/BBC Studios

All other images courtesy of the author.